Dear
Brownlee's

Hope this comes in
handy on your travels.

Carole, Duncan
&
Ross

Christmas 1985

THE
PALACE
UNDER
THE ALPS

THE PALACE UNDER THE ALPS

And Over 200 Other
Unusual, Unspoiled, and
Infrequently Visited Spots
in 16 European Countries

WILLIAM BRYSON

 CONGDON & WEED, INC. NEW YORK

To Cynthia

Copyright © 1985 by William Bryson

Library of Congress Cataloging in Publication Data

Bryson, William.
    The palace under the Alps.

    Includes index.
    1. Europe—Description and travel—1971–   —Guide-
books.   I. Title.
D909.B79   1985   914'.04558   84-27458
ISBN 0-86553-144-7
ISBN 0-312-92635-9 (St. Martin's Press)

Published by Congdon & Weed, Inc.
298 Fifth Avenue, New York, N.Y. 10001
Distributed by St. Martin's Press
175 Fifth Avenue, New York, N.Y. 10010
Published simultaneously in Canada by Methuen Publications
2330 Midland Avenue, Agincourt, Ontario M1S 1P7

Designed by Irving Perkins
Maps by David Lindroth

CONTENTS

INTRODUCTION

This is a book for people who want more from a trip to Europe than just to see the Eiffel Tower, Buckingham Palace, the Colosseum at Rome, and 25,000 Japanese tourists. Although no reasonable person would ever suggest that you skip these sights (well, you might give the Japanese tourists a miss), your trip will be infinitely more rewarding if you can occasionally slip off from the throngs and strike out on your own. The following pages describe some 200 sights that most travelers never see—little-known museums, unspoiled towns and villages, out-of-the-way resorts, and unusual attractions—where one can experience European life firsthand rather than from the back of a crowd. Although a few are fairly remote—like the northernmost golf course in the world at Boden, Sweden, and the Aran Islands in Ireland—most lie slightly off the main tourist routes. This book offers options and brief detours, rewarding places to explore in addition to, rather than instead of, the main tourist centers.

Obviously you can't expect to have many of these places entirely to yourself. Europe is, after all, a densely populated continent whose residents are enthusiastic travelers. I don't suppose you'll ever have to fight your way through crowds to see the German National Bread Museum at Ulm or the Swedish Match Museum at Jönköping. But if you head for a coastal resort in July or August—however obscure it may appear on the map, however formidable it may be to get to—you will find crowds.

The simplest way to avoid this is to visit out of season. I'm amazed that so few people do this. Unless you are absolutely determined to return home with a deep Mediterranean suntan, my advice is to travel in spring or early summer or fall. Even in the depths of winter most of Europe enjoys a gratifyingly temperate climate (and in Britain, I can tell you from painful experience, there's often little to choose between February and August). Off season you'll find the prices cheaper, the people more hospitable, and the hoteliers, restaurateurs, and museum keepers almost lonely for your company.

The following attractions have been chosen to help you avoid other tourists, whatever the season, yet this isn't their only merit: they are also good fun. A few, of course, are of purely specialized interest—the world's largest nudist colony at Cap d'Agde in France springs instantly to mind—but each is historic or fascinating or beautiful (and often all three). That they have managed to escape the attentions of most travelers is an incidental benefit—and an enduring oversight for which we should be grateful.

At this point many travel books trot out a string of disclaimers, saying that while every care has been taken to ensure that prices, opening times, and other such details were accurate at the time of going to press, things may have changed since then and you really ought to check them. The same goes for this book, of course. But here the warning is particularly heartfelt. It's one thing to stroll four blocks and find the British Museum closed on a Sunday when the guidebook clearly said that it was open on Sundays, but infinitely more painful to travel halfway across a continent to some obscure (but rewarding) museum or monument only to find that the head person, in a moment of whimsy, has decided to close the place for the whole of July. So be sure to check with local tourist offices, particularly for those attractions that require you to travel some distance. And bear in mind that prices given here are intended only as rough guidelines. You've lived with inflation long enough to know that they can rarely be more than inspired estimates.

I would like to thank all those who helped with this book, most notably Sandra Choron and Lea Gordon, my colleagues Lindsay Bray, Alan Howe, Peter Elman, Bob Dyson, Allen Kingsland, Peter Blacklock, Caroline Double, Tony Sikkima, and Bob Ballantyne, and, above all, my wife, Cynthia.

AUSTRIA

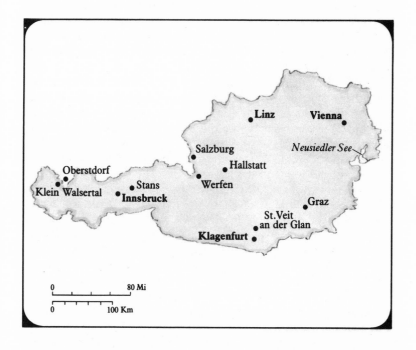

Linz

Vienna

Salzburg

Neusiedler See

Oberstdorf

Hallstatt

Klein Walsertal

Stans

Werfen

Innsbruck

Graz

St. Veit
an der Glan

Klagenfurt

0   80 Mi

0   100 Km

Austria's "Lost" Valley, Klein Walsertal

The compact and tidy valley of Klein Walsertal is sometimes called Austria's only colony. Although it's clearly in Austria, a horseshoe-shaped wall of mountains cuts it off from the rest of the country. The mouth faces out into Germany. The only other way in from Austria is on foot through the intimidating Rochalp and Gemstel passes, an arduous slog best suited for professional climbers. The only other way in is to leave Austria, drive through Germany, and enter on the road from Oberstdorf. Thus, although the Austrian village of Schrocken is only four miles away as the crow flies, to get there by car requires a journey of about 110 miles and a passport.

This curious geography has given the seven-mile-long valley and its four villages a somewhat schizoid air. The citizenry are loyal Austrians governed by Austrian law but they pay import duties on Austrian goods and none on those from Germany; their police are Austrian but their customs officials are German; their postage stamps are Austrian but paid for with German money while their mail is delivered by German vans. To top it all, these people, who originally came from Switzerland, speak a dialect that is equally incomprehensible to the Germans, Austrians, and Swiss.

Quite apart from these peculiarities, Klein Walsertal is special. Its setting of farmlands, towering mountains, and villages is as glorious as any in the region, and infinitely less trammeled. Guesthouses are comparatively cheap, the people are friendly, and there's excellent walking along the paths leading off the main road. Just don't try to get there from Austria.

Details: Klein Walsertal is in Voralberg and contains four villages: Riezlern, Hirschegg, Baad, and Mittelberg. It lies just north of the main road between Liechtenstein and Innsbruck and is approximately 30 miles west of Lake Constance. You'll need a good map to find it. The only approach is through the West German town of Oberstdorf (itself an attractive resort), about 2 hours and 15 minutes southwest of Munich by train.

Schloss Tratzberg, Stans

In a part of the world dense with old castles, Schloss Tratzberg is easily overlooked. It shouldn't be. Though a dour gray fortress that lacks fairy-tale charm from without, its setting on the slopes of a Tyrolean valley is magnificent and beneath its dull exterior are treasures to be found nowhere else in this part of Europe.

The richly carved mahogany ceiling of the Queen's Room alone justifies the trip. It is said that seven carpenters and seven apprentices spent seven years and seven months carving the ornate patterns. True or not, the wooden detail throughout the castle is superb.

Tratzberg was built in about 1500 by the brothers Jacob and Simon Tänzl and contains everything you might hope for in a castle of that period—heavy wooden doors and furniture, rich tapestries, knights' armor, and even a secret passageway through a cupboard in one of the bedrooms. The great hall is notable for its fresco—a family tree for the House of Hapsburg holding 148 half-length portraits with biographies in exquisite gothic script under each. Painted in 1508 and running 150 feet overall, with seven life-sized stags scattered around the walls wearing real sets of antlers, it creates a stunning effect—as do the views over the valley of the River Inn.

Details: Schloss Tratzberg, near Stans, is about 20 miles northwest of Innsbruck just off the motorway to Salzburg, and is open daily from Easter to the end of August from 10 A.M. to 3 P.M. Guided tours only. The closest rail connection is Jenbach. Nearby is the Wolfsklamm, a gorge through which there is a lovely walk up to a cloister on the rocks and the pilgrimage church of St. Georgenburg.

The World's Largest Ice Cave, Werfen

Austria has 4,300 caves and more are being discovered all the time. If your interest runs in that direction, 20 of them are open for public viewing. One of the most awesome and accessible is the Eisriesenwelt, south of Salzburg, a vast ice cave system running for 26 miles under the Alps, making it the biggest in the world.

The view from the mouth of the cave over the valley 3,300 feet below is ample reward for the effort of getting there. Once inside even the most reluctant visitor will be impressed by the scale of the cave system and the eerieness of the ice formations. These are made by water trickling down from the surface and freezing as it reaches the chill air of the cave, forming incredible curtains, pillars, and cascades. Subtle backlighting gives the formations a luminous, unearthly glow. Most unsettling. The mandatory guided tour covers only a tiny part of the system, but takes in all the highlights—the famous Ice Palace, immense ramparts, and the vast domed halls. Even so, the tours last two hours, a fact you should bear in mind if you're traveling with small children. And since it is also quite cold, a sweater, heavy socks, and stout walking shoes are recommended.

If you are interested in speleology or geology, or simply seeking an escape from a summer downpour, the Eisriesenwelt provides an unusual and absorbing alternative to a long, wet afternoon spent in museums.

Details: The Eisriesenwelt Ice Caves are open daily from May 1 until October 15. In July and August guided tours start every hour on the half hour. At other times the tours are at 9:30, 11:30, and 3:30. The caves can be reached via the Eisriesenwelt cable car at Werfen. Tours start from the Dr. Friedrick-Oedle-Haus refuge at the top. For those interested in exploring caves elsewhere in the country, the Austrian National Tourist Office publishes a very good booklet in English called *Showcaves in Austria.*

The Water Tricks at Schloss Hellbrunn, near Salzburg

Marcus Sitticus, a seventeenth-century archbishop of Salzburg, was by all accounts a good and noble man, but he must have made a trying friend. He loved nothing so much as to soak others with water. To that end, from 1613–19 he built Schloss Hellbrunn, a magnificent baroque residence whose grounds incorporated the most elaborate fountains and water jokes in the world. Today, you may be pleased to hear, they are all still in perfect working order.

At every turn you will find yourself being sprayed by streams of water from unexpected places—sometimes from above, sometimes from below, sometimes from the sides, and occasionally from all directions at once. With every hedge, paving stone, and piece of statuary holding a potential aquatic surprise, you soon find yourself creeping around cautiously. The most famous of the water jokes is the carved stone outdoor dining table where Sitticus would dine with his friends (among whom there must have been an exceptionally high

turnover) on warm summer evenings. Every seat, with the predict-
able exception of Marcus Sitticus' own, contained a small hole through
which the archbishop could send a surprisingly fierce jet of water
when the conversation lulled.

Less threatening is a wide assortment of animated models—serpents, mermaids, and the like—that perform a variety of stunts in
the little grottoes and ponds. Most amazing of these is a miniature
theater, built in 1750 by an unemployed miner, where 100 or so
small wooden figures do their complicated business to the accom-
paniment of a hurdy-gurdy: a band plays, a guard marches up and
down in front of a town hall, and gypsies dance with a bear while a
butcher kills a calf. Like everything on the grounds, the whole,
including the hurdy-gurdy, is entirely driven by running water. Endlessly fascinating.

Also on the grounds is a folk museum in the little Monatschlössen
(so called because it was built in a month) and a zoo. Both are very
good, but there is a separate admission charge for each.

Details: Schloss Hellbrunn is open daily from May 1 to August 31
from 8 A.M. to 5:30 P.M., and in April, September, and October
from 9 A.M. to 4 P.M. Admission is 25 schillings for adults and 14
schillings for children aged 4 to 15. From central Salzburg take the
"H" bus.

Hallstatt

This is the longest continuously inhabited village in Europe and
home of the oldest salt mine on earth. But that's not all. In the local
museum are unique Iron Age relics—remnants of a prehistoric tribe
so advanced that it practiced democracy, using its weapons only as
ornaments. And don't miss the ice caves, or the sixteenth-century
parish church with its famed winged altar, or the macabre charnel
house decorated with human skulls and bones—unless you wish to.

But the beauty of the place will stay with you. Hallstatt is astonishingly, unremittingly lovely. A tightly packed cluster of balconied
houses, it hugs a narrow spit of land overlooking the dark waters of
the Hallstatter See (or lake) and is surrounded by towering mountains. Few places of its size can match it for beauty and none that
I know of can even approach its range of diversions.

Your first stop should be the local museum. Archeological finds
in Hallstatt for the period 800–400 B.C. were so important that the

era is known as the Hallstatt Epoch, and the best of the artifacts—a 2,500-year-old leather pouch in amazingly good condition, plus an assortment of brooches and pottery—are displayed there. The museum also chronicles the history of salt, and thus serves as a useful introduction to what should come next: a visit to the local salt mine. After donning pale blue or red overalls and an absurd little hat (the effect of which is to make you and the other tourists look like a party of Smurfs), you enter the mines, a trifle unceremoniously, by sliding down a chute. Kids love it. The mine is the oldest in the world and its complex of interconnected tunnels is vast, the longest stretching 32 kilometers into the mountains. You can see how salt was once mined and watch brine being extracted. There are still more artifacts from the Iron Age, including the rush lanterns used by the first miners 2,500 years ago. You return to the real world on a miner's train. However unpromising all this may sound, it's interesting and a lot of fun.

If time allows, try to see the winged altarpiece in the village church with its nine exquisitely carved panels. A short trip across the lake by steamer takes you to Obertraun, where a cable car up the mountainside provides spectacular views and deposits you near the entrance to the local ice caves. You can also take a rowboat out on the lake, stroll for miles through the Echern Valley, play tennis, go fishing, attend a lakeside concert, or simply eat and drink at one of the village's many restaurants and cafes. Don't miss it.

Details: Hallstatt (pop. 1,500) is about 30 miles southeast of Salzburg just off the main highway to Graz. It can be reached by train from Salzburg (change at Bad Ischl) or direct from Linz. The town possesses only one hotel, the Seehotel Gruener Baum, but it's a knockout. Built in 1670 and commanding a prime setting between the lake and small market square, it has 21 rooms, a bar, and two restaurants. Charges range from about 200–600 schillings a night depending on the time of year and size of the room. Reservations are strongly recommended.

Hochosterwitz Castle, near St. Veit an der Glan

When you travel around Europe, even for a short time, you tend to get a bit jaded by castles. Even so, Hochosterwitz in Carinthia will take your breath away. Easily the most beautiful castle in the country, it crowns the summit of a steep hill that rises explosively out of the surrounding plain, interrupting the sky with a profusion of turrets, towers, sheer walls, and crenelations. With its dramatic setting and romantic air it is the archetypal fairy-tale castle, so it should come as no surprise that this is the one Walt Disney chose, after examining hundreds of schlosses and chateaux all over Europe, as his model castle for Snow White and the Seven Dwarfs.

Hochosterwitz is approached by a long, steep, winding walk up the hill through 14 arched gateways and drawbridges, each a masterpiece of defensive design. The castle was built about 1500 by the Khevenhöller family, which has owned it without interruption for almost 500 years—though not without challenges. Around 1600 a certain Countess Maultasch tried to acquire the property through the simple expedient of starving out the residents. After months of siege, the occupants were down to their last cow. In a bold attempt to convince the marauders that they were not short of food, the occupants hurled the unfortunate animal over the parapet. Happily, the ruse worked and the dispirited countess and her men withdrew. Today, the present Count Khevenhöller lives in a smaller castle lower down the hill.

Although there isn't a great deal to see at Hochosterwitz besides the armory and portrait gallery, there is a good terrace restaurant with outstanding views.

Details: Hochosterwitz is about 10 miles north of Klagenfurt, from which there are frequent buses. It is open daily from 9 A.M. to 6 P.M. from early May to late October.

The Armory Museum, Graz

The Austrians are a wonderful people and I won't hear a word said against them, but it can't be denied that they are a teutonic race with all the regimentation that entails. Consequently, one of the best museums in the country—the largest of its kind in the world—will open its doors to you only if you are willing to see it as part of a guided tour and then only if there are at least seven, but no more than 50, people prepared to go with you.

With such ground rules I can hardly urge you to head off through cloudbursts or blizzards, but if you are in Graz and are willing to chance that there will be at least seven other people clustered at the entrance (a quite likely proposition, in fact), then by all means go there.

The armory occupies a four-story sixteenth-century building next door to the Landhaus, or provincial parliament, itself a renaissance building of some note. From the seventeenth to the nineteenth centuries the armory, or Zeughaus, served as the local storehouse for arms and munitions. The contents are of an exceptionally high quality, yet what makes the collection notable is the sheer wealth of items on display, some 30,000. Objects that other museums proudly set out singly or in pairs here march across the walls and hang from the ceilings in hundreds and sometimes thousands. Inlaid pistols, racks of guns, lances for jousting, powder horns, breastplates, swords, maces and armor for horses are laid out in neat rows and in magnificent profusion. The suits of armor, many bearing delicate inlays, are among the world's finest. The museum is open for only seven months a year. The rest of the year, I'm told, the staff spend their time polishing and de-rusting.

Details: The Graz Armory is at Herrengasse 16 and is open daily from the beginning of April to the end of October from 9 A.M. to noon, and from 2 to 5 P.M. on Monday, Tuesday, and Thursday. In July and August it is also open on Wednesday afternoons. Graz, capital of Styria and the second largest city in Austria with a population of about 250,000, is old and appealing and certainly worth a visit in its own right. The town's focal point is Schlossberg, which is reached by a funicular railway. Most of the castle was destroyed by Napoleon in 1810, but the clock tower is still standing and there are panoramic views from the summit. Interestingly, the castle dungeons have been converted into a theater; guests sit in former cells. Graz is about three hours southwest of Vienna by train.

The World's Strangest Lake, Burgenland

The Neusiedler See (or Lake Neusiedl) in eastern Austria is certainly the most bizarre and mysterious body of water in the world. It is the third largest lake in Europe, yet it is shallow enough to walk across. When the local prevailing wind, called the "windstau," blows steadily for several days, all the water rolls over to the westernmost corner, leaving the rest of the lakebed high and dry. Every century or so, the lake quietly disappears. (The last time was for two years in 1865–66.) Why it goes away no one knows. Nor does anyone know why the lake is salty, or how it maintains its depth; the only river flowing into it is tiny and replaces only 25 percent of the water lost daily through evaporation. Despite its size—22 miles long and up to nine miles wide—the Neusiedler See can be exceedingly difficult to find. Because of the tall dense reeds around its perimeter, you can be a few yards away from it without knowing it's there.

At some of the lakeside villages, notably Podersdorf, the reeds have been cleared away to provide beaches for swimming. But for the truly energetic, the place to go is Mörbisch on the first weekend in August for the annual footrace across the lake. Hundreds of contestants slog, swim, or flounder the two miles across the water to Illmitz. The record is 49 minutes and 35 seconds.

Unless you are accompanied by someone in a boat (which can be rented at most lakeside villages), you should not try the crossing. It's seven feet deep in places and, even if you manage to avoid the deeper pockets, three or four miles from shore is no place to get a cramp. Also beware that the southernmost quarter of the lake lies in Hungary. If you stray very far off course, you may find yourself encircled by armed patrol boats.

Details: The Neusiedler See is an easy trip by bus or train from Vienna or Graz. The principal lakeside communities—Podersdorf, Neusiedl am See, Rust, Mörbisch, and Illmitz—are linked by buses and motorboats. For bird-watchers, the area is the richest in Europe and at Neusiedl am See you'll find a museum containing more than 250 stuffed birds from the region. Another nearby curiosity is the hamlet of Chicago on the road to Bratislava—so named because 25,000 people emigrated from here to the Windy City around the turn of the century. For a few years the flow of dollars back to the region was so great that the greenback superseded the Austrian schilling as the local currency. Today Chicago is noted for being the easternmost community in Western Europe.

Vienna's Small Museums

London is perhaps the only city in Europe that can rival Vienna for the number of its museums, but none can approach it for the spread of interests that they cover. The city's 65 museums and galleries range from such famous attractions as the Museum of Fine Arts and Ephesus Museum to such decidedly specialized interests as the Esperanto Museum (at 1 Hofburg; open Monday, Wednesday, and Friday from 9–3:30) and the Undertaker's Museum (at Goldegasse 19; by appointment only). In between there's the Museum of the

History of Medicine, the Sigmund Freud Museum, the Museum of Folklore, and the Circus and Clown Museum—all fascinating. Add in the city's antique markets, coffee houses, concerts, and imperial architecture and you may be excused for wondering why anyone goes anywhere else.

Two of the very best small museums, usually overlooked, are the Clock and Watch Museum and the Tobacco Museum. The first houses an extraordinary collection of timepieces from the fifteenth century to the present day. Displayed over three floors in a charming old house are some 3,000 clocks and watches of every description, from the very tiniest wristwatch to a huge old clock that once graced the tower of a local cathedral. Perhaps the most remarkable is an astronomical clock from 1769 which makes a complete revolution once every 20,904 years.

Then there's the Tobacco Museum on Messepalast. Here you'll find everything connected with one of mankind's oldest and most peculiar habits. There are intricate cigar cases, the oldest pipe in Europe (carved in 1601), displays of live tobacco plants, paintings chronicling the history of smoking, and some absolutely knockout meerschaum pipes, for starters.

Space considerations preclude a discussion of the city's other museums, but the Austrian National Tourist Board publishes two excellent brochures in English—both, somewhat confusingly, called *Museums Vienna*—which provide brief descriptions, addresses, and opening times of all the city's museums. Get one, read it, and you will probably want to double the time you had planned to spend in Vienna.

Details: The Clock Museum (in German, Uhrenmuseum) is at Schulhof 2 (Tel. 63 22 65) and is open Tuesday through Friday from 10 A.M. to 4 P.M., Saturday from 2–6 P.M. and Sunday from 9 A.M. to 1 P.M. The Tobacco Museum is on Messepalast, but the entrance is at 2 Mariahilfer Strasse (Tel. 96 17 16). It's open on Tuesday from 10–7, Wednesday to Friday from 1–3 P.M. and Saturday and Sunday from 9 A.M. to 1 P.M.

BELGIUM

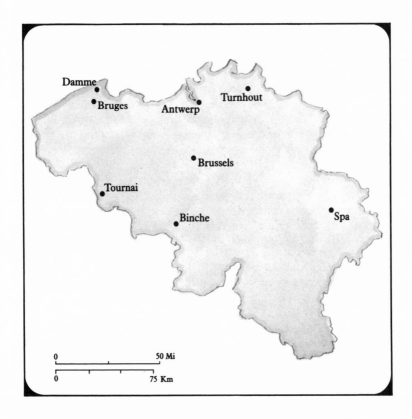

Damme

Bruges

Antwerp

Turnhout

Brussels

Tournai

Binche

Spa

0   50 Mi

0   75 Km

Museum of Musical Instruments, Brussels

Just off the picturesque Place du Petit Sablon in Brussels, in the Royal Conservatory of Music, is one of the city's best kept secrets—the Museum of Musical Instruments. Even the Belgian tourist authorities probably won't be able to tell you much about it without consulting their files. The museum houses 5,000 rare instruments from all over the world, dating from man's very earliest attempts at making music down to the present, with approximately 600 items on display at any one time. Here are trumpets from ancient Rome, old pianos, rare violins, harpsichords, spinets, and clavichords, all notable as much for their superb craftsmanship as for their historical value. And here also is the private collection of Adolphe Sax, the Belgian who invented the saxophone. In short, this is one of the most superb museums of its kind in the world. On alternate Wednesdays, concerts are held in the splendid concert hall using the original instruments. For anyone with even a passing interest in music, this collection is a must. It's free, but note below that its hours are a trifle bizarre.

Details: The Museum of Musical Instruments is open on Sunday mornings from 10:30–12:30, on Wednesdays from 5 P.M.–7 P.M., and on Tuesdays, Thursdays, and Fridays from 2:30 P.M.–4:30 P.M. For those with a deeper interest in the history of music, guided tours can be arranged by applying to the curator, Mr. R. de Maeyer. Tours cost 300 francs (125 francs for students).

While you're in the neighborhood, take time to stroll over to the Palais de Justice on the nearby Rue de la Regence—the most enormous building in the world in the nineteenth century. Rising to a height of 385 feet and containing 280,000 square feet of office space in its 245 rooms, this huge construction offers commanding views from its terraces.

Plantin-Moretus Museum, Antwerp

In a country as hard pressed for first-rate tourist attractions as Belgium it is astonishing that the Plantin-Moretus Museum in Antwerp remains in relative obscurity. This sixteenth-century townhouse on a quiet street in the heart of the city is one of the finest surviving examples of patrician Renaissance architecture in northern Europe. More than that, it is perhaps the best museum of the history of printing in the world.

The museum was the home and workshop of one Christoph Plantin, and it remained in the family from the founding of the business in 1549 until it was sold to the nation in 1876. In 1570, Plantin became typographer-in-chief to Philip II of Spain and his family thereafter enjoyed the sort of prosperity that only such a monopoly could bring.

The combination of a wealthy residence with a noisy, grimy workshop may seem a little odd to us today, but it was common enough in the fifteenth and sixteenth centuries. The living quarters, with their beamed ceilings and parquet floors, hand-tooled leather walls and splendid furniture, exude prosperity. But even so, the business of printing is everywhere. At each turn are priceless manuscripts, engravings, and ancient first editions, including a 1450 Bible attributed to Gutenberg. On the walls are several works by Rubens.

The workshops consist of a printing room with seven old presses, a proofreaders' room, composing room, and type room, as well as a display of the processes involved in making a book in the fifteenth to eighteenth centuries. Nowhere is there a better place to see how a middle-class family worked and lived over three centuries.

Details: The Plantin-Moretus Museum, at No. 22 Vrijdagmarkt (Friday Market) between Hoogstraat and Nationale Straat in central Antwerp, is open every day except national holidays from 10 A.M. to 5 P.M. Admission, as with other museums in the city, is free.

Bicycling Along the Bruges-Sluis Canal

For anyone who wants to savor the Belgian countryside—not always easy in a country as densely populated as this one—there is no better place to do it than on the Bruges-Sluis Canal and no better way than on bicycle. This tree-lined waterway runs through some tranquil (and blessedly flat) countryside and connects two of Belgium's loveliest towns, Bruges and Damme. The trip is only 8 kilometers but the energetic can follow the canal 5 kilometers farther into Holland to the market town of Sluis.

Bruges (Flemish: Brugge) is justly famous for its canals and medieval atmosphere and should be included on any Belgian itinerary. Damme, however, is now largely and surprisingly forgotten. The legendary home of Tijl Uilenspiegel, it is today a sleepy community of about 1,000 people, but its massive Church of Our Lady and Stadhuis (Town Hall) stand testimony to the fact that it was once one of the most important towns in northern Europe.

Renting bicycles is a breeze almost anywhere in Belgium. Thanks to a commendable scheme run by the national railways, you can rent a bike at any of 44 stations around the country and return it at any of 149, sparing you the necessity of retracing your steps. There are some curious omissions—you can, for instance, return a bike in Antwerp but you can't rent one there, and you can neither rent nor return in Brussels—but on the whole the country is well served by the arrangement. Damme, unfortunately, is not part of the system, so you'll either have to return the bike to Bruges or cycle on about six miles to the coastal resort of Knokke-Heist.

Details: Tourist offices throughout Belgium have leaflets on renting bicycles. The cost is 80–125 francs a day depending on how many days you're renting for. There are additional discounts for those with a valid rail ticket or rail pass. You can both hire and return in Bruges. Alternatively, but more expensively, bicycles can also be rented in Bruges from 't Koffiebootje, a tea room on Hallestraat, alongside the belfry tower near the market square. The cost is 180 francs a day plus a refundable deposit of 320 francs.

Belgium's Oldest Cathedral, Tournai

The Romanesque Cathedrale de Notre-Dame in Tournai is one of the most beautiful ecclesiastical structures in northern Europe. That it exists at all is something of a miracle since concentrated German bombing in World War II destroyed more than a thousand ancient buildings in Tournai—virtually the whole town. But Belgium's loss is the modern tourist's gain. After the war the city decreed that none of the surrounding buildings could be more than one story high. Thus the gray cathedral with its five towers (the tallest is 272 feet) escapes the claustrophobic clustering that obscures so many European churches.

The cathedral, built in 1110–1170, is the oldest in Belgium. Inside, you are struck immediately by the beauty of the stained glass windows and by how much vaster the structure seems from inside than out. (Portico to ambulatory is 440 feet.) Two other treasures are the restored Rubens painting *Souls in Purgatory* and the very ornate Renaissance rood screen, carved in colored marble by Cornelis de Vriendt in 1570–73. Note that in one of the reliefs a naked Jonah is seen disappearing into the mouth of the whale, but in the next emerges with his shirt on.

The real treasures of Tournai are, appropriately, to be found in the Treasury. These include some exquisite gold and silver chalices, carved ivories, a fifteenth-century Aras tapestry, a reliquary cross from the sixth or seventh century, and rare illuminated manuscripts.

Details: Tournai (pop. 70,000) is in the province of Hainaut about 40 miles west of Brussels near the French border and on the main road and rail line to Lille. Also of interest in town is a twelfth-century belfry, oldest in the country, at the far end of the main square across from the cathedral. It's a 260-step climb to the top, but the view is rewarding. At the Museum of Fine Arts can be found paintings by Breughel, Van Gogh, Manet, and David.

The Annual Mardi Gras at Binche

Every year just before Shrove Tuesday, the ancient community of Binche takes on the air of a city under siege. Shopkeepers and residents board up their windows. Mounted police arrive. A hushed air of expectancy descends over this town of 11,000 people midway between Mons and Charlerois. Very soon, everyone knows, there will be an attack by the Gilles—an army of 1,000 preposterously attired men with rhythm in their feet and a touch of malice in their hearts. The occasion is the annual Mardi Gras, the largest, noisiest, and in some ways most painful celebration in Europe. If you like your spectacles laced with physical abuse, then Binche on Shrove Tuesday is the place for you.

For more than four centuries, since a feast in 1549 to mark Pizarro's victory over the Incas in Peru, people have been congregating in Binche each year for three days of music and revelry. The highlight comes on Tuesday with the procession of Gilles, or clowns. As many as 1,000 of them dressed in intensely gaudy costumes with bells around their waists and four-foot-high plumed headdresses dance their way through the streets to the main square to the ceaseless cacophony of brass bands. An advance party of youths sprint ahead whacking the hapless with inflated sheeps' bladders (yes, it stings).

The Gilles themselves carry baskets full of oranges (Incas' gold) that they hurl—not lob—at the crowds as they pass. This explains the boarded windows and why people remove their eyeglasses and shelter small children as the procession approaches.

Depending on your inclination, the Binche Mardi Gras can be seen as an occasion for a bit of wanton revelry or as providing insight into a rather alarming side of the Walloon character. In any event, there's nothing to rival it this side of Rio.

Details: Binche is about 40 miles (or an hour's train trip) south of Brussels, near the French border. It's an interesting and historic old town enclosed by a twelfth-century fortified wall. If you miss the carnival, the Gilles' costumes can be seen at the International Carnival Museum (Le Musee International du Carnaval et du Masque) just off the Grand-Place in the heart of Binche. As its name suggests, the museum displays costumes not only from the local carnival but from carnivals throughout the world. If you do attend the carnival, watch your step. Squashed oranges are very slippery.

Spa

When you consider that health resorts have always been big business in Europe, it is somewhat surprising that the oldest of them all— the one from which all others derive their name—is now scarcely known. Although the days of greatness are long past for this little city tucked in a fold of the Belgian Ardennes, it clings to its charms.

The curative powers of the springs (or pouhons) at Spa were first noted by Pliny the Elder, and from the seventeenth to nineteenth centuries royalty from all over Europe flocked here, from Charles II of England to Peter the Great of Russia—attracted first by the spring water and later (and more sensibly) by its famous gambling casinos. In 1918, the town was headquarters of the German army; the Kaiser abdicated from here.

Though you can still drink a glass of spring water in the town's pump room (it tastes awful), you needn't have rheumatism or lumbago to make a visit worthwhile. Today Spa is simply a small, charming inland resort full of elegant villas and hotels and a whiff of anachronism. The flower-bedecked Avenue Reine Astrid, the town's main street, is cluttered with agreeable sidewalk cafes, and the Parc de Sept Heures, just off the Place Royale, is exceptionally pleasant for a stroll. The more energetic can wander into the local forests, heavily scented with pine and liberally dotted with welcoming inns, or down to the banks of Lake Warfaz, Belgium's loveliest lake. For children, a miniature train called Baladeuses circles the town. There's also tennis and horseback riding and a golf course said to be one of the most beautiful in Europe. And if all this palls, the elegant Casino, rebuilt in the first decade of the century, remains as good a place as any in Europe to lose your shirt.

Details: Spa (pop. 9,500) is 15 miles from Liege in southeastern Belgium and can be reached by train from Liege or Brussels (change at Pepinster). The local tourist office is at Rue Royale 2.

National Playing Card Museum, Turnhout

Since 1826, Turnhout's modest claim to fame has been as the playing card capital of Belgium, if not the world. Four factories (there were once six) produce playing cards by the billion. In 1977, the directors of the remaining factories decided to capitalize on this civic expertise by opening a National Playing Card Museum. Don't cancel all plans to get there, but if you're in the neighborhood on one of the three days each week that the museum is open, it offers a diverting and possibly unique way to pass an hour.

Playing cards have been distracting humanity from more serious matters since the second half of the fourteenth century. Originally they were painted by hand, often on blocks of wood, but it wasn't until the invention of lithography in the late eighteenth century that they really took off. The museum at Turnhout contains many rare examples of the earliest playing cards, including some from as far away as America and China, and the machinery used to make them. Although the traditional division of decks into four suits of 13 cards was a long time coming (and even now is by no means universal) it is remarkable that a 400-year-old jack of spades is clearly recognizable. If you've ever wondered why we have a jack of spades and king of diamonds instead of, say, an earl of rubies or a lord of roses, here's the place to find out.

Details: The National Playing Card Museum (National Museum van de Speelkaart) is in central Turnhout at Begijnenstraat 28, just north of the Grand-Place. It's open only 11 hours a week—on Sundays from 10–12 and 2–5, and on Wednesday and Friday afternoons from 2–5. Admission is 20 francs for adults and 15 francs for children. Turnhout is in northeastern Belgium about 6 miles from the Dutch border and only about 12 miles from Baarle-Hertog/Baarle-Nassau (see page 192).

DENMARK

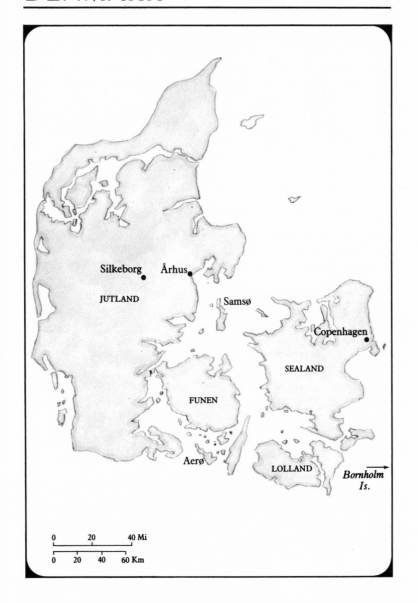

Silkeborg   Århus

JUTLAND

Samsø

Copenhagen

SEALAND

FUNEN

Aerø

LOLLAND

Bornholm Is.

| 0 | 20 | | 40 Mi |
| 0 | 20 | 40 | 60 Km |

World's Oldest Amusement Park, Copenhagen

Tivoli, in the heart of Copenhagen, is Europe's most famous amusement park and ought to be seen for this reason alone. But few people outside Denmark realize that the city boasts a much older and—dare I say?—rather less commercialized place to play on its northern fringe. Called Bakken, it is the oldest amusement park in the world. When the pilgrim fathers first set foot on Plymouth Rock, Bakken had already been around for a generation. Tivoli, some 250 years younger, is a mere infant in comparison.

Bakken may lack Tivoli's fame and rather self-conscious charm, but its air of conviviality is more genuine and its pleasures more spontaneous. More important, its rides are among the scariest in Europe. The roller coaster is perhaps a trifle tame by American standards, but Sky Lab, Alpine Races, and Big Octopus are all commendably terrifying while the Viking Ship and bone-shaking Rainbow are certified puddle-producers. If you're an amusement park freak or simply want to see the Danes at play, you'll leave Tivoli for your retirement trip.

Details: Bakken is open until midnight from mid-April to the end of August. Unlike Tivoli, admission is free, as are the stage performances, though you'll have to pay for the rides. It's a 20-minute journey on an S-train from the Central Station in Copenhagen to Klampenborg. From there it's a 10-minute stroll to the park. Bars, beer cellars, cafes, and restaurants abound. For a sit-down meal both the Lille Pater and Skovly restaurants on the grounds are very good.

A Visit to the Stone Age, Sealand

Most of what we know about early humans is based on a scattering of relics, a few cave paintings, a relative handful of primitive tools. From such fragments scientists have had to piece together a picture of what life was like in prehistory. But it was left to the vision of a Danish schoolboy to show whether there was any real basis for these sometimes elaborate conjectures. In 1954, Hans-Ole Hansen, then just 15, got the idea of building a stone age community using stone-age tools to test the hypotheses of how early humans worked and lived. The result today is the Historical-Archeological Experimental Center at Lejre, a unique and sprawling open-air laboratory and museum that covers almost every aspect of daily life from the stone age to the nineteenth century.

Here you'll find farms, workshops, and dwelling places inhabited by volunteers who live, work, dress, and even eat as the people of the time did. You can see how early roads were built, crops culti-vated, animals domesticated, and foods cooked. In the stone field you can watch experiments designed to discover how primitive tools were used to build such vast monuments as Stonehenge and Carnac; at Fire Valley children can participate in a variety of activities under supervision. A 3-kilometer path through the wooded countryside links the sites. There's a film show at the entrance and throughout the summer various demonstrations of ancient crafts like weaving, pottery, and flint-working. Not to be missed.

Details: The Research Center is open from May 1–September 26 and October 16–24 from 10 A.M. to 5 P.M. Admission is Kr25 for adults, Kr10 for children. You should allow a minimum of two hours to see all the sites.

There are trains from Copenhagen to Lejre and in the summer special bus connections run from Lejre Station to the Research Cen-ter. By car from Copenhagen, take the A1 motorway to the Roskilde exit. Turn right almost immediately onto the Holbaek road and then take the first left at the signpost for Ledreborg. From Ledreborg the route to the Research Center is well signposted.

Aalholm Castle and Car Museum, Lolland

This is probably the only place in the world where you can ride on a nineteenth-century steam train driven by a member of the European aristocracy. Aalholm Castle goes so far back in history that no one is quite sure just how old it is. Its 62 acres of grounds, which belong to Baron Johan Otto Raben-Levetzau, include one of Europe's largest vintage car museums, a ravishing model railway, and the baron's own steam train, on which you can take a 20-minute ride through the grounds and down to the Baltic and back. Evidently a fun-loving man, the baron often climbs into the locomotive himself to take a trainload of tourists for a spin. The car museum is one of the finest in the world and contains 200 automobiles, among them a very rare

Decauville, the car that inspired Henry Royce to design the Rolls-Royce.

But for my money the real winner is the 34 mm gauge model railway. The little trains run charmingly, if a bit predictably, through a panorama of towns and countryside. What's unique, however, is that the layout incorporates cycles of day and night, each lasting for a few minutes. Very effective.

You can also visit the castle itself. The first recorded mention of it was in 1328 when its owner, King Christopher II, suffered the not inconsiderable indignity of being poisoned in his own dungeon. The dungeon is still there to be seen, as are the vast dining room, knights' hall, ballroom, kitchens, and much else. This is a great spot to bring a child (or to pretend to be one).

Details: Aalholm Castle is just west of Nysted on the Rødby road, about two hours by road or rail from Copenhagen, on the island of Lolland. The grounds are open all year, but the castle, car museum, and model railway display are open only from May 29 to September 4 from 11 A.M. to 6 P.M.

Also in the area is Knuthenborg, the largest park in Europe. Among its 1,500 acres you'll find a safari park, a deer park, lots of rare trees, and open space.

The Bottle Ship Museum, Aerøskøbing

I don't suppose I'll get invited to many parties in Århus or Odense once I've said this, but Aerøskøbing, on the Isle of Aerø, is the most charming town in Denmark. It's a small (pop. 1,300), carefully preserved seventeenth-century seafaring community, full of quaint streets and brightly painted houses with overflowing flower boxes and intricately carved front doors, all clustered around a thirteenth-century church.

The preservation everywhere is remarkable. The Post Office dates from 1749 and the town is illuminated by cast iron gaslights. Even the public lavatory is neatly hidden away in an old cookhouse. Note as you stroll around the "busybody" mirrors on many of the houses. These jut out at carefully positioned angles so that the occupants can watch the doings of their street without actually exposing their faces at the windows.

On grounds of charm alone, Aerøskøbing is worth a long detour, but its main attraction—for me, at any rate—is the small, enchanting Bottle Ship Museum. A local retired ship's cook named Peter Jacobsen, known to one and all as Bottle Peter, painstakingly built more than 1,600 ships in bottles before his death in 1960. Some 750 of these small works, no two of which are quite the same, are now housed in the museum, along with a fascinating collection of seamen's pipes and other relics of the days when Aerøskøbing was home port for more than 100 windjammers.

Also not to be missed is Gunnar Hammerich's House, actually three seventeenth-century cottages knocked into one by a sculptor of some note who came to the island in 1914. Hammerich spent the next 39 years cramming his house almost to overflowing with antiques, fine porcelain, old maps, and rare prints. In 1943, he abruptly turned the whole lot over to the nation as a museum and moved on. Although many of the contents are exceptional, the real lure is the house itself—filled with incredibly narrow staircases and passages and tiny doorways. Unless you're a dwarf, you are guaranteed to bump your head at least a dozen times before you emerge into daylight and safety.

Details: Aerø lies off the south coast of Funen. There are frequent ferries between Aerøskøbing and Svendborg in Funen (a journey of about an hour and 15 minutes) and also from other points on the island to Jutland and Langeland. The tourist office is on Torvet, near the church. The Bottle Ship Museum is open June 1–August 31 from 9–11:45 A.M. and 1–5 P.M., and from September 1–30 from 10–12 and 2–4. Admission is Kr6. Hammerich's House is open in June, July, and August only, from 2–4 P.M. At the height of the season, from about June 20 to August 5, it is also open from 10–12 in the mornings. Admission is Kr3.

Egeskov Castle, Funen

Although Egeskov Castle is the most handsome moated fortress in Denmark—and possibly in Europe—relatively few non-Danes visit it. That the public isn't allowed into the building is probably the reason. But don't let this put you off. Just to see the outside is a memorable experience. Rising sheer from its little lake, the vast redbrick fortress, with its rounded towers and steep gables, seems to float eerily on the still waters. There's a sad story connected with it. In the seventeenth century, the owner had his sixteen-year-old daughter bricked up in a tower room after she had given birth to an illegitimate child. For five years her only communication with the outside world was via a small hole through which food and water were passed. Happily, upon her father's death her brothers let her out.

Surrounding the castle are 35 acres of exceptionally lovely gardens. Peacocks strut on the expansive lawns. Flowerbeds burst with color. There's a rose garden, a French style garden of box hedges, some wonderful topiary, and even a "biodynamic" herb garden. In a large former barn there's also a good collection of old cars, motorcycles, and aircraft—though with a separate entrance charge. One caveat: Egeskov is about two miles from the nearest railway station (at Kvarendrup) and bus services from there are poor.

Details: The park is open daily in the summer from 9 A.M. to 5:30 P.M. and from 9 A.M. to sunset in winter. The car and aircraft museum is open daily 9–6 from June 18 to August 31 and 10–5 from May 1–June 17, September 1–30, and October 15–23. It's also open on Saturdays and Sundays in April and October, but closed the rest of the year.

The whole area around Egeskov is rich with castles and manor houses. In fact, the triangle formed by Nyborg, Odense, and Svendborg contains more castles per square mile than anywhere else in the world apart from the Loire valley. The Danish Tourist Board produces an excellent booklet, *Danish Castles and Manor Houses*, which gives details of about 170 properties open to the public throughout the country.

Legoland, Billund

On a continent where land is often at a premium, Europeans have approached the matter of amusement parks with a compact alternative—the miniature village. Perhaps the best of these, and certainly the most unusual, is Legoland in central Jutland, which was started about 15 years ago as an eccentrically stunning way of demonstrating the almost limitless potential of the famous Lego toy brick. Using only the basic plastic brick and its 1,499 variants (windows, tiles, etc.), craftsmen from the Lego factory next door have constructed dozens of scrupulously accurate scale models of such monuments as the Taj Mahal, the Acropolis, the Amalienborg Palace in Copenhagen, the Temple of Rameses II, and most of central Amsterdam. There is an entire English market town, villages from Sweden, Germany, and Austria, an airport, and a Chinese pagoda. An Arab city from *A Thousand and One Nights* so enchanted one Arab visitor that he bought it on the spot and carted it home with him. Most stunning of all is a 45-foot-high model of Mount Rushmore, which took nine months to build and consumed 1.5 million toy bricks. Everything, right down to the pair of pince-nez spectacles on Teddy Roosevelt's nose, has been made entirely of standard Lego materials.

From this modestly ambitious beginning, the park has now sprawled to include rides for children (all modeled on Lego toys), a marionette theater, a cowboy town called Legoredo, a collection of antique dolls and dollhouses, educational exhibits, and even a museum of ephemera. For many visitors the most memorable attraction is Titania's Palace, the world's most elaborate and expensive dollhouse. Bought for almost $250,000 at an auction in London in 1979, it contains miniature paintings by leading nineteenth-century British painters, musical instruments that can actually be played, and other exquisite tiny treasures—all of it built as a birthday present for one very rich and lucky little English girl a century ago. If you're traveling with children, plan to devote a full day here—it could well be the high point of their trip.

Details: Legoland is in Billund in central Jutland between Århus and Esbjerg. It is open from May 1 to the last Sunday of September from 10 A.M. to 5:30 P.M. At the height of the season, from mid-June to mid-August, it stays open until 7:30 P.M. Its restaurants stay open slightly later. Admission is Kr25 for adults and Kr15 for children. The rides cost Kr6 apiece, but you can save by buying a book of 10 tickets for Kr40.

The Peat Men, Jutland

In 1950, two men digging peat in a bog near Silkeborg stumbled on one of the most remarkable archeological finds of the century. Nine feet below ground level they unearthed the perfectly preserved body of a man who had died 2,000 years before during the early Iron Age. Called the Tollund Man after the spot where he was discovered, he had been strangled in what was apparently a ritual execution in about his fortieth year. The leather plait he had been killed with still dangled around his neck.

Two years later a group of peat diggers near Graubelle came across a younger man who had lain undisturbed since having his neck cut from ear to ear 1,600 years before. Again, the murder was apparently inspired by ritual. As with the earlier discovery, the body was perfectly preserved—so well preserved, in fact, that scientists from Copenhagen were able to determine that he had eaten a bowl of scalded porridge for his last meal.

Today these two corpses form somewhat macabre but perennially fascinating centerpieces for two of the most remarkable museums in Denmark. The Tollund Man can be found in the local museum at Silkeborg, about 15 miles west of Århus. Only his head, still wearing the small leather cap he had on when he died, is on display, inside a glass case. The tannic acid from centuries in a peat bog has given his face a deep copper color, but otherwise the skin is unflawed. The expression he wears is strangely serene, almost holy. So startling is his appearance that upon seeing him most visitors fall immediately into an awed hush.

His younger counterpart, the Graubelle Man, can be found a few miles away at the Århus Museum at Moesgard, five miles south of the city. He lies naked in a reclining position. Again, the skin is copper colored and the state of preservation extraordinary. Of the two museums the one at Moesgard is unquestionably the finer. Its collection of Stone and Iron Age artifacts, runic stones, and Viking relics is one of the best in northern Europe. A two-mile "prehistoric trackway" leads off through the grounds past recreated prehistoric settlements from the Stone Age to Viking times emerging at a beach where you can swim. (You can also catch a bus back to Århus from there to avoid having to retrace your steps.)

The home of the Tollund Man, in contrast, is essentially a local museum, with a collection of old pottery, glassware, and furniture, though upstairs there is a more unusual collection of old door ornaments—hinges, doorknobs, locks, and keyholes. Yet the Tollund Man is somehow more moving and, given the choice of just one, I'd plump for him. The sight is one that will stay with you for a long time.

Details: The Silkeborg Museum is in the town's oldest building, on Hovegården. It's open April 15–October 15 from 10–12; the rest of the year it is open Wednesdays, Saturdays, and Sundays from 10–12 and 2–4. The town, which is about an hour's train journey from Århus, makes an excellent base for exploring the Danish lake district. Moesgard, set in the lovely grounds of an old manor house, can be reached by a No. 6 bus from Arhus Rail Station. It is open from 10 A.M. to 5 P.M.

Touring Samsø by Horse-drawn Wagon

The island of Samsø, sheltering in the pocket of sea between Jutland, Funen, and Sealand, is sometimes called the best of Denmark in miniature. A smallish place (it's about 20 miles long and five miles wide at its widest point), it is a pretty island of beech forests, quiet roads, and fertile farmland rolling down to a glistening sea. This part of the world begs to be explored at a gentle pace and there's probably no better way to do it than by horse-drawn wagon.

For your money, you get a simple wooden "prairie schooner," a Conestoga-type wagon under a canvas roof hitched to a pair of placid horses who will lead you on your prescribed daily route. The wagons can accommodate up to four people and come complete with cooking and eating utensils, fridge, and tiny stove. Familiarity with horses is helpful but not essential. As long as you know which end the oats go in you can't go too far wrong. You will in any case be given some instruction in their care before you set out. The daily route covers about 10 miles and delivers you each afternoon to a campsite where food and water are provided for the horses and a seaside setting for you. If you don't mind sleeping under canvas and have a week to spare, Samsø provides a wonderfully peaceful interlude for anyone making a hectic circuit of Europe.

Details: Further details and booking forms from Samsø Turistfor-ening, Turistbureauet, 8791 Tranebjerg, Samsø, Jutland. Tel. (06) 59 14 00. The cost of a wagon per week is Kr1800 from April 28–May 26 and from August 18–September 15; Kr2300 from May 26–June 23; and Kr2600 from June 23–August 18.

Samsø can be reached by ferry from Hov in Jutland (just south of Århus) and from Kalundborg in Sealand. Both voyages take between one and two hours. The tours begin every Saturday from Strandskoven Campground about a mile north of Ballen on Samsø.

Similar prairie wagons can also be rented on the island of Lange-lands (write to Langelands Turistbureau, Gåsetorvet 1, DK-5900 Rudkøbing) and on south Funen (write to Dantourist A/S, Hulgade 21, DK-5700 Svendborg).

Cycling on Bornholm

In a country whose highest hill is 416 feet shorter than the Eiffel Tower and whose mightiest waterfall drops just four feet, it should come as no surprise that cycling is a relatively effortless endeavor. Nowhere is this truer than on the handsome island of Bornholm. Not only is the topography comparatively undemanding, but the island is also well off the beaten track and liberally adorned with bicycle paths. A roughly circular island some 70 miles in circumference, cast adrift from Denmark and floating in the Baltic off the southern coast of Sweden, Bornholm is an eight-hour boat trip from Copenhagen (but less than two hours by boat from Simrishamm in Sweden). Its tranquil forests, farmlands, and two dozen or so little towns are home to about 50,000 people, with wide sandy beaches on the south coast and a more rugged coastline to the north.

At Rønne, the island's capital and principal port, you can rent bicycles from the local tourist office for exploring the island. Using the bike paths, you could make a three-day trip taking you up the west coast to the dramatically positioned ruins of Hammershus Castle, back down the opposite coast, and across country to Rønne through the beautiful Almindingen forest (Denmark's third largest) with its famous echo valley and ruined twelfth-century castle of Lilleborg.

In addition to bikes, the tourist office in Rønne can provide you with maps and detailed itineraries, advice on accommodation along the way, and help finding a place to stow any unwanted luggage for a couple of days. If you're looking to stretch your legs, this is an excellent place to do it.

Details: Bicycles can be rented for about Kr25 per day, plus deposit, from most of the larger Danish Tourist Board offices throughout the country. The one at Rønne is at Havnen, DK-3700 Rønne. Tel. (03) 95 08 10. It's open all year.

FINLAND

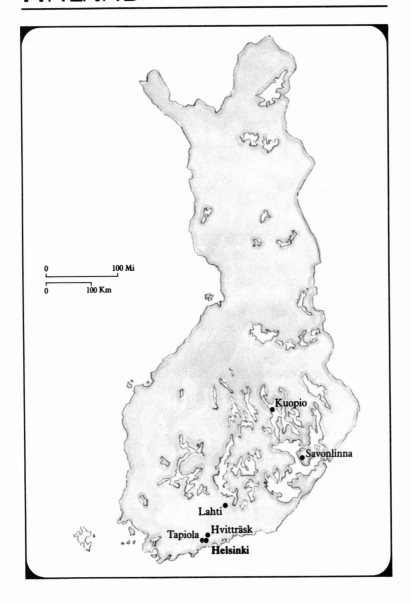

0   100 Mi

0   100 Km

• Kuopio

• Savonlinna

Lahti •

Tapiola • Hvitträsk
• Helsinki

The World's Best Suburb, Tapiola

One of the great curses of twentieth-century life is the development of the suburb. In a world teeming with these dreary, soulless places, Tapiola Garden City comes as a refreshing—and probably unique—change. In the 1950s, 12 Finnish architects were chosen to build a model community six miles west of Helsinki. The result was Tapiola (pop. 16,000), a perfect blend of homes and apartment houses, parks and fountains, shopping centers and small factories. If Walt Disney had seen this place, he'd have canceled Epcot.

Although Tapiola is widely famed among architects and city planners, it is scarcely known to tourists—no doubt because there are no traditional tourist attractions. One doesn't go to see museums or historic sights, but simply to stroll around randomly, admire the architecture, and savor a community that has been a stunning success from concept to execution. After 30 years, the architecture that was once a trifle stark and daring is now mellowing into a serene middle age.

An easy bus ride from Helsinki, Tapiola is definitely worth visiting. Or it could serve as your base with Helsinki as the place for outings.

Details: From the central bus station in Helsinki take any bus from platform 52 or 53. It's about a 20-minute ride.

Hvitträsk

In 1902, three young Finnish architects decided to undertake a unique joint enterprise—building a communal studio and three separate homes in one large structure on a woodland setting overlooking Lake Vitträsk, about 15 miles west of Helsinki. The architects were Armas Lindgren, Herman Gesellius, and Eliel Saarinen (the father of Eero Saarinen, designer of the Gateway Arch in St. Louis). Today their rambling home, called Hvitträsk, serves as museum, conference center, showcase for Finnish handicrafts, and monument to one of the most felicitous undertakings in modern architecture. Made of natural stone and wood and abounding with cupolas, gables, and latticed

30

windows, it dips and rises across the natural contours of the landscape and serves as a perfect complement to the surrounding forest and lake. The grounds are graced with the architects' own sculpture and there is an excellent restaurant in one of the many outbuildings. A path leads to a small beach on the lake.

Inside, the house is also redolent of wood and stone. Saarinen's portion is preserved much as he left it, with examples of embroidery by his wife, a vast ceramic fireplace designed by Louis Sparr, and furniture crafted by the architect himself. Elsewhere in the house are frequent exhibits of Finnish handicrafts. For anyone interested in domestic architecture or modern design, Hvitträsk is a must.

Details: Hvitträsk is open in summer from 10 A.M. to 8 P.M. on weekdays and from 12 P.M. to 7 P.M. on weekends. The restaurant is open from 12 P.M. to 10 P.M. on weekdays and until 8 P.M. weekends.

From Helsinki, you can take a bus from platform 62 of the central station (a 45-minute ride) or an electric train to Masala or Kauklahti stations; both are about a mile from the home, but taxis are available if you don't want to walk. By car, take the Jorvas motorway to the Kivenlahti exit, then drive about three miles to Kauklahti and follow the signs to Hvitträsk.

Seurasaari Open Air Museum, Helsinki

Scandinavians have a passion for open air museums, no doubt because they have a passion for the open air. One of the biggest in Scandinavia—and probably the most accessible for those not wandering very far from the main tourist routes—is Seurasaari. Founded in 1909, it consists of more than 100 buildings, from primitive turf-roofed huts to a rococo manor house, gathered from all over Finland.

More than most other open air museums, Seurasaari goes in for demonstrations: at almost every turn you'll find groups of people in contemporary costumes performing traditional dances, playing folk music, or giving dramatic renderings of historical plays. In the farm buildings and houses artisans are engaged in traditional crafts such as spinning, weaving, and lacemaking—making it seem very much a living community. Even in the seventeenth-century church, the oldest building in the park, religious services are still held every Sunday. Midsummer is the biggest day of the year here, as in the rest of Scandinavia, and bonfires burn throughout the night, and the air is filled with music and revelry.

Seurasaari is on a wooded island, connected to the mainland by a wooden footbridge. Even before the museum was thought of, this was a traditional haunt for Helsinki office workers seeking fresh air and an escape from city life. Today it's a national park. The museum takes up only about a third of the island's space; the rest consists of wooded walks and small beaches for swimming.

Details From June 1 to August 31, the museum is open from 11:30 A.M. to 5:30 P.M. (and till 7 P.M. on Wednesdays). At other times, hours vary and only some buildings are open. Check with the tourist offices or phone 484-712. From central Helsinki, take the number 24 bus to the end of the line (a 15-minute ride).

Gallen-Kallela Museum, Helsinki

Askeli Gallen-Kallela (1865–1931) was a leading force in modern Finnish art who painted in the haunting style of his good friend Edvard Munch. If you're not familiar with his work, don't worry. The principal attraction of his studio home in suburban Helsinki is not so much the paintings as the house itself. In spirit it is similar to the more famous studio-home at Hvitträsk (see earlier entry). Eliel Saarinen, one of Hvitträsk's founders, actually drew the original plans, which Gallen-Kallela later discarded in favor of his own. From the outside, the house looks deceptively like a medieval Finnish church with its arched veranda and octagonal belfry. But inside it couldn't be more secular.

Like many Victorians, Gallen-Kallela was a man of boundless energies, an inveterate traveler and relentless dabbler. He filled his house with souvenirs of his travels—African drums, crocodile skins, inlaid boxes from the Far East—and with his own manifold handiworks: paintings, tapestries, stained glass, posters, pieces of furniture, all arranged with almost obsessive care.

The home's focal point is a large studio with a bank of sloping windows taking up the whole of one wall and a long pine refectory table dominating the middle. The other walls are littered with an extraordinary, but strangely harmonious, assortment of knickknacks—a pair of snowshoes, the skull of a caribou, a pickaxe, a rack of skis. In front of a walk-in fireplace there's a rocking chair and an easel with a painting of a nude and brushes at the ready, as if the artist had only just been called away. You'll feel more like a secret intruder than a visitor to a museum.

Details: The museum is open from mid-May to mid-September from 10 A.M. to 10 P.M. Tuesday to Thursday and from 10 A.M. to 5 P.M. Friday to Sunday. It's closed Mondays. From central Helsinki, take a bus from platform 31B at the bus station (to Leppävaara) or the number 4 tram to the end of the line. From both destinations the museum is a pleasant walk of about a mile.

Poster Museum, Lahti

Of all the applied arts, perhaps none has attracted less acclaim than the advertising poster. In 1975, the Finns, who are among the world's leaders in the field, decided to do something about this oversight by establishing an international poster museum at Lahti, a small industrial city of 95,000 people about 64 miles north of Helsinki. Today, the Lahti Poster Museum, an annex of the city's art museum, has 13,000 posters from all over the world.

The range of inventiveness is astonishing. Consider for a moment what a good poster must do: attract attention, convey a message at a glance, invite more studied reflection, and, in general, amuse and inspire. Not an easy challenge. Many of the posters at Lahti achieve all this in indecipherable tongues, making them no less arresting but infinitely more intriguing. What, for instance, does a photograph of a white mouse on a hunk of Swiss cheese under the message "Vuoden Huippukirja" signify? And a globe of the earth in a chamber pot under the message "Pallo on nyt meilla"?

To increase its poster stock, the museum has hit on a canny scheme. In odd-numbered years it holds an international contest, the Lahti Poster Biennale, which runs from mid-May to early September. After the judging, the best posters become part of the permanent collection.

Details: Lahti is about 1½ hours by train from Helsinki on the main line to Leningrad. The museum is at Vapaudenkatu 22 and is open daily from 11 A.M. to 7 P.M.

Orthodox Church Museum, Kuopio

Linguistically and historically the Finns are more closely related to Estonia and Hungary than to the rest of Scandinavia. For evidence, you have only to look at the language—a bewildering agglomeration of vowels that bears almost no relation to any other Western European language—and to the continued presence in Finland of the Orthodox Church.

Although only one percent of Finland's 4.7 million people belong to the church, it is still an important force, particularly in the country's eastern parts. The small, modern city of Kuopio (pop. 72,000) is the seat of Orthodoxy in Finland and there, in the Orthodox Church Museum, you will find the finest collection of Orthodox treasures in Western Europe.

The museum, an elegant modern building on two floors, was opened in 1969. Its most treasured relic is a stunningly beautiful seventeenth-century icon of the Virgin Mary, but more than 2,000 icons, vestments, and other objects are on display in the museum's 13 rooms. Watch in particular for the very fine communion set in Room 3, originally intended as a gift to Ethiopia by Ivan the Terrible. He decided it wasn't impressive enough and gave it to the Finns instead.

Even if you have no interest at all in the Orthodox Church or religious art, don't bypass this museum if you're in Kuopio.

Details: The Orthodox Church Museum is at 10 Venemiehenkatu in the northern part of central Kuopio. Kuopio itself is a cultural and economic center and the largest town in the Saimaa Lakeland district. Lake steamers from there can take you to most other communities in the district, including Savonlinna (see next entry).

Savonlinna Opera Festival

What does it take to make a perfect opera festival? Well, first you must build a castle of massive ramparts and brooding towers, then allow it to mellow for 500 years, and, finally, invite some of the world's leading opera companies to perform there in the open air for three weeks every July. It's a foolproof formula.

Those who consider a night at the opera about as pleasurable as major surgery have to be impressed by the majestic setting of Savonlinna's annual musical outburst. The festival is held in the courtyard of Olavinlinna Castle, a commanding fortress built in 1475 on an island in the Kyronsalmi Straits. The castle, claimed as the finest medieval building in Scandinavia, is compelling even when there is no opera. Its three towers, thick stone walls, and lakeside setting impart a romantic air that belies the building's violent history and invite comparisons with the smaller but more famous Chillon Castle in Switzerland. Reached either by boat from Tallisaari Island in the old section of town or by wooden footbridge, Olavinlinna Castle contains a number of large and carefully restored rooms and a chapel still frequently used for church services and weddings. Views across Finland's largest lake are memorable.

Savonlinna, a handsome town of 29,000 people and vacation resort about 225 miles northeast of Helsinki, makes an excellent base for anyone touring the Saimaa Lakeland district. Called the Land of a Thousand Islands (actually a misnomer; there are 33,000 islands), Saimaa is a complex system of interconnected waterways. Lake steamers connect Savonlinna to the other important lake towns, most notably Kuopio (see previous entry) and Lappeenranta.

Details Olavinlinna Castle is open from 8 A.M. to 8 P.M. throughout the summer. The opera festival, normally held in the first three weeks of July, includes more than 50 events—concerts, lectures, and exhibitions, as well as about 15 opera performances. Reservations (strongly urged) and details are available from the Savonlinna Opera Festival, Olavinkatu 35, SF-57130 Savonlinna 13, Finland (Tel. 957 22 684).

FRANCE

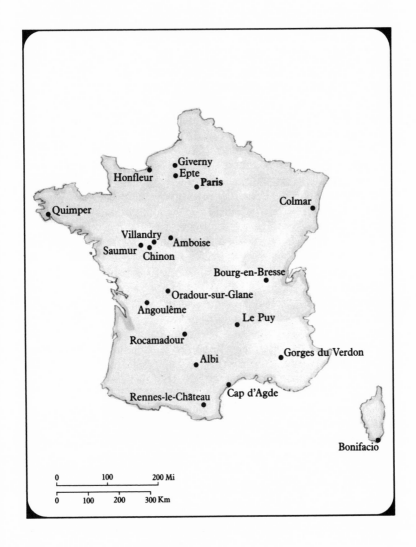

Giverny
Honfleur
Epte
Paris

Quimper

Colmar

Villandry
Saumur
Chinon
Amboise

Bourg-en-Bresse

Oradour-sur-Glane
Angoulême

Le Puy

Rocamadour

Gorges du Verdon

Albi

Rennes-le-Château
Cap d'Agde

Bonifacio

0   100   200 Mi

0   100   200   300 Km

Père Lachaise Cemetery, Paris

Père Lachaise has long been a magnet for an eccentric assortment of little old ladies, hero worshipers, necrophiliacs, families out for a Sunday stroll, and the romantic young of Paris. It is infrequently visited by outsiders, which is both surprising and unfortunate because, quite simply, it's one of the most remarkable cemeteries in the world.

Spread across 100 acres on a hillside in the unfashionable 20th arrondissement, Père Lachaise is a densely packed jumble of tombs, necropolises, temples, mausoleums, and tiny chapels, some no bigger than a phone booth. There's even a small-scale version of the Taj Mahal, built for the one Indian among the almost one million people who have been buried here since the cemetery opened in 1804.

Strolling along the curving pathways you'll find the graves of some of the most famous—and often most notorious—names of the last two centuries. Oscar Wilde, Isadora Duncan, Gertrude Stein, Cyrano de Bergerac, Edith Piaf, and the rock star Jim Morrison are all buried here. So too are Chopin, Delacroix, and the playwright Alfred de Musset, all lovers of George Sand (who is, curiously, buried elsewhere). Modigliani is interred alongside his mistress, Jeanne Hebuterne, who committed suicide on the news of her lover's death. Marcel Proust, more circumspectly, is tucked up snugly in a granite tomb with his father and brother. Oscar Wilde can be found in a grave topped by a life-sized statue that is, you'll note, devoid of private parts. These were lopped off some years ago by a pair of scandalized English spinsters and are now rumored to be serving as a paperweight in the cemetery warden's office. Many other Frenchmen and women who died earlier—among them Molière, Balzac, and the lovers Héloise and Abelard—were transferred here later.

For Parisiens, the most famous monument is that of Victor Noir, a nineteenth-century journalist shot down on the streets of Paris at the age of 22 after writing an article critical of the emperor. He no doubt would have been forgotten long ago except that the artist who sculptured his memorial gave Noir a bulge in his breeches that can only be described as awesome. Women come from miles around to touch the statue in the hope of becoming pregnant.

Details: Père Lachaise Cemetery, just by the Metro station of the same name, is open from 7:30 A.M. to 6 P.M. from mid-March to November 5 and from 8:30 A.M. to 5 P.M. the rest of the year. On Sundays throughout the year it is open from 9 A.M. to 5 P.M. Admission is free. Maps of the more famous graves are available for about 4 francs from the wardens at the entrance gate.

Perfume Museum, Paris

For those of us always darkly suspicious about perfume, and who blanch at forking over a large stack of money for a teensy bottle of what is after all mostly scented water, the Musée de la Parfumerie Fragonard in Paris is something of an eye-opener. It may not convince us Philistines that perfume really is a good deal and money well spent, but it does demonstrate quite convincingly that the making of perfume is a complicated and painstaking business with a long and noble history.

Opened in 1983, the perfume museum is one of the newest and most elegant small attractions in Paris. It resides above the equally elegant premises of La Parfumerie Fragonard at 9 rue Scribe, where the stately salesroom has more the air of a private salon than a place of commerce, and the museum, with its chandeliers, parquet floors, and Louis Quatorze trimmings, reinforces the impression with cool assurance.

Here you'll find old copper stills standing incongruously amid the finery, along with almost everything else connected with the exceedingly ancient art of aromatics. Fragonard's own products are actually made in Grasse, far away in the south of France, but by an effective blend of old implements, raw ingredients, books, ancient recipes, and photographs the museum is able to provide a pretty thorough explanation of the history and manufacture of perfume.

The objects on display date from 3000 B.C. to the present. Particularly impressive are the phials, jugs, and bottles that once contained perfumes, many of them from ancient Greece, Rome, and Egypt. The one shortcoming of the museum is that all the explanatory notes are in French, yet the displays themselves will give you a clear enough idea of how perfume is made. Best of all—and a great rarity in Paris—the museum is free, a consideration that can help to soften the blow considerably if you should pause to make a purchase in the store below on your way out.

Details: La Parfumerie Fragonard (Tel. 742 04 56) is at 9 rue Scribe, just across from the Opera House.

Monet's Garden, Giverny

In 1883, after much searching, the artist Claude Monet took his wife and eight children to live in the village of Giverny in the Epté valley of Normandy. The family was desperately poor. As Monet himself recalled years later: "There was nothing but a farmhouse and a poor orchard. Little by little I enlarged and organized it. I dug, planted, weeded it myself. In the evenings the children watered."

What eventually emerged was one of the loveliest small gardens in France—nearly as valuable, to my mind, as anything the artist ever committed to canvas. After Monet's death the garden fell into neglect. But, in 1981, Monet enthusiasts began to restore it to its original state, using Monet's own paintings and photographs for guidance. Today it is as glorious as it was in the artist's lifetime and open to the public.

Monet crammed in his flowers almost to choking point. The garden around the low farmhouse is a riot of color—pinks, oranges, reds, whites, yellows, and blues mingle in splendid confusion. It is as if an English garden had been transplanted to France, creating an infinitely more relaxed and inviting effect than the formalized geometrical layouts more characteristic of the country. Across the road, reached by a tunnel, is the water lily pond immortalized by Monet in his famous painting of 1899. A Japanese-style bridge arches gracefully over the water and a path meanders around the pond's edge. Here the effect is more subtle—of cool greens and muted tranquility. If you can't remember the famous painting offhand, you'll almost certainly recall it the instant you emerge from the tunnel. (If your memory still deserts you, copies of *The Water Lily Pond* and other paintings inspired by the garden are on sale in the artist's former studio.)

The pink farmhouse with its green shutters and steps has been restored too and is open for inspection. Inside, the kitchen's polished range and copper pans show that Monet was a man who took his food seriously. A dining room entirely in yellow leads into a tiny sitting room containing Monet's treasured collection of Japanese prints. But in every room it is the garden that beckons to you through the open doors and windows. This is an enchanting place.

Details: Giverny is near Vernon, just off the main road and rail links between Paris and Rouen. From the station at Vernon it's a three-mile walk or taxi ride to Monet's house. The garden and house are open from early April to the end of October from 10–12 and 2–6. Closed Mondays. Admission is 15 francs.

Church of Ste. Catherine, Honfleur

If you think time sometimes has a habit of getting away from you, consider the people of Honfleur in Normandy. In 1468, at the end of the Hundred Years War, they erected the wooden church of Ste. Catherine and its separate bell tower as a temporary measure until something more permanent could be built in stone. Today, half a millennium later, Ste. Catherine is still awaiting its replacement— and still looking more than a little impermanent. Much of the air of transience comes from the lean-to wooden struts that rather clumsily prop up the weatherboarded belfry, as if holding it in place until the workmen come back from lunch. Superficially, the church is similar to a Scandinavian stave church, but its architectural details also convey a decidedly nautical air—not surprising perhaps since it was built by unemployed ships' carpenters. This is especially apparent in the spacious interior where the vaulting resembles an upturned ship's hull.

Apart from this curious old church, Honfleur offers much else. In the sixteenth and seventeenth centuries it was one of the most important ports in Europe, and its age of greatness lives on in the old quarter by the harbor with its tall, narrow houses, some up to seven stories high, and rich shipbuilders' homes. A plaque on one notes that from here the town's most famous native son, Samuel de Champlain, set sail in 1608 to found Quebec. The area is a gift to the stroller and littered with agreeable sidewalk cafes. Honfleur was also a center of the impressionist movement in art. Monet, Renoir, Pissarro, Corot, and Cézanne all worked here, influenced by another local, the artist Eugene Louis Boudin. As a result, the Boudin Museum in Honfleur now has an outstanding collection of paintings from that period. The town makes an excellent starting point for exploring the Corniche Normande, Côte Fleurie, and the graceful countryside of Normandy, but if you are pressed for time you need go no farther than the celebrated local beauty spot known as the

Côte de Grace with its beautiful views across the Seine estuary and up the river to the big bridge at Tancarville.

Details: Honfleur (pop. 10,000) is not on a railway line, but it can be reached by bus in about an hour from the railway stations in Le Havre or Caen.

France's Cornwall, Quimper, Brittany

Quimper is a handsome and, uncharacteristically for Brittany, rather elegant little city of bridges, cobbled streets, and spired vistas set in a valley on the westernmost prong of France. It is the political capital of the department of Finistere and the spiritual capital of a part of France more closely linked by tradition to Britain and Ireland than to Paris. Celtic invaders 1,500 years ago gave the region bagpipe music, a language (Breton, still spoken by about a million people), a fierce sense of independence, and many place names—most notably the ancient name for the region, Cornouaille, which is simply Cornwall rendered into French.

Quimper's principal landmark is its Cathedral of St. Corentin (who, like many other Breton saints, is not recognized by the Vatican), which dates from the thirteenth century, although its most felicitous features, twin gothic spires, were not added until 1856. As you step inside, you'll immediately notice that the choir and nave are noticeably out of alignment—a remarkable piece of bodging in a structure that took 300 years to build. Quimper is also the home of a very good museum, the Beaux Arts (in the Place St. Corentin by the cathedral), which possesses works by Rubens, Boucher, and Fragonard. If time is at a premium, simply head for the old part of town, the vieux quartier, for lunch at a creperie and a very pleasant hour's wandering along the narrow streets.

As a base for excursions Quimper is practically unbeatable. A boat trip down the River Odet to the seaside resort of Benedot (very pretty with good beaches) and on to the fishing port of Loctudy is wonderful. Try also to find time to take in the lovely village of Locronan and the ancient walled town of Concarneau. A bit to the west is Pointe du Raz, Brittany's Land's End—the westernmost point in the country. It can be blustery at times (people have in fact been blown off the cliffs), but the rocky outcroppings and thundery surf are memorable. Public transportation in the area ranges from erratic to appalling, but bicycles can be rented reasonably at Locavelo

107, Avenue Ty-Bos. This whole area is a jewel and shouldn't be missed.

Details: Quimper is about six hours from Paris by train. As with anywhere in France within sniffing distance of the sea, it becomes packed in late July and the whole of August, but is extremely quiet the rest of the year. The best time for a visit is the fall, which lingers seductively in this part of the country for weeks and weeks.

Leonardo da Vinci Museum, Amboise

Few men are more indelibly associated with a time and place than Leonardo da Vinci with Renaissance Italy. If you wish to see his works of art, then of course you should go to Italy. But if it is the man himself you are after, head instead for the Loire valley and the fetching riverside town of Amboise. Leonardo spent three contented years here up to his death in 1519 under the patronage of the youthful King Francois I, who lodged him in the Chateau Clos-Lucé (then called Chateau Cloux), a small but very attractive fifeenth-century manor house. Though Leonardo executed no great works in his time here, he may have designed parts of the chateau at Chambord and the famous staircase at Blois.

Clos-Lucé has been restored and refurnished much as it was in Leonardo's time. Some of the contents are quite rare (a Dürer portrait of Maximilian I) and some simply very appealing (a huge chest in the kitchen designed as part breadbin, part servant's bed). But the heart of the museum is found in three basement rooms that house a fascinating collection of working models faithful to the famous sketches in Leonardo's notebooks. These include a flying machine, a swingbridge, an air-conditioning system, a turbine engine, and a parachute, among much else. Nothing I know of more visibly demonstrates the fertile range of Leonardo's genius. With the exception of the flying machine, all could have been made to work if the craftsmen of Leonardo's day had possessed the necessary skills and materials.

An underground tunnel, still in existence but not open to the public, links Clos-Lucé to Francois' own chateau down the road. In the fifteenth century this was the largest building in the Loire valley, though much of it was destroyed in the Revolution. It continues to dominate the town and is well worth a visit if only to see the small and exquisite chapel of Saint-Hubert, built in 1493 in an exuberant style. Inside, a simple stone claims to mark Leonardo's burial place, but you should regard it with some skepticism. His original burial place, also on the castle grounds, was destroyed and several years later workmen searching the original graveyard found a skull with a "notable brow"; on the basis of that evidence alone they concluded it was Leonardo's. The bones in Leonardo's grave belong, likely as not, to someone else.

Details: Amboise (pop. 8,000) is about 120 miles southwest of Paris on the main rail line to Bordeaux. Express trains will get you there in about two hours. The chateau, which dominates the town, is closed in February but otherwise is open daily from 9–12 and 2–7 (until 6 in winter). Clos-Lucé is an easy stroll from the chateau along the Rue Victor Hugo and has the same opening times.

World's Most Unusual Vegetable Garden, Villandry

The gardens of the Chateau Villandry in the Loire valley are among the most elaborate and unusual in Europe. Although originally laid out during the Renaissance, their present appearance dates only from 1906 when a certain Dr. Carvalho took over the chateau and began the long project of restoring them to their original glory. The gardens are set in a series of formal terraces. The most interesting and unusual is the vegetable garden where the main fruits and vegetables of the sixteenth century—cabbages, chicory, leeks, strawberries, lettuces, and the like—are arranged in formal patterns to delight the eye rather than the palate. There's nothing like it anywhere else.

On another terrace scrupulously clipped box hedges are arrayed in ornate patterns—a Maltese cross, a fleur de lys, and so on—interspersed with decorated boxes representing the four kinds of medieval love: tender, tragic, adulterous, and fickle. In the third terrace are fountains and a lake. From the highest of the terraces, lined with 300-year-old lime trees, good views of the garden abound and span across the valley to three other chateaux—Langeais, Cinq-Mars, and Luynes.

To my mind, this sort of gardening represents not so much a love for nature as a determination to beat it into submission. Not a leaf is out of place; the hedges and rows of yew trees are so exquisitely cropped they seem almost artificial. At the same time you cannot fail to be impressed by the scale of the project, and its clipped, formal precision is undeniably awesome. If you are at all interested in the history of gardening, Villandry is one of the three or four gardens of Europe you must see.

Details: Chateau Villandry is just west of Tours on the D7 road. It is open throughout the year from 9 A.M. to 7 P.M.

Chinon, Loire Valley

If you're in the market for memorable experiences, come to Chinon on an early spring morning and pause for a moment by the handsome stone bridge across the River Vienne. Ahead of you lies a sleepy, prosperous wine town largely unchanged since the fifteenth and sixteenth centuries, overshadowed by a vast fortress, its dazzling white stone gleaming in the morning sun. Wander into the town and you'll find steep narrow streets and alleys that command exploration. Ancient half-timbered houses with turreted roofs and projecting overhangs jostle together. Most are 500 years old; a few date from the twelfth century. Select a sidewalk cafe overlooking the river on the Quai Charles VII, order croissants and a big cup of coffee as the town stirs to life, and, with any luck at all, you might just think you've died and gone to heaven. Fortified, you can then consider the steep climb up through the twisting lanes to the chateau.

Chinon chateau is one of the most historic in France—in fact, from here we can trace the long association of French kings with the Loire valley. The chateau was built by Henry II, who died here in 1190. Here also, in 1429, the young Joan of Arc had her first meeting with Charles VII. Thinking he would make sport of an 18-year-old country girl, the king secreted himself among his 300 courtiers in the vast Grand Salle. But Joan, on being shown into the hall, strode up to the king without a flicker of hesitation—a display of astuteness that had a profound effect on Charles and on French history. The hall is now mostly in ruins—a fireplace hanging on one wall shows the former floor level—but still strangely evocative. One of the towers houses a small Joan of Arc museum. Much of the rest of the chateau—actually three chateaux melded into a harmonious whole—was despoiled by Cardinal Richelieu, who took the stone to build his nearby dream city of Richelieu. But it still retains its majestic scale and glorious views and—as added incentive—is one of the few monuments in France you can visit without being hectored by a guide.

Details: Chinon (pop. 6,000) is about 25 miles southwest of Tours on the N751, but it is more memorably approached from the direction of Loudon or Poitiers. The chateau is open in summer from 9–12 and 2–7 and every day but Wednesday from 9–12 and 2–5:30 in the off season. Closed December and January. The local campground, on the south side of the bridge over the Vienne, is one of the loveliest settings in Europe. Some guidebooks wrongly give Chinon as the birthplace of Rabelais. Although he lived for a time in Chinon (at 15 Rue Lamproie), his birthplace was the nearby village of La Deviniere, in a simple stone farmhouse, now a museum. Open from 9–12 and 2–7 (9–12 and 2–5 off season; closed December and January), it's an interesting diversion.

Chateau Museum, Saumur

Before you mutter, "Oh, God, another chateau" and start flipping pages, hold on. The Chateau of Saumur, a fourteenth-century fortress-like building, contains two of the most fascinating small museums in France, both the result of local bequests. The more unusual is the Museum of the Horse, which has a floor to itself upstairs. Its contents, bequeathed to the town by a veterinarian in 1911, trace the history of the horse from prehistoric times to the present. The centerpiece is the enormous skeleton of one of history's greatest racehorses, Flying Fox from Britain, which won every race it ran around the turn of the century. You won't doubt the record when you see the horse's size. There's also an eclectic assortment of intriguing odds and ends—a cowboy saddle from the American West, one from Samurai Japan, another designed by Catherine de Medici, riding bits from ancient Greece, the fossilized skeleton of an early North American horse no bigger than a dog, and much, much else. On one wall is a very fine engraving of another great horse, Godolphin Arabian, given as a gift to Louis XIV. The king, normally a shrewd judge of horseflesh, didn't like Godolphin and sold it. An astonished English tourist spotted the horse pulling a water cart in Paris, bought it for a pittance, and took it home. Today every thoroughbred in Britain and most of America are its descendants. Even if your experience of equestrianism goes no further than rocking horses and merry-go-rounds, you won't fail to be fascinated by this museum.

Downstairs is the Museum of the Decorative Arts, which houses not the usual worthy but boring assortment of bits and pieces, but some really quite fascinating old furniture, tapestries, paintings, and carved wooden statuettes, plus an excellent collection of fine china, some 1,300 pieces, all left to the museum by a local benefactor in 1919. Predictably, but tiresomely, you will be escorted around the premises by a guide, who will lock doors behind her and whisk you through in about an hour. But if you smile sweetly and look honest, you may be allowed back in for a more leisurely perusal.

The grounds of the chateau offer pleasant gardens with a picnic area and good views over the town. It all looks so peaceful you'll find it hard to believe that for three days in 1940 more than a thousand bombs rained down on the city. If you're still in the mood for offbeat attractions, a few miles outside town on the D751, at Chênehutte-les-Tuffe, there is an interesting little mushroom museum in a cave dug into the hills. A guided tour takes you about half a mile into the hillside where you witness the whole process of production from the spreading of sterilized mycelium (the spores) to the development of full-sized mushrooms up to five inches across.

Details: Saumur (pop. 23,000) is about 30 miles west of Tours (a 40-minute journey by train) and about 10 miles from Chinon (see page 45). The chateau museum is open April 1 to September 30 from 9–12 and 2–6, and the rest of the year from 10–12 and 2–5. Closed Tuesdays throughout the year. The mushroom museum is open from 9–12 and 2–6 from mid-March to mid-November.

Monument to a Massacre, Oradour-sur-Glane

On June 10, 1944, four days after the Allied forces landed in Normandy, a detachment of German soldiers, assisted by 13 Frenchmen, rolled into the small town of Oradour-sur-Glane in the sleepy Limousin countryside near Limoges. It was a warm, sunny day, just after noon. The soldiers herded the village's 445 women and children into the church and its 197 men into a barn and garage, then systematically set fire to every house and cold bloodedly shot all the villagers—642 people, 205 of them children. To this day no one knows why. Oradour had no connections with the Resistance movement and was so far removed from the war that in three years of occupation not one German soldier had been to the town. Only about two dozen villagers survived—a few because they hid, others because they were out of town. One woman lost 23 members of her family.

Today Oradour stands virtually unchanged from that day, a stark and silent memorial to a heartless massacre. A large sign over the entrance carries a simple message in French and English: "Souviens-Toi. Remember." Walking through the empty, burnt-out streets you find rusting cars sitting where their owners left them, bicycles still propped against walls, a baby carriage hauntingly forlorn. In the rubble you'll spy pieces of scarred furniture, a sewing machine, old bed frames. The effect is unutterably sad. On a continent filled with shameful memorials to the ferocity of war, Oradour is perhaps the most moving and least visited. Remember.

Details: Oradour-sur-Glane is about 10 miles northwest of Limoges on the D9 road and a 40-minute trip by bus from the Place des Charentes in central Limoges. The memorial is open during daylight hours throughout the year, with free admission. Allow two hours to see the site.

Cruising on the River Charente

This one is so good I was tempted to keep it to myself. The River Charente, which winds for about 120 miles through the cognac country of west-central France, was until about five years ago a "lost" river. Stretches of it were choked with weeds and overgrowth, and its locks were neglected and unworkable. Then in 1979 a British-based company called Holiday Charente, with assistance from the French government, reopened the upper part of the river for boating. Today you can explore almost its whole length, from just west of Angoulême to the Atlantic estuary at Rochefort, in one of the company's four classes of cruise boat or by canoe.

On a continent where every inch of navigable waterway is clogged with weekend sailors, the Charente is breathtakingly peaceful and unspoiled; it's possible to go all day without seeing another boat. The water is clear, safe for swimming, and—unusual for European rivers—completely pollution-free. When you've had enough of the river for one day, simply moor by the bank, unload your bicycles (an optional extra), and pedal off to explore the forgotten villages and gentle countryside of the region or sample the excellent, and gratifyingly cheap, local cuisine. Along the way you'll pass the famous distilleries of Jarnac and Cognac, where the air is heavy with the aroma of distilling brandy—described by one visitor as "the ultimate soporific" for anyone who moors alongside for the night. (There are tours, in English, by day.)

How long all this serenity can last is anyone's guess. But for the moment, make the most of it.

Details: Holiday Charente's cruisers can accommodate three to six adults and come equiped with everything you need for cooking, sleeping, and washing. Costs range from about $250 a week for a two-berth boat in low season (April and May) to about $700 a week for the six-berther in high season (July to early September), with a 10 percent discount on the rental cost if you take the boat for a second week. There are small additional charges for bicycles and fishing permits. You must be over 21 to take out a cruiser and, because some of the locks are still a bit hard to work, it's more or less essential that there be at least two fairly fit adults in your party.

Canoe charges start at about $30 a week per person, and include tents, lifejackets, maps, and a full set of camping equipment. At the end of the week a company representative will pick you up wherever you happen to be on the river and take you back to the train station at Angoulême.

Holiday Charente has developed a reputation for being outstandingly helpful and because it's an English company language problems are greatly obviated—no small consideration if you have trouble with your boat or you get sick. Brochures and booking forms are available from Holiday Charante, Wardington, Banbury, Oxfordshire, OX17 1SA, England (Tel. 029575 8282) or from Les Garbariers, St. Simeux, Chateauneuf, 16120 Angoulême, France (Tel. 45 62-56-98).

Rocamadour, Dordogne

Few towns command a more spectacular setting than Rocamadour. Strung out along a steep valley, it climbs almost vertically up a cliff face, its stone houses perched precariously on footholds in the rock. Since the Middle Ages, Rocamadour has been a famous place of pilgrimage, though exactly why has never been clear. The most convincing explanation is that a certain St. Amadour, who is buried there, is said to have been responsible for a number of miracles. For whatever reasons, pilgrims still come today to climb on their knees the 216 steps that lead from the town's one street to the upper Cité Religieuse, where seven churches cluster around a small square and are interconnected by a series of staircases and tortuous passageways. The less hardy, or reverent, can ascend in an elevator. Farther up still, at the summit of the cliff, is a chateau, ancient in appearance but actually only about 100 years old. The views, not surprisingly, are fabulous.

Rocamadour is occasionally (and, I'm afraid, rightly) criticized for the touristy tattiness of its single main street, but don't let that put you off. The view from across the valley is one of unrelieved splendor, and in any case it would take more than an assortment of shops selling crummy trinkets to spoil this place.

Details: Rocamadour is in the heart of the Dordogne about 90 miles north of Toulouse on the D673 road. By train, it's a journey of about 3½ hours from Toulouse or 45 minutes from Brive, the main interchange to the north. The station is about 3 miles from the town itself, but it's a pleasant walk. About 10 miles northeast of Rocamadour is the Gouffre de Padirac, a series of fantastic caves (open daily from April to October).

Albi, Languedoc

It is a curious fact that the two principal attractions of Albi owe their existence to a bizarre religious sect and an artistic dwarf. The town, which with its red tiled roofs and arched bridges over the River Tarn looks rather more Italian than French, was in the Middle Ages the seat of Catharism, an austere and peculiar religious sect whose adherents believed that God was essentially evil and the world was the creation of the devil. The Church responded to this heresy by slaughtering the Cathars wholesale and, just to put the matter beyond argument, building a massive and daunting cathedral on a hilltop overlooking Albi. It is a remarkable building, built (from 1282–1390) like a fortress with thick brick walls and inaccessible windows. A porchway was later added in an ineffectual attempt to soften the lines, yet there can be no doubt that the purpose of this mighty building is to assert authority over the little city and surrounding countryside.

This grim exterior scarcely prepares you for the splendors within. Brilliant frescoes and rich gothic sculptures hit you like a glorious smack in the face—there is an explosion of color and light and ornamentation everywhere. The rood screen that bisects the nave is said to be the finest in France despite its heavy vandalization during the Revolution. The fresco on the west wall, *The Last Judgment*, painted by a forgotten artist in the late fifteenth century, is the largest painting in the country. If you're wondering what became of Christ, he was obliterated by an ill-considered alteration in the seventeenth century when a window was inserted in the wall. This is one of the most magnificent churches in France and should not be missed.

Across the way is the Palais de Berbie, formerly the bishop's palace, which was also built to resemble a fortress but now contains the world's finest collection of works by the artist Henri de Toulouse-Lautrec, Albi's most famous son. The paintings include not only the familiar renderings of belle epoque Paris, but also more gentle landscapes and other little known works. The earliest of the paintings, called *Gunner Saddling His Horse*, was painted when the artist was just 16. Even if you're not a great Toulouse-Lautrec fan, the size of the collection is impressive (the paintings were donated by his mother) and the museum affords a rare chance to examine the work of a great artist from his first faltering efforts to the peak of his fluency.

Details: Albi is about 20 miles northeast of Toulouse on the N88. There are train services in summer only from Lyon, Le Puy (see page 53), and Toulouse. The Toulouse-Lautrec Museum is open from July to September from 9–12 and 2–6, and from 10–12 and 2–5 the rest of the year. It's closed on Tuesdays in the off season.

The Most Mysterious Church in France, Rennes-le-Château

In 1891, in mysterious circumstances, an obscure provincial priest named Berengar Saunière found something in his church in the hilltop village of Rennes-le-Château, near Carcassonne. What he found has never been revealed. What we do know, however, is that Saunière's life was instantly and dramatically transformed. Suddenly he was being visited by the rich and noble of France; actresses, philosophers, businessmen, and aristocrats hastened to his impoverished eyrie in an atmosphere of great secrecy and urgency. At the same time it became obvious that Saunière had acquired considerable wealth. He was able to make generous donations to the village, build himself a lavish house, and redecorate his little church in the most bizarre way imaginable.

Various investigators have suggested that what Saunière found may have been the lost treasure of Jerusalem, or of the Cathars, or of the Knights Templar. The most intriguing theory, posited in the book *The Holy Blood and the Holy Grail,* is that Saunière's find was no less than the Holy Grail itself—the bloodline of Christ, whose descendants are, according to this theory, still flourishing today and at the head of a powerful secret society. Saunière himself refused to say even when intensively questioned by his superiors. As a result he was unfrocked, though he continued to live in Rennes-le-Château and to spend lavishly until his death in 1917.

Of all the mysteries surrounding Saunière, perhaps the deepest—and certainly the most visibly evident today—concerns the odd decorations he chose for his church. Over the lintel is the strange sentiment "Terribilis est locus iste" ("This place is terrible"). Inside, demons cavort alongside saints. A hideous devil holds up the holy water font with clawed fingers. Representations of Christ's death and resurrection feature inexplicable and intentional errors. In one, for instance, Jesus is shown being taken out of his tomb in darkness rather than daylight. In another, he addresses a crowd while a bag of money lies unnoticed in the foreground. These adornments supposedly offer clues to Saunière's sudden rise to wealth and influence. But be warned: it is said that all those who try to uncover the mystery meet an untimely death.

However much or little of this you accept, there is no doubt that the little church of Rennes-le-Château is the most sinister and mysterious in France.

Details: Rennes-le-Château is 20 miles from Carcossonne on the D613 in the Pyrenean foothills. It sits on a commanding position high on a hill overlooking the village of Cuiza, with wonderful views across the valley of the River Aude.

The World's Largest Nudist Colony, Cap d'Agde

If you've ever wondered what it would be like to do your banking in the altogether or to dine in a restaurant full of naked people, you may be interested to know that there is a place where you can gratify your curiosity. The Quartier Naturiste at Cap d'Agde, on the Mediterranean coast of France, is the largest nudist resort in the world. This is no seedy retreat of high hedges and furtive-looking volleyballers, but a small, cosmopolitan city with boutiques, discotheques, supermarkets, bars, restaurants, a movie theater, and, of course, acres and acres of naked flesh. At the height of the season up to 20,000 devotees flock here.

To my mind, so much nudity does little but confirm that the human body is (a) on the whole not terribly attractive and (b) notably lacking in places to store billfolds, combs, and loose change. On the other hand if you find this sort of thing appealing or are simply in the mood to give your buttocks that rare treat—a few days of sunshine—Cap d'Agde is certainly the place to do it. The complex consists of four interlocking resorts—Port Nature, Heliopolis, Port Ambonne, and Center Helio Marin—built alongside the old fishing village of Cap d'Agde (itself an attractive but non-nudist resort).

The naturist quarter has two miles of very good beaches, swimming pools, tennis courts, and all the other facilities you would expect at a first-class resort, including its own marina. Here is also France's only nudist hotel, The Eve, but most visitors stay in small apartments or villas, available at a wide range of prices. If you don't mind the surprise that comes when you slide bare flesh onto a cold leatherette bar seat or encounter other sometimes all too literal snags, Cap d'Agde does offer an unusual experience. If nothing else, the sight of a supermarket full of naked shoppers is one you won't forget in a hurry—though you will, of course, have to shed your own clothes to see it.

Details: Cap d'Agde is southwest of Montpellier, between Marseilles and the Spanish border, in the Languedoc-Rousillon region. Prices for a small studio apartment for two with kitchenette and shower start at about $120 a week in low season. Booking forms and details can be acquired from Genevieve Naturisme, Port Ambonne, BP 539 France, or Eden Holidays, 47 Brunswick Centre, London, WC1N 1AF, England, and Emsdale Travel, 91–93 Cranbrook Road, Ilford, Essex, 1G1 4PG, England. For the last two, be sure to specify whether you wish to include the costs of round trip travel from England.

Le Puy, Auvergne

Le Puy is an extraordinary marriage between nature at its most bizarre and humans at their most unpredictable. Its name means "the peak" and when you get here you will see instantly the title's justification. Soaring volcanic pinnacles jut out of the fertile plain and loom over the town like blunt daggers. Perched precariously atop one of these, covering almost the entire tiny summit, is the eleventh-century chapel of St.-Michel d'Aiguilhe. It's a taxing climb up some 260 steps, but the views are superb and the little chapel is a marvel. With its colorful mosaics and minaret-like tower it looks more like a misplaced mosque than a church. The arabesque influences in the chapel, and in the lovely Cathedral of Notre Dame in the town below, are accounted for by Le Puy's location as an important resting place for crusaders returning from Byzantium.

On the highest of the volcanic outcroppings, the Rocher Corneille, stands an enormous statue of the Virgin Mary, made in 1860 from Russian cannons captured in the Crimea and melted down. Again, the views are splendid—and better still if you squeeze up the narrow steps to the viewing platform in the statue's halo.

Le Puy was long the central worshiping place of the cult of the Black Virgin. A wooden statue of the virgin, destroyed by fire in the eighteenth century, made the Cathedral of Notre Dame an important shrine. Today it is notable primarily for its arabesque touches and commanding position overlooking the narrow streets of the town. Try to see the beautiful eighth-century bible of Theodulph, bishop to Charlemagne, in the sacristy. The town has also long been an important lacemaking center and on warm days you can still see little old ladies sitting in doorways practicing the ancient craft. If your interest goes deeper, the Crozatier Museum in the Vinay Gardens on the southeast side of town contains an excellent collection of handmade lace, some of it extremely old, as well as items relating to local and regional history.

Details: Le Puy is about 70 miles southwest of Lyon on the N88. It can be reached by frequent trains from Lyon (three hours) and St. Etienne (80 minutes). In summer only, there are connections to Rocamadour (see page 49). The Cathedral of Notre Dame and Chapel of St.-Michel d'Aiguilhe are both open daily in summer from 9–12 and 2–6, but on Sundays and Wednesdays only in winter. The Crozatier Museum is open throughout the year from 10–12 and 2–6; closed Tuesdays.

The Gorges du Verdon, Provence

The gorges of Verdon are sometimes compared, a bit unfairly, to the Grand Canyon. Although this series of gorges north of St. Tropez cannot begin to match the scale of their American counterpart, they are wild, spectacular, and unrelentingly beautiful. There's nothing like it anywhere else in Europe.

Like a deep, narrow wound, the main gorge runs for about 13

miles between Moustiers and Castellane. In some places it's so narrow
you almost feel you could bound across it. Yet peer over the edge
and you can look down practically perpendicular granite walls to the
River Verdon crashing along up to 2,000 feet below. The best viewing
point is along the road leading out of the village of Comps where a
stone platform called the Balcons de la Mescla hangs out over the
precipice at the point where the Verdon merges with the little Ar-
tuby. The setting captures nature at its most dramatic and the sheer
walls of the canyon sides glow with color—golds, reds, oranges, and
purples—in the rich Provençal sunlight. Note the house across the
way: perched on the most precipitous of ledges, it must be one of
the most inaccessible-looking buildings on earth.

Apart from the visual glories confronting you at every turn, this
is one of the few places where you're likely to notice the air you
breathe. The atmosphere in this part of Provence is said to be the
purest on earth—a claim at least partly confirmed by the nearby
Observatoire Nationale d'Astrophysique average of 250 clear viewing
nights a year (against 80 for the Mount Wilson Observatory in America).

Details: The Gorges du Verdon are in the southeast corner of France
about 20 miles inland from the Côte d'Azur. The nearest rail connection is at St. Andre-les-Alpes on the narrow-gauge railway between Nice and Digne, though this still leaves you several miles
short of the gorges. For those without a car, take a bus to Castellane
or Moustiers from Sisteron to the north or one of the coastal resorts
to the south.

Church of Brou, Bourg-en-Bresse

It sometimes seems as if the most certain guarantee of premature
death is to build a lasting memorial to yourself. Time and again
throughout history kings and queens have lavished years of attention
on castles and cathedrals only to abruptly snuff it just as work is
nearing completion. Such was the case at the remarkable Church of
Brou, which was built from 1513–32 by Margaret of Austria in
fulfillment of a vow made years before by her mother-in-law, Margaret of Bourbon. Two years before its completion, and just as she
was about to make her first trip from Flanders to see her memorial,
Margaret cut her foot on a piece of glass, contracted gangrene, and
with embarrassing haste expired.

Today Brou stands as perhaps the most elaborate mausoleum in Europe. Almost everything about it is astonishing—its convoluted history, its beauty, its remarkable state of preservation, its wealth of architectural detail, and, not least, its relative lack of fame. What strikes you first on entering it is the luminosity of the milky white stone, quarried from the nearby Jura foothills. Isolated from the soot and smoke of cities, the church has not once needed cleaning in more than 400 years. Its high windows, up among the delicate fan vaulting, fill the nave with light and command respect, both for the builders and the Christian church. But, strangely, throughout its long history Brou has been used only fitfully as a place of worship. After Margaret's death it became successively a stable for pigs, a prison for wayward priests, a barracks, a home for beggars, and a lunatic asylum. Today it is deconsecrated and no services are offered there.

The chancel offers an abrupt, almost startling change from the relative simplicity of the nave. Here is found an incomparable riot of fretwork, arabesques, balustrades, finials, and accolades, more suggestive of starched lace than stonework. The craftsmanship is staggering. As one observer put it: "Everything which would seem difficult to execute in metal has here been executed in marble."

The 74 ornate choir stalls—carved, incredibly, in just two years— are a tour de force of intricate realism. You could easily spend a day examining their Rabelaisian details. Also here are the tombs of Margaret, her husband, Philibert, and his mother, their effigies laid out on slabs of black marble. Philibert is represented twice, once in life and once as a corpse in a shroud. (If you look closely at the corpse you'll notice that the artist, in an outburst of macabre realism, covered parts of his flesh with maggots.) So too is Margaret. Note the fatal foot wound on the rendering of her corpse. Note also the neat but ambiguous pun on the canopy above: "Fortune infortune fortune," which can be translated either as "Fortune is cruel to one woman" or "In fortune or misfortune, I remain strong."

Next door, in the former monastic quarters, is the Musee de l'Ain, which houses furniture and costumes of the region as well as a fully reconstructed interior of a Bressane house. As an incongruous touch, three rooms are given over to the unlikely theme of poultry in art.

Details: The Church of Brou is on the N75 about a mile from the center of Bourg (pronounced *berk*) in a southeastern suburb. It's open March 15–June 30 from 8:30–12 and 2–6; July 1–September 30 from 8–12 and 1:30–6:30; October 1–31 from 9–12 and 2–5;

and November 1–March 14 from 10–12 and 2–4:30. At Easter and on Thursdays, Sundays, and public holidays from late May to late September there is a very good son et lumière. Bourg-en-Bresse is about 15 miles northeast of Lyon and can be reached by frequent trains from there and Dijon.

Colmar, Alsace

Anyone driving along the bleak industrial outskirts of north Colmar could be forgiven for whispering "Pittsburgh" and pressing on to more salubrious parts. But head into the center of town and you'll find a city as far removed from the squalor of industrial life as it can be. Colmar (pop. 70,000) is one of the world's loveliest towns and one of the few in Alsace to escape the war unscathed.

Most visitors make immediately for the Unterlinden Museum (at the Place des Unterlinden), a former Dominican convent, which was built in the thirteenth century but since 1849 has been the home of perhaps the finest provincial museum in France. It contains Mathias Grunewald's famous Issenheim altarpiece—possibly *the* masterwork of German art—but also has an outstanding collection of works by modern artists like Picasso and Leger, a number of Roman artifacts, some Alsatian odds and ends, and much else. For opera lovers, there is a beautiful, well-preserved, and justly famed theater. But for me, Colmar is simply a place to wander. At every corner you're met with an inviting vista of narrow and irregular streets, ancient (and often crazily leaning) half-timbered houses, and quiet waterways laced with graceful bridges. The whole is broadly suggestive of Bruges or Amsterdam, but with the additional virtue that most of the town center has been closed to traffic. Go down beyond the Customs House to where the little River Lauch flows serenely under tiny bridges and past centuries-old houses, or meander along the Avenue de la Republique for a woodland stroll through the Champ de Mars. If you're feeling particularly ambitious, continue on to the southern side of the city where broad, leafy residential streets are as handsome as any in the world.

Then, famished, head back into town and enter a restaurant— any restaurant (well, almost)—because one of the glories of Alsace in general and Colmar in particular is the food. Both Michelin and Gault Millau, the leading French guidebooks, have to provide map enlargements to cover all the first-rate dining spots in the area. For a splurge, try Schillinger, at 16 Rue Stanislas, which is unimpressive looking from the outside and very expensive within (about $40 a head for lunch with wine), but by common consent the best restaurant in an area of outstanding eateries. For a more modest splashout, try La Taupe or the Maison des Têtes.

Details: Colmar is about five hours by train from Paris and about 30 minutes from Strasbourg. Bus services, both local and regional, are terrible. If you are driving, there is a vast parking lot off the Place Rapp; parking elsewhere in the town is generally difficult.

Bonifacio, Corsica

From the seaward side, the southernmost tip of Corsica ends in a sheer and spectacular wall of rock, rising a dizzying 200 feet from the sea and presenting a defiant face to the world. At its summit, jutting out from the cleft of rocks, is a jumble of ancient houses. This is Bonifacio, the most spectacularly sited town in the Mediterranean. Houses here are not merely built on the cliff's edge, but in many cases actually overhang it. Below them it is a 20-second plummet to big boulders and frothy seas. The people who live in these houses are, of course, quite insane. Even to enter such a residence would be an act of questionable daring. To live in one is simply to admit that you have no capacity for rational thought. Residents would no doubt calmly point out that their houses have maintained their tenuous grip on the cliff top for centuries, but even so, in private, I have no doubt that they shut their eyes and genuflect meaningfully every time someone sneezes.

As well as offering a refuge for the insane, Bonifacio is an ideal outpost for paranoiacs. Few places in the world can match it for its siege mentality architecture, though given its long and turbulent history this much at least is understandable. Most houses in the old part of the town, the Haut Ville, were built without entrances at ground level; many still contain little drawbridges that can be pulled up in case of attack. That may seem a remote possibility these days, but throughout most of the last eleven centuries foreign armies have shown a curious compulsion to try to storm the place. The most famous incident was in 1420 when the locals successfully beat back Spanish invaders by pouring boiling oil onto them—generally a pretty effective defense, I'd have thought.

Today Bonifacio remains a garrison town for the French army and still has its vast Citadel, built in 829 and little changed in 1,100 years. Even its drawbridge, it is said, is the original. I find that a bit hard to swallow, but certainly there's no argument that the place is magnificently ancient and that the views are splendid; in all but the worst weather you can see Sardinia, seven miles away.

Details: Bonifacio (pop. 3,000) is a 45-minute bus trip from Porto Vecchio or a one- to two-hour boat trip from Sardinia. The hotels, cafes, and restaurants are clustered around the Quai Camparetti at the foot of the cliffs by the harbor. Because of the town's peculiar geography, getting a view of the overhanging houses of the Haute Ville is not easy. You can see them a bit if you wander down to the lighthouse at Pertusato, but to savor them properly you must take one of the boat excursions to the nearby grottoes, in themselves quite interesting. For sandy beaches and decent swimming, you'll have to go to Calalonga, about five miles to the east, or Tonnara, about six miles to the northwest.

WEST GERMANY

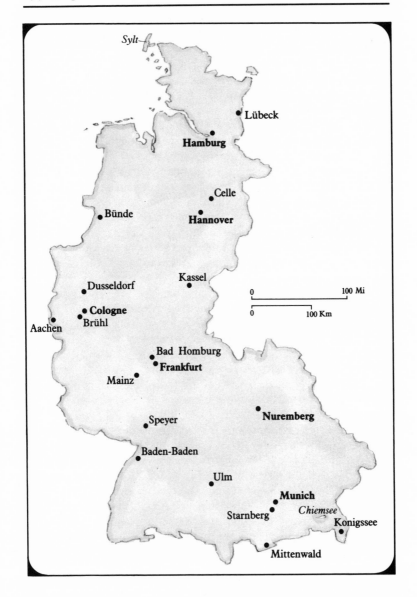

Sylt

Lübeck

Hamburg

Celle

Bünde

Hannover

Dusseldorf

Kassel

0   100 Mi

Cologne

Brühl

0   100 Km

Aachen

Bad Homburg

Frankfurt

Mainz

Speyer

Nuremberg

Baden-Baden

Ulm

Munich

Starnberg   *Chiemsee*

Konigssee

Mittenwald

Konigssee, Bavaria

Berchtesgaden is one of those places that are as lovely as you hoped and as commercialized as you feared. It is, on the whole, a bit of a disappointment. What is even more disappointing is the number of people who flock there, mill around, and depart without ever knowing that just a couple of miles away is one of the most beautiful and unspoiled small lakes in Europe—Konigssee.

Konigssee is sometimes called Germany's only fjord, and when you get there you'll see why: snowcapped mountains plunge straight into it, leaving it almost no shore, à la Norway. The lake is only about five miles long and perhaps half a mile wide, but its setting is astonishingly beautiful and the dark green water incredibly pure. No motorboats are allowed to disturb the lake's tranquility. Even the tourist vessels that ply the calm water (and take you on a short, memorable trip to the castle and chapel of St. Bartholomä) are required by law to use silent electric motors.

Apart from a tidy cluster of hotels at the northern end, no development has been allowed to despoil the lake's natural beauty. Incredibly, even Hitler was refused permission to build here. He went a bit farther up the mountain to erect his famous retreat, Berghof. It is now destroyed, but one of his other ambitious projects, the Adlerhorst, or Eagle's Nest, is still there, high up on Mt. Kehlstein. From Obersalzburg, a bus takes you on a hair-raising journey up a single-lane road carved out of the rock to a tunnel into the mountain. From there you walk into what must be one of the world's most incredible elevators. About the size of a living room, it is lined with gilt mirrors and gleaming art deco brasswork. Silently it takes you up 300 feet through a shaft cut from solid rock to the summit. This was Hitler's teahouse, though he used it just five times. The building has been carefully stripped of all associations with the Third Reich, but the heavy panelling and ornate fireplaces still hint at its former grandeur. Its rooms are now occupied by a restaurant and snack bar. The view on a clear day is fantastic.

Details: Konigssee is a very pleasant three-mile walk from Berchtesgaden, though it can also be reached by bus or electric train.

Berchtesgaden itself is served by frequent trains from Munich and Salzburg (change at Freilassing).

Schloss Herrenchiemsee, Bavaria

Chiemsee, about an hour's drive south of Munich, is the largest lake in Bavaria and, like Konigssee a few miles to the south, intensely beautiful. It is therefore no surprise that Ludwig II, the famed Bavarian monarch whom fate endowed with extravagant tastes and a proclivity for insanity in roughly equal measure, should have chosen it as the setting for one of his castles, Schloss Herrenchiemsee (or Herreninsel, as it is sometimes called). I can't guarantee that you will have the place to yourself, but it is immeasurably quieter than his nearby and more famous folly of Neuschwanstein (built at the same time) and no less impressive in scale. This was, in fact, his most ambitious project—and the one that at last proved his undoing.

Sited on an island on the lake, the palace was envisioned as Ludwig's answer to Versailles, but its interiors were never quite finished. One grand staircase is completed, but its twin has stood for a century with bare bricks and wood, thus providing a rare glimpse of what these stately homes look like beneath the plasterwork and ornamentation. Ludwig spent just 23 nights at Herrenchiemsee, in a bedroom of astounding gaudiness in which the decor suggests an international convention of gold cupids and nymphs meeting on a field of velvet. The house, built from 1878–86, contains a number of unusual features—a dining room table that could be winched up through a trap door from the kitchens below so that the reclusive king needn't suffer the attentions of a servant, a chandelier made not from crystal but from Meissen china—but the most notable is the Hall of Mirrors, even bigger and grander than the one at Versailles. The gleaming rosewood floor seems to run for miles (it's actually just under a hundred yards) and twin rows of towering, heavily ornamented candelabras provide a long diminishing perspective, surmounted by a high vaulted ceiling of rich frescoes and baroque scrollery. You'll gasp, I promise you. On summer Saturdays the hall's 2,188 candles are lit (the palace still has no electric lights) and concerts of chamber music are held there. Tickets can be hard to come by, but are well worth fighting for.

Herrenchiemsee is reached by boat from the lakeside town of Prien, itself a charming place that deserves a lingering look. From Prien you can also take a boat to Chiemsee's other island, Fraueninsel, which has a beautiful village and an ancient Benedictine monastery, founded in 782 but later destroyed and rebuilt in the tenth century. The island is the site of an impressive water festival on the Feast of Corpus Christi.

Details: Prien is on the main rail line between Munich and Salzburg, about an hour's journey from either.

Mittenwald, Bavaria

Mittenwald (pop. 9,900) is one of the most beautiful towns in the Bavarian Alps, which is saying a lot, and one of the quietest, which is saying even more. Spread out along the banks of the little Isar River, it is towered over by the practically sheer wall of Mount Karwendel (2,400 meters). At its back are more gentle slopes leading to the Wetterstein-Gebirge range, which includes Mount Zugspitze, the highest peak in Germany (2,966 meters). In between are 60 miles of woodland walks and a scattering of small, appealing lakes.

Even without its glorious setting, Mittenwald would be a winner. In the area around the eighteenth-century parish church, on Obermarktstrasse and Die Gries, are dozens of charming baroque houses with overhanging eaves, most bearing colorful and quite beautiful frescoes. Everywhere you go in town you will notice violins—hanging in windows, on sale in shops, cradled in schoolchildren's arms. Mittenwald is the center of the violin-making industry in Germany and has been since 1684 when one Mathias Klotz set up his workshops here. There is a small but interesting museum, the Geigenbau, at Obermarkt 7, containing dozens of violins and other stringed instruments from the seventeenth century to the present.

The museum and town are certainly worth exploring, but everywhere the mountains, lakes, and woodland paths beckon to you irresistibly. This is a place for loading up a rucksack with bread and cheese and a bottle of wine and heading off for a day of random wandering through the Alpine meadows and along the wooded paths. Even if pressed for time or short on energy, you will come across at least 15 beauty spots within an hour's stroll of the town. You could, for instance, make for the lake of Ferchensee (about 75 minutes on foot), where you'll find facilities for swimming, boating, and fishing, or head for the Lautasch Valley (60 minutes) with its dramatic gorge and 82-foot-high waterfall. Wherever you go, take your passport because Mittenwald is built right on the border with Austria and you're likely to be suddenly confronted with a customs post.

For the more sedentary, there are two cable car systems (the one up Karwendel, taking you almost to the summit, is one of the most spectacular anywhere), trips by horse and cart, summer concerts in the town's music pavilion, and 24 acres of idyllic resting spots in the town's Kurpark at the far end of Grunkopf Strasse.

Details: Mittenwald is about 10 miles south of Garmisch Parten-kirchen and 10 miles north of Innsbruck and is easily reached by train or bus from either.

House of 101 Beers, Starnberg, Bavaria

In the perhaps unlikely event that you've ever wondered how Tsing-tao Beer from China compares with, say, Fix Hellas from Greece, or whether Yugoslavia's Bip Pivo might just have the edge over Mexico's Cervezo, you may be interested to know that you can run a taste test at the House of 101 Beers (Haus der 101 Biere) in Starn-berg.

The name is actually a misnomer. This beerhouse stocks some-thing like 130 beers from all over the world, from Africa to Australia and Iceland to Argentina. The number would be larger except that West Germany's stringent laws on additives, which date from the seventeenth century, make it illegal to sell many beers in the country, including all of those brewed in North America. Even so, there's enough variety here to keep even the most heroic drinkers busy for a month. Once you've plowed your way through the international list, you can start on the German beers. You might want to try a bottle of Treuchtlingen, the world's most expensive beer, which is allowed to mature for seven years and comes in a bottle with its own serial number. On the other hand, if all you're interested in is the shortest route to dribbling incomprehensibility, ask for the special Kulmbach brew, the world's strongest beer with an alcohol content of 28 percent.

If you should happen to miss the last train back to Munich—always a very real danger once you've started tasting—you may find it useful to know that Starnberg is also an exceptionally recuperative place to nurse a hangover. As the playground and weekend retreat for Munich's bourgeoisie, Starnberg is a pleasant resort built on terraced slopes overlooking the lake of Starnbergersee. Lake steam-ers will convey you gently to the other resorts scattered around the lake. For those suffering acutely from the previous evening's revelries, the sedate village of Seeshaupt, and in particular its lakeside promenade, provides one of the pleasantest settings in Germany to simply sit very quietly. The less critically wounded should head to the nearby lake of Ammersee, where a woodland walk will take you on an easy climb to the Benedictine priory at Andechs. The views en route are terrific, and at the end—assuming you are your old self again—you can reward yourself with the special dark beer the monks have brewed in their mountain retreat for centuries.

Details: Starnberg is a short trip by S-Bahn No.16 from the Marienplatz in Munich. There are 160 miles of marked trails in the area, including, for the really energetic, a 60-mile-long King Ludwig Trail, which starts at Berg on the Starnbergersee and takes you to the famous castles at Neuschwanstein and Hohenschwangau. Alternatively, you can rent bicycles at the station in Starnberg and return them at a number of other stations in the area.

Deutsches Museum, Munich

This amazing museum is strangely overlooked by a lot of English-speaking travelers even though almost every guidebook mentions it, at least in passing. The idea of a museum of science and technology may sound a trifle boring or perhaps tourists are overwhelmed by the wealth of other outstanding attractions in Munich. If you entertain either possibility, dismiss it instantly—you will enjoy this museum.

The full name of the place in English is The German Museum of Masterworks of Natural Science and Technology (in German it is even more intimidating) and it stands on its own island in the River Isar. It is the world's largest technological museum and the scale is staggering. Covering six floors, the museum has 300 rooms, 45,000 exhibits, and ten miles of corridors. To see it all even fleetingly takes a full day. The displays encompass every conceivable aspect of science and technology, from particle physics to making movies. Whole rooms deal with weights and measures, transportation, chemistry, aeronautics, metallurgy, photography, time measurement, writing and printing, civil engineering, and much, much more. There are coal mines, salt mines and iron mines, cars, airplanes and rocket ships, scale models, dioramas, an alpine chalet, musical instruments, oceangoing ships, and the first diesel engine.

The museum's most remarkable achievement is to have made it all endlessly fascinating. If, like me, you have stumbled through life without even the tiniest discernible spark of interest in science, you'll find yourself marvelling at the achievements of mankind and playing with the gadgets (there are hundreds of buttons to push and handles to crank) with increasing absorption. The museum endeavors to present its displays in a way that neither patronizes the intelligent nor mystifies the stupid—and it succeeds admirably. If you are traveling with children, this is one of those rare attractions that you can both enjoy in equal measure.

Details: The Deutsches Museum is open from 9 A.M. to 5 P.M. daily. Take the S-Bahn to Isartoplatz or tram No. 9 to Ludwigsbrücke.

German Bread Museum, Ulm

In Hamburg, there used to be a Message in a Bottle Museum, containing a large collection of bottles that had drifted vast distances across the seas after being cast overboard from passing ships. Now, alas, it is closed and the mantle of the most unlikely of Germany's small museums has passed to the unique Deutsches Brotmuseum, or German Bread Museum, in Ulm. Opened in 1955, it tells you everything there is to know about the history of bread—and, no doubt, rather more than you were probably hoping to know. But when you see the displays, and begin to consider the vital role bread has played in religion, politics, and economics for more than 5,000 years, you may just find yourself succumbing to an unexpected fascination.

There are hundreds of loaves on display (all reproductions of course), in all shapes and sizes, representing virtually every kind of bread in the world from the Stone Age to the present, plus a large and diverse collection of historic implements and documents associated with the long and noble history of baking. There are ancient Roman bread-making implements, metal and clay bread molds, flour-grinding tools, seals, stamps, and coins, works of art, and even some of the very oldest grain on earth. The collection of carved wooden molds is particularly handsome, and eight very good dioramas chronicle the development of milling and baking. I wouldn't suggest that you're likely to want to spend hours and hours here, but if you're in Ulm it's worth peeking in on. And it's free.

Ulm itself is an exceptional place. An ancient town on the Danube, it is home of the second largest gothic cathedral in Germany (after Cologne) and one of the most beautiful anywhere. The cathedral, large enough to accommodate 11,000 people, was built from 1377–1543, but its most famous features, its twin towers and soaring spire, were not added until 1890. At 528 feet, the steeple is the highest in the world (nearly the height of the Washington Monument). The 768-step walk to the top provides more exercise than some of us get in a year, but the view from the summit over the ancient town, river, and (on a clear day) Lake Constance and the Alps beyond is well worth risking a coronary for.

Details: Ulm is roughly midway between Stuttgart and Munich, about a 75-minute train journey from either. The Bread Museum is at Fuersteneckerstrasse 17, just off the riverfront. From central Ulm take bus No. 4 or 8 to the Hasslerstrasse stop, then walk toward the river.

Baden-Baden

Ideally, to get the most from a visit to Baden-Baden you should be filthy rich, titled, and suffering from a series of debilitating ailments. Happily, however, none of this is compulsory. It is enough simply to like charming towns, glorious woodland settings, and quiet, elegant living, even if only from a distance. The curative waters hereabouts have been famous since pre-Roman times, yet Baden-Baden's days of greatness really began in the early nineteenth century, when the town became a fashionable watering hole for royalty. Rich little old ladies still flock here with their mink coats and abominable dachsunds in a futile effort to recapture the glow of youth. For those with a basket full of money (about $150 a night, plus food and spa costs), the Brenner's Park Hotel—the place where Cesar Ritz got his start and now generally considered one of the world's six best hotels—offers unrivaled elegance and a rather terrifying sounding regimen of health treatment, which ranges from hydrotherapy in mildly radioactive waters to instruction in how to drain your own lymph glands.

For the less daring or desperate, the appeal of Baden-Baden lies in its own handsome presence. Set among darkly wooded hills, it offers a succession of broad avenues and meticulously tended parks where the atmosphere of elegance hangs as heavily in the air as the scent of azaleas in June. Almost every street presents a pleasing tree-lined prospect of big houses and discreet hotels, charming enough to melt an anarchist's heart. This is a town for strolling, particularly along the Lichtentaler Allee, where the Brenner's Park and other nineteenth-century hotels overlook the shallow River Osback (known familiarly as the Oos). The town's focal point is the 200-year-old casino, the oldest in Europe and even more elegant than its famous cousin in Monte Carlo. There are two castles for exploring (one now the home of the Baden Historical Museum, with a fine collection of china and porcelain, and good views of the town from the terraces), some ruined Roman baths (on the Römerplatz), and a cable railway called the Merkur that takes you up a mountainside for an unforgettable look at the town and surrounding Black Forest. In clear weather you can see as far as the cathedral at Strasbourg and the mountains on the far side of Heidelburg.

Baden-Baden also makes an ideal base for forays in to the Black Forest. The famous Black Forest High Road (the Schwarzwald Hochstrasse) starts here and will lead you through a breathtaking succession of lovely villages, most notably Freudenstadt, where there are 100 miles of marked footpaths. This is one of the few parts of the world where it is actually possible to overdose on beauty.

Details: Baden-Baden (pop. 45,000) is just across the French border from Strasbourg (just over an hour by train) and about 20 miles south of Karlsruhe (20 minutes by train) in Baden-Württemberg.

German Wine Museum, Speyer

Even among discerning travelers, Speyer tends to be overlooked—an odd fact for a town that offers as much as it does. For starters, there's a broad and handsome main street with an agreeable mixture of modern shops and baroque buildings running from an imposing thirteenth-century town gateway at one end to its large cathedral at the other. The cathedral, dating from 1030, is the largest romanesque church in Europe and one of the most historic in Germany. Here the term Protestant was first used, in a decree confirming the Diet of Worms. The cathedral's massive crypt (the biggest and most splendid in the country) contains the tombs of eight Holy Roman emperors and four queens.

Speyer has long been known for its wine production. This region of Germany, the Palatinate, or Pfalz, still produces more wine than any other part of the country—although the total is only about a quarter of what it was in 1500. So it is only fitting that Speyer should house the German Wine Museum, probably the best such museum in Europe. Here you will find everything to do with viticulture over the last 2,000 years. The most imposing item on display is a 43-foot-long wine press of 1702, but there are countless other flasks, flagons, glasses, and implements, including an extremely rare vintner's knife from ancient Greece, and a fascinating reconstructed old wine tavern. Among the elaborately decorated casks is one from about 1800 showing the devil carting off an astonished woman who has refused her husband a drink. The rarest item in the collection is the oldest bottle of wine in existence, dating from about A.D. 300. It was found intact, and, against all odds, in a Roman burial chamber in Berghausen. A simple glass bottle with two pierced lugs to accommodate a strap, it contains no cork or stopper; the wine is preserved under a simple plug of dried olive oil.

In the same building is the Palatinate Historical Museum, which has an outstanding collection of treasures dating from prehistoric times. Particularly notable are its collections of medieval art and works in gold and bronze.

Details: The German Wine Museum is at Grosse Pfaffengasse 10 and is open Monday to Friday from 9–12 and 2–5 and on Saturdays from 2–3. There are no rail services to Speyer, but there are frequent buses from Ludwigshafen, about 15 miles away.

World Printing Museum, Mainz

For most people, Mainz is a place to hurry through on the way to or from a Rhine cruise. Although there isn't a great deal to captivate the hurried traveler here, one museum is worth sticking around for—the World Printing Museum, formerly the Gutenberg Museum, founded in 1900 as a memorial to the town's most famous offspring, Johannes Gensfleisch zum Gutenberg.

Gutenberg was born in Mainz in 1397, the illegitimate son of a local canon, but until the age of 40 he spent most of his working life in Strasbourg as a stone cutter and mirror polisher. It wasn't until he returned to Mainz in about 1450 that he invented movable type. The first Bible, which you can see at the museum, followed in 1455. Several other of the earliest printed books are also included, among them the Book of Hours of Charles the Bold, the Mainzer Psalterium of 1459, and a Gutenberg Bible of 1462, as well as Gutenberg's first handprinting press, which was adapted, ingeniously if a bit surprisingly, from a wine press. Other curiosities include the oldest printing block in existence (from eighth-century Japan) and what is claimed to be the smallest book in the world, a rendering of the Lord's Prayer in seven languages, which can be read only with a strong magnifying glass. But the heart of the museum is a replica of Gutenberg's workshop with demonstrations of printing as it was first carried out 500 years ago. If you have any interest at all in books—and you must have or you'd be watching television now—you won't be disappointed.

Details: The International Press Museum is at Liebfrauenplatz 5 and is open from Tuesday to Saturday from 10 A.M. to 6 P.M. and on Sunday from 10 A.M. to 1 P.M. Admission is free. Mainz is about 30 minutes by train from Frankfurt and two hours from Cologne.

Bad Homburg, near Frankfurt

Bad Homburg has everything you would expect from a German spa—curative waters, spacious and appealing parks, a soothing ambiance—but with a bit more in the way of unusual attractions. Its reputation as a healing center goes back to Roman times and for a long while in the nineteenth century it was a favorite haunt of the world's royalty. King Chulalonghorn of Siam (of *King and I* fame) was so taken with the place that he had a Siamese temple erected in the Kurpark. Czar Nicholas II of Russia, not to be outdone, built an onion-domed Russian chapel nearby.

Another frequent visitor was Britain's King Edward VII. In 1880, in need of a hat to cover his head while hunting, he had a local hatmaker design him a little something out of the ordinary. The result was the famous homburg with its distinctive rolled side brims. With its fame so intimately tied up in the history of headwear, it is perhaps no surprise that Bad Homburg should be the home of the German Heimatmuseum, or Hat Museum. Here you will find three rooms full of hats from four centuries—top hats, three-cornered hats, extravagant ladies' hats, hats worn by famous people, and, of course, the homburg. I can't pretend that it's my idea of a great day out, but among those interested in costume or millinery, the museum is very well respected.

A much more appealing attraction to me—and one for which we can again thank Bad Homburg's links with royalty—is at the neighboring town of Saalberg, about four miles away. When the remains of a Roman settlement were found there, Kaiser Wilhelm II took a great interest. Thanks largely to his encouragement, the whole complex—in effect, a fortified village—has been carefully reconstructed. There are shops, arsenals, baths, temples, and a museum containing 30,000 objects found on the site. Nowhere else is it possible to get a better feeling for what life was like in a Roman outpost during its centuries of European domination—as singular and moving in its way as Pompeii, but infinitely less thronged by tourists.

Details: Bad Homburg is 12 miles north of Frankfurt. The Hat Museum, at Louisenstrasse 120, is open Tuesday to Friday from 4:30 to 6:30 P.M. and on Sunday from 10 to 12. Closed Mondays and Saturdays.

International Press Museum, Aachen

I have to admit a certain professional bias here, but, even so, the International Press Museum in Aachen is an exceptional place. Housed in a fifteenth-century residence, it contains 100,000 newspapers from all over the world, many of them unique. Although there is an understandable slant toward German publications, a great deal exists for the English-speaking monoglot. The collection includes the oldest newspaper in the world, the *Sin Pao* of Peking, printed on delicate rice paper, as well as newspapers in Sanskrit and ones written by hand. There is also the smallest paper in the world, the *Telegrama* of Guadalajara, Spain, measuring just 3½ by 4½ inches, and the largest newspaper ever printed, *The Constellation*, spanning three feet by just over four feet and printed in New York in 1895. There are also many historic editions, including the *Neue Rheinische Zeitung* of May 19, 1849, announcing rather melodramatically in red ink the banishment of its editor, Karl Marx. Even if your interest in newspapers normally goes back no farther than this morning's edition, I don't think you'll fail to be fascinated.

Even if you are, there is also always Aachen itself—or Aix-la-Chapelle, as the French know it. Founded in 795, it's one of Germany's oldest and most historic cities. Aachen was Charlemagne's capital, the seat of the Holy Roman Empire. There are reminders of his reign everywhere, most notably in his impressive cathedral, built about 800. The stained-glass windows here are a marvel and the church's treasures are among the richest in Germany. A gold-

and-silver bust of Charlemagne is perhaps the most magnificent—so magnificent, in fact, that of all the objects from 20 centuries of Western art Kenneth Clark chose it to grace the cover of his book *Civilisation*. Also in the Treasury is the famous Cross of Lothar, heavily emblazoned with gold filigree and jewels. Lord Clark called it, with more reverence than grammar, "one of the most moving objects that has come down to us from the distant past." These and the other objects were tributes paid long after Charlemagne's death. The man himself lived simply, wearing only a plain cloak rather than regal finery. Nothing perhaps catches the essence of Charlemagne better than the simple marble throne from which he directed the destiny of much of Europe. It's on display upstairs and you can see it only in the presence of a guide (ask in the Treasury), but it's definitely worth the trouble.

Details: Aachen (pop. 180,000) is in Nordhein-Westfalen near the point where the German, Dutch, and Belgian borders meet. It is about 40 miles west of Cologne and can be reached by frequent trains between there and Brussels or Liege. The International Press Museum is at Pontstrasse 13.

Schloss Benrath, near Dusseldorf

This may sound a little strange, but I would like to suggest that you catch a tram to the outskirts of Dusseldorf, and spend a couple of hours looking at some floors. You may thank me for it. The place is Schloss Benrath, an eighteenth-century manor house built on an estate overlooking the Rhine. From the roadside it doesn't seem like anything much, which no doubt helps explain why it isn't better known. Your first view of it, from across a small private lake, reveals a smallish pink house with white shutters, gray trim, and a rounded roof. If it weren't for the two freestanding wings flanking it, you might almost think this was the guests' lodge and that the real schloss was simply hidden away in the trees. But move closer and you'll see how easily you are fooled.

First you notice that the house is actually three stories high (underground is a fourth) and not one story, as it appeared from the roadside. It's also clearly larger than you thought, though you still won't believe it could possibly contain 84 rooms. But step inside and suddenly, magically, you're met with an inexplicable spaciousness. At a time (1755–73) when architects all over Europe were flaunting their clients' wealth by throwing up grandiose piles, Schloss Benrath was designed to provide an appearance of modesty, simplicity, and good taste. This is probably the most handsome rococo building every built—in my view, perhaps the only really handsome rococo building ever built—and thus one of the most important eighteenth-century structures in Europe.

You will be asked to slip on some felt slippers for the floors here are perhaps the finest in the world. In the first two rooms—the grand entrance and the domed Kuppersaal—they are of multicolored marble, cut into discrete but intricate patterns. Elsewhere they are of wooden parquet, again in highly intricate patterns. Complicated arabesques outline some of the floors in black. You'll swear the lines were painted, but look closer and you can see inlaid ebony. In other places flowers bloom. The effect was achieved entirely with natural woods; staining was never allowed.

Despite the intimate allure of its rooms, Benrath has hardly ever been lived in. Its only real residents, the German elector Karl Theodor and his wife, had the house designed with the two halves as exact mirror images of each other. All the rooms to the right of the main hall were Karl Theodor's and all the rooms to the left were his wife's. Their bedrooms were at the two most distant points in the house. The explanation for this is quite simple: the elector and his wife couldn't stand each other.

Outside are grounds of 157 acres (including the lake), with a long, pleasant walk through formal gardens down to the Rhine.

Details: Schloss Benrath is open every day but Monday from 10 A.M. to 5 P.M. From the central station in Dusseldorf, take tram No. 1 or 18.

The Ugliest Staircase in the World, Brühl

In the eighteenth century, a taste for rococo swept across Germany like a great fever. The interiors of every great country house became a riot of intense filigree and wrought ironwork, with celestial paintings splashed across every ceiling and plaster cupids peeking out from each pilaster. For most people the height of this architectural excess is to be found at the famous Wurzburg Residenz in Bavaria. But the true connoisseur will head instead for the farming and orchard country south of Cologne to the much less well-known Augustburg Palace at Brühl. There you will find an imposing but discreet country house whose tasteful exterior gives no hint of the marvel that lurks inside—the ugliest staircase in the history of humanity.

Ugliness is, of course, subjective, and students of the Caesar's Palace school of interior design may find it quite fetching. But even for an enthusiast, the sweeping grandeur and manic profusion of the staircase at Brühl are likely to be a trifle overpowering. Every surface drips with ornate plasterwork. Life-sized statues of Grecian figures cluster around the supporting pillars—themselves a bilious combination of green and orange marble—and sprout from every pediment on the walls. Cupids race around the upper balustrades. The ceiling painting by Tiepelo only adds to the liveliness. The whole is indescribable—like a walk-up wedding cake or a hallucinogenic nightmare depicted in stone.

In contrast, the rest of the house seems remarkably subdued. Designed by Balthasar Neumann in 1724 for Archbishop Clemens August, it offers everything you would expect in a palace of the period—dozens of vast rooms, all opulently decorated on a grand scale—yet it is the staircase that will stay with you for a long, long time. Neumann, the leading exponent of rococo, considered this staircase one of his finest achievements. Certainly it was his most ambitious and worth seeing for that reason alone. For anyone seriously interested in the history of architecture, Schloss Augustburg offers the chance to observe the height of rococo excess without the crowds of Wurzburg.

Details: Brühl is an industrial town nine miles south of Cologne. Also in the town is Phantasialand, the largest amusement park in Europe. Schloss Augustburg is open daily from 9 to 12 and from 2 to 4.

Schloss Wilhelmshöhe, Kassel

Schloss Wilhelmshöhe is one of Germany's largest and handsomest buildings, contains one of Europe's finest but most unsung art collections, and backs onto one of the world's most surprising and appealing parks. And you've never heard of it, have you? Don't feel ashamed. There is, I'm convinced, a conspiracy among travel writers to keep it secret.

Kassel itself, though generally dismissed as an industrial town, is not at all a bad place. Heavily bombed during the war, it has been sensitively rebuilt and liberally strewn with parks. Its glory, however, lies in the Habicht forest on its western edge, where the great schloss spreads out across a broad sweep of lawn at the crest of a hill. Here is a vast Palladian structure built from 1786–98, which at various times served as the home of Napoleon III and Kaiser Wilhelm I. Wander inside and you'll find what is quite simply one of the most extraordinary museums in Germany.

This is the Staatliche Kunstsammlungen, or Provincial Art Collection. Seventeen Rembrandts—the largest assemblage, I think, outside the Netherlands—including the famous *Blessing of Jacob*, as well as a stunning array of works by Rubens, Van Dyck, Hals, Titian, Tinteretto, Poussin, and many others not normally encountered in such profusion outside the world's capitals. Dürer's portrait of a woman you may reconize as the one gracing the German 20-mark bill. There's also a vast collection of etchings and other graphics—some 35,000 items in all—and several rooms preserved as they were in the eighteenth century. Behind the palace is perhaps the most enjoyable treasure of all, the massive Bergpark Wilhelmshöhe, an incredible oasis filled with waterfalls, temples, grottoes, pyramids, and fountains. There's a mock ruined castle called Lowenburg and a colossal monument to Hercules, the symbol of the city. The statue itself stands 30 feet high and rests on an even more enormous plinth. Absolutely not to be missed.

Among its other modest claims to fame, Kassel numbers the invention of logarithms and wallpaper, so it is perhaps only fitting that the town should be the home of the world's only wallpaper museum. (Logarithms, mercifully, go uncommemorated.) The label is somewhat deceptive because the museum's collection of wallcoverings goes back much farther than the invention of wallpaper in 1789. There are dozens of examples of ornate tooled leathering and oilskins, flock-tapete from the eighteenth century (in which bronzed wool dust was gently blown onto linen to form intricate patterns) and handpainted coverings of linen and silk. The earliest real wallpapers were made using blocks of wood and paint and there is a vast collection of these, along with an assortment of printing tools and old machinery.

Kassel was also the home of the Brothers Grimm and there is a museum dedicated to them. But it concerns itself as much with their studies of linguistics as with their fairy tales and, unless your interest in the brothers is scholarly, you'll probably find it disappointing.

Details: Kassel is in Hesse in central Germany and has direct rail links to most of the country's larger cities. To reach Schloss Wilhelmshöhe (open every day but Monday from 10–5 in summer and 10–4 in winter), take tram No. 6 from the central station. The Wallpaper Museum (Deutsches Tapetenmuseum) is in the Hessen State Museum (Hessisches Landesmuseum) at Brüder Grimm-Platz 5 in central Kassel, and is open Tuesday to Friday from 10 to 5 and on Saturdays and Sundays from 10 to 1. Admission to both museums is free, but there's a small charge to see the state apartments at Wilhelmshöhe. The Hessen State Museum is itself worth looking around; it has a particularly good astronomy section.

Celle, Niedersachsen

Celle (pop. 60,000) is a storybook town of half-timbered, high-gabled sixteenth- and seventeenth-century houses, as lovely as any of the smaller cities of Bavaria but, thanks to its relative remoteness in the unbeaten pathways of Niedersachsen, blissfully free of the hordes of tourists who swamp so much of the rest of the country. Celle not only managed to escape the ravages of the last war, it has also escaped the ravages of time. Its old houses are so uniformly free of the cracking and listing characteristic of other ancient towns that you would almost swear they were reconstructed fakes (as they are in many German towns), but these are quite genuine.

The town's focal point is the imposing ducal palace with its distinctive towers gracing each corner. Inside you'll find an ornate chapel, the oldest theater in Germany (dating from 1674), and a magnificent hall of mirrors. But perhaps the best bet in town is the Bomann Museum, across from the castle and town church. Often called the finest provincial museum in Germany, its collections include a complete sixteenth-century farmhouse, a large assortment of Hannoverian army uniforms, folk handicrafts, and much else relating to the culture and history of lower Saxony—all more interesting than a bare description can make it sound.

For anyone traveling between southern Germany and Hamburg or Scandinavia, Celle makes an ideal place to break the journey. It is also an excellent base for exploring the Lüneberg Heath, a 300-square-mile heather-covered expanse of moorlands where sheep wander through unfenced fields and a pastoral way of life has been preserved unchanged for almost 1,000 years. August and September, when the heather is in bloom, are the best months to see it, and bicycles (which can be rented from Schollmeyer's on Kanzleistrasse in Celle) the best way since large parts of the heath are closed to

motor vehicles. One warning, however: much of the heath is sometimes shut to the public because of NATO exercises. Inquire at the
local tourist office before you pedal off.

Details: Celle is roughly midway between Hamburg and Hannover
and can be reached by train from either. The Bomann Museum is
open Monday to Saturday from 10 to 5 and on Sunday from 10 to
1. The palace (guided tours only) is open daily from 9 to 12 and 2
to 4.

Lübeck

For 600 years, Lübeck was "the Queen of the Hansa," one of the
most important cities in the world, playing as pivotal a role in the
affairs of the Baltic as Venice did in the Adriatic. But the eighteenth
century abruptly ended its days of greatness when the commerce of
northern Europe shifted from Baltic ports to North Sea ones. Ever
since, in architectural terms at least, time has stood still here.

Perhaps no other city of its size—Venice apart—can match it for
medieval and Renaissance treasures. Wander through the cobbled
streets and squares of its old town and you are confronted with a
seemingly endless succession of gothic buildings, patrician houses,
and tall, noble warehouses. Seven spires dramatically punctuate the
sky from the old town's cathedral and four churches, all built between 1160 and 1500. From the tower of the cathedral, Petrikirche
(St. Peter's), are splendid views across the rooftops and to the streets
165 feet below. The church fathers have thoughtfully provided an
elevator to spare you a long trudge to the top—a true act of Christian
charity.

Among Lübeck's other notable structures are the thirteenth-
century Town Hall, the squat but formidable capped towers of the
fifteenth-century Holstentor, or Holsten Gate, and the thirteenth-
century Hospital of the Holy Ghost, one of the oldest hospices in
Europe. Perhaps the most memorable sight is to be found in the
Marienkirche (St. Mary's Church), built in 1250. During World War
II, bombing—which destroyed about a third of the city—brought
the church's bells crashing down onto the floor below, where they
became embedded and have been left as an unusual but evocative
reminder of war's ferocity.

With its seductive courtyards and extensive pedestrian precincts,
Lübeck is a town for walking—and for working up an appetite,

since it's also home for two of the best and most atmospheric restaurants in Germany. One is Schabbelhaus at 48–52 Mengstrasse, built in two fine old houses and once the haunt of Thomas Mann, Lübeck's most famous native son. The restaurant, both expensive and elegant, is spread over several rooms filled with antiques and bronze chandeliers plus one wall of tall windows looking out onto a little garden. The food is excellent, though the service is sometimes a bit impersonal. A cheaper alternative is the Haus der Schiffergesellschaft at 2 Breitestrasse near the church of St. Jakobi (St. James), which specializes in seafood. From its founding in 1535 until fairly recent times it was a hostel and club for seamen and retains a decidedly nautical atmosphere with ships' models hanging from the ceiling beams, tables built from old ships' planks, and walls littered with souvenirs brought back from long ocean voyages. It is a particularly good place to go if all you want is a snack or just a beer.

Details: Lübeck (pop. 240,000) is built almost up against the East German border in northern Germany, and can be reached by frequent trains from Hamburg, about 40 miles to the west.

Sylt

The Frisian island of Sylt is Germany's northernmost outpost and most battered bit of landscape. It is also the most fashionable seaside resort in the country—in July and August more Mercedes per square mile are found here than anywhere else in the world—and consequently it can be one of the most expensive. History and the sea have not been very kind to the Frisians, an island chain stretching from Denmark to Holland. In 1250 these islands covered an area of more than 1,000 square miles. But by 1850, six centuries of storms and erosion had reduced them to their present size of just over 100 square miles.

This ceaseless pounding has, not surprisingly, given Sylt a rugged, windswept look. Half the island's surface is sand, particularly along the west coast where miles and miles of expansive beaches and rolling dunes unfold before you. Sylt has two small claims to fame. First, the inordinately high salt content of its air makes it among the most invigorating, healthful, and (so it is claimed) aphrodisiacal in the world. Second—and perhaps not entirely unrelated—the modern movement to nudism began here, at the Klappholttal beach near Kampen in 1921.

Nudists still account for about half of Sylt's annual visitors—they come even in March to have their skin rubbed raw by the blustery winds—but Sylt also attracts an odd admixture of writers and artists and wealthy industrialists and aristocrats. Both groups congregate in Kampen—the writers and artists at the Kupferkanne (Copper Kettle), a hangout/restaurant with a slightly nautical air, and the wealthy in their villas, which are required by law to be built in the Frisian style, with thatched roofs and low eaves, making them look like the world's most fabulous peasant cottages. Kampen is a lovely place, but the liveliest resort on the island is Westerland, its capital. With a population of 11,000, Westerland is home for about half the island's people and boasts a very attractive promenade, a casino, and Kurhaus (health spa), as well as an inviting assortment of bars, restaurants, and nightclubs. Sylt is a small, weirdly shaped island (roughly in the form of a T), lying half off the Danish coast and half off Germany. Apart from Kampen, the prettiest villages are Keitum (whose sheltered aspect makes it the only place on the island with trees) and Rampun, which both feature the island's typical and appealing thatch-roofed architecture. The romantic should head for Wenningstedt, where the low cliffs take on an enchanting reddish glow at sunset. Afterwards, if you have any sense at all, you'll retire to a bar and order a Sylterwelle, the island's famous drink (well, famous on the island). A fortifying concoction of rum, arrack, and red wine, it is served hot with a spoon balanced across the top on which rest a slice of lemon and a burning lump of rum-soaked sugar. What this adds apart from a spark of theatricality I don't know, but it's a drink that helps justify this detour.

Details: Although Sylt is an island, the Hindenburg viaduct from the mainland provides access to the island for trains. From Hamburg it's about a 3½ hour trip to Westerland. For those coming from or traveling on to Denmark, a boat service runs between Sylt and the Danish island of Rømø (a 45-minute trip), which in turn is connected to the Danish mainland by a road bridge.

The German Tobacco and Cigar Museum, Bünde

This is the only museum I know of that positively encourages you to smoke as you stroll around it. An obscure little town hard up against the Dutch border in northern Germany may seem an unlikely place for a tobacco museum, but the explanation is simple: Bünde has 40 cigar factories, making it the cigar capital of Europe, if not the world. The museum's proudest possession is the world's largest cigar, almost six feet in length and packing enough tobacco to provide 600 hours of smoking pleasure—not counting time off for lung surgery. But in its seven rooms there are also hundreds of pipes from all over the world and as far back as the eighteenth century, including some very fine hand-painted porcelain pipes, a large selection of clay churchwardens, and some really knockout meerschaums. There are also the pipes of famous German smokers, among them Johann Bach and Frederick Schiller, as well as a wide assortment of tobacco tins, boxes, and implements, ancient and modern cigarette-making machinery, and a handsome but stolid-looking carved figure of an African native—the equivalent of an American cigar store Indian—that actually smokes cigarettes. The whole is nicely set out and really quite diverting. I wouldn't suggest you break a leg to get there, but you might find it an interesting interlude on your way to somewhere else.

Details: The German Tobacco and Cigar Museum (Deutsches Tabak- und Zigarrenmuseum) is at Funfhausenstrasse 8–12 in Bünde. It is open Monday to Saturday from 10 to 12 and from 3 to 5, and on Sundays and public holidays from 11 to 12:30 only.

GREAT BRITAIN

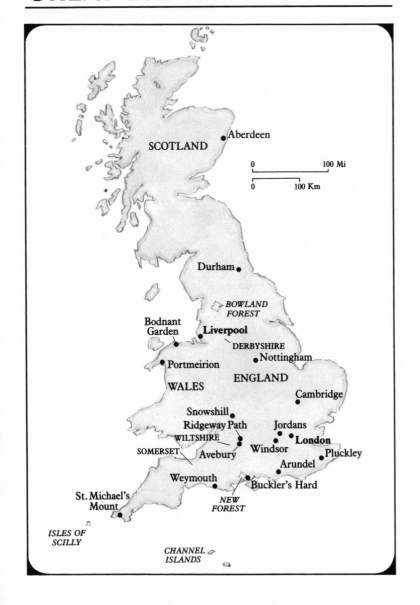

SCOTLAND

Aberdeen

0   100 Mi

0   100 Km

Durham

BOWLAND FOREST

Bodnant Garden

Liverpool

DERBYSHIRE

Nottingham

Portmeirion

ENGLAND

WALES

Cambridge

Snowshill

Ridgeway Path

Jordans

WILTSHIRE

London

SOMERSET

Windsor

Pluckley

Avebury

Arundel

Weymouth

Buckler's Hard

St. Michael's Mount

NEW FOREST

ISLES OF SCILLY

CHANNEL ISLANDS

The Most Unusual Museum in London

Down a silent, shadowy street in Spitalfields, the area of East London where Jack the Ripper once roamed, in a neighborhood of derelict buildings and warehouses, stands a four-story, seventeenth-century house, forlorn and anomalous and loomed over on all sides by abandoned factories. Step through the front door on any night of the week and you leave the twentieth century behind. Inside it is 1766 and you are in the home of the Jervises, a family of prosperous French Huguenot weavers. Outside, a horse and carriage can be heard clopping by in the street; from a back room comes the tinkling sound of a clavichord.

A young American named Dennis Severs greets you and takes you on a two-hour trip through time. Following him into rooms lit only by candles and open fires, you find a house not only miraculously preserved but clearly lived in. Each room seems to have been vacated only a moment before: in the sitting room, beside an open book and blazing fire, a pipe still smolders in its bowl; in the kitchen, amid the unmistakable aroma of recently baked bread, a cup of tea sits steaming on a table. All the while Severs immerses you in four generations of the Jervis family, from 1766 to 1850: their hates, their ambitions, their fears, what they ate, how they cooked it, how they dressed and slept and passed their days.

If the house seems convincingly lived in, it is. Severs resides here as if in another century, without electricity or running water, allowing the outside world to intrude only for two hours each evening when he takes a group of six people on a trip through time to let them see and feel exactly what life was like from the reigns of George II to Queen Victoria. The Jervises are a fiction, created to heighten the effect, but everything else—the furniture and ephemera, the clothes and keepsakes—is real.

Each tour is meticulously plotted and takes Severs four and a half hours to prepare. The 93 candles he uses are timed to burn out just as you leave each room. Sound effects from hidden speakers—footsteps upstairs, mumured voices from the room next door, passing horses outside—have you half convinced that what you're seeing is real. The result is both remarkable and eerie. One writer for the

London Sunday Telegraph called it "the most astonishing evening I have ever spent." He wasn't exaggerating.

Details: An evening with Dennis Severs is, at £12.50 per person, not cheap. But then Severs couldn't offer such intimate tours and still keep up the house by charging any less. You certainly won't go away feeling shortchanged. The house is at 18 Folgate Street, London E1, and the telephone—Severs' one concession to modern life—is 247–4013 (dial 01 first if calling from outside London). Because numbers are strictly limited to six people a night, reservations are essential (by telephone only). Tours start at 8 P.M. sharp—with the careful timing involved, latecomers simply aren't admitted.

Sir John Soane's Museum, London

Wend your way through the noise and crowds of Holborn in central London, turn down a narrow passageway called Great Turnstile and suddenly you find yourself in one of those green and sudden pockets of serenity the city specializes in. This is Lincoln's Inn Fields, once an area of meadowland but now a small park bounded by mostly Victorian office buildings. Along its northern edge, to your right, is a row of dignified but unimposing eighteenth-century townhouses. Midway down is No. 13, a four-story building of tall windows. Except for a small sign announcing it as a museum, nothing indicates that this is one of the world's most remarkable treasure houses.

The Sir John Soane in question was an eighteenth-century laborer's son who, thanks to his skills as an architect (he designed the Bank of England building) and, more important, a prudent marriage, acquired the wealth to follow that great fashion of his age: random and extravagant collecting. Anything of note he could lay his hands on, from an elephant's tooth to Sir Christopher Wren's walking stick to an Egyptian sarcophagus, he would purchase and bring home to squirrel away in his house. So vast did his collection grow, and so deep his obsession, he had to buy the houses on either side to accommodate his sprawling empire of antiquities. The result today is a succession of ponderously furnished rooms crammed with all kinds of objects—Egyptian vases, Grecian urns, almost 8,000 books, many fine paintings (among them three Canalettos, a Watteau, and 12 Hogarths, including the whole of *The Rake's Progress*), the shackles of an African slave, a giant fungus from Sumatra, Greek and Roman statuary, and other unquantifiable plunder from the dusty graves of the ancient world. So neatly is it all crammed in that you begin to wonder if the later items were acquired less for their intrinsic value than for their being the right size to fit a particular gap in the wall or space on the shelves.

As an architect, Soane had not only the wealth but also the skills to indulge his fancies, and many of the structural features are superb, most notably the canopied wooden ceiling of the breakfast room. More impressive still is the 30-foot-high domed rotunda he built at the back of the house to display his statuary, its walls packed with busts (including one of Soane himself about halfway up), urns, plaster casts, fragments of ancient temples, and the priceless sarcophagus of the Egyptian Pharoah Seti I. Equally remarkable is the Picture Room, where Soane's acquisitive instincts very quickly outstripped the available wall space. To get around this, he ingeniously built into the walls hinged panels that open out to reveal still more pictures beneath. The effect of the whole is marvelous—like a bizarre cross between a gentlemen's club, a warehouse, and a museum. Definitely not to be missed.

Details: Sir John Soane's Museum is at 13 Lincoln's Inn Fields and is open Tuesday to Saturday from 10 A.M. to 5 P.M. but is closed for the whole of August. Admission is free. On Saturdays lecture tours start at 2:30 P.M. On the opposite side of the park and just around the corner is The Old Curiosity Shop, said to have been the inspiration for the book by Charles Dickens. Now filled with a predictably dire assortment of souvenirs, it is still a charming building and provides an irresistible backdrop for photographs.

The Most Hapless Art Museum in the World, London

Stealing Rembrandt's *Portrait of Jacob Van Gheyn* from the Dulwich College Picture Gallery has become something of a sport in south London in recent years. Since 1966, the painting has been spirited off four times, an undisputed record in the art world. Although the museum has clearly been unfortunate to be so assiduously singled out by art thieves, it's difficult to rule out suspicions of incompetence entirely. In 1973, a visitor to the gallery simply took the painting off the wall and walked off with it. The police stopped him a few blocks away, on a bicycle, and found the painting in a paper bag on his bike rack. Eight years later, another visitor tucked the painting under his raincoat and again sauntered out. But he bungled his ransom demand and the work was quickly recovered. The most recent, and serious, robbery was in May 1983 when thieves broke in through a skylight, ignored all the other paintings in the gallery, and took the one magnetic Rembrandt. At the time of writing, it was still missing.

In between the outbursts of publicity that attend these periodic thefts the gallery slides back into a curious and no doubt welcome obscurity. In 1983, despite making the headlines yet again, it attracted barely 26,000 visitors. Yet even without the *Portrait of Jacob Van Gheyn,* the Dulwich College Picture Gallery is one of the most outstanding in Europe— "more important," in the words of the British newspaper *The Guardian,* "than the national collections of some European countries." Its possessions include other works by Rembrandt, as well as a stunningly diverse collection of paintings and drawings by Van Dyck, Canaletto, Hogarth, Rubens, Raphael, Murillo, Gainsborough, and Reynolds, among many, many others. Several works represent the artists' best or most famous paintings, as with Reynolds' portrait of Mrs. Siddons or Watteau's *Les Plaisirs du Bal.*

The gallery is also one of Europe's oldest public museums. It dates from 1626 when a Shakespearean actor named Edward Alleyn donated his paintings and the funds to found Dulwich College, one of Britain's leading public schools. But the bulk of the collection was given by an expatriate Frenchman named Desenfans, who insisted that he, his wife, and best friend be interred on the site, so the gallery also incorporates, a bit bizarrely, an elaborate mausoleum. The building was designed by Sir John Soane—he of Soane Museum fame (see page 85)—and was considered one of his finest achievements. It was more or less destroyed by a bomb in World War II, but was faithfully rebuilt.

Even if you're not wildly enthusiastic about Old Masters, Dulwich rewards a morning's visit. An easy train ride from Victoria Station, it is one of the few parts of London to have retained a village-like atmosphere. Old almshouses stand beside an ancient park, famous for its azaleas and rhododendrons, and the only remaining toll road in London. The whole is a surprising—and refreshing—intrusion of green in one of the world's busiest cities.

Details: The Dulwich College Picture Gallery is on College Road, a 10-minute and well-signposted walk from Dulwich Station. It is open from Tuesday to Saturday from 10 to 6 in the summer (until 4 or 5 in the off season) and on Sundays from 2 to 5 in the summer only.

An Evening at Sutton Hall, Surrey

Let me say at the outset that this is not an attraction for paupers or the uncultured—which pretty much excludes me for a start. However, for anyone with £50 or so and an ear for chamber music, an evening concert at Sutton Hall provides an unforgettable experience, comparable in spirit and quality to that other great British musical tradition, opera at Glyndebourne, but much less well known.

Sutton Hall, built in 1525 in what is now the suburban stockbroker belt of Surrey, is one of the largest and most appealing Tudor houses in England and has been called one of the dozen or so most beautiful private residences in the world. Once the home of Sir Francis Weston, who gained an uncomfortable sort of fame by being beheaded by Henry VIII for an alleged dalliance with Anne Boleyn, it is now best remembered as the longtime residence of the reclusive oilman J. Paul Getty. After Getty's death, another American, Stanley Seeger, bought it and set up a trust to preserve the fabric of the place. Not one for stinting, Seeger employed Sir Hugh Casson, president of the Royal Academy, to preside over the restoration and the famous landscape artist Sir Geoffrey Jellicoe to work similar wonders outside. His gardening project is in fact the most ambitious undertaken in Britain this century.

To help fund the enormous costs, the Sutton Place Trust offers concerts throughout the year. On arrival you are greeted with a glass of wine and given the chance to explore the vast house or wander through the grounds. At about 7:30 you will be summoned indoors for a concert by such leading artists as Julian Bream or the Allgeri String Quartet. This is followed at about 9:30 by dinner in the opulent surroundings of the Great Hall. The food is first rate— especially the partridges and vegetables, both of which are produced on the estate—and the surroundings incomparable. Throughout the evening you will be made to feel more like an invited guest than a paying visitor. The music, food, and stately home make an inspired combination, and one that can't easily be matched.

Including train tickets from London and a taxi ride from Woking Station, an evening at Sutton Place won't leave you much change out of £50. But when you consider what a good night out in London costs, you'll wonder how the Sutton Place Trust can offer so much at the price.

Details: For reservations and concert information, write to the Sutton Place Trust, near Woking, Surrey, England, or telephone (0483) 504455. For those who don't wish to partake of a concert and meal, the house and grounds can be toured during the day for £4, but only by appointment. Tickets for concerts can be hard to come by, so make reservations as far in advance as possible. Formal dress is more or less de rigueur.

Windsor Great Park, Berkshire

When you consider that Windsor Great Park is one of the world's oldest and most historic parks and that almost eight million people live within an hour's drive of its perimeters, you might be excused for expecting it to be a trifle overcrowded. To be sure, on a Sunday afternoon in August the vast lawns and paths around its manmade lake, Virginia Water, can become dense with strollers and picnickers. But wander half a mile into the park's vast interior and you can claim 10 or 20 acres for your own.

No one knows just how old the park is. Its present boundaries date from 1365, but it was mentioned in the Domesday Book of 1086 and it was thought old even then. For centuries it was the preserve of Britain's kings and queens, who would ride out from Windsor Castle at its northern edge to exercise their horses and themselves. The crazed George III was said to have wandered around addressing the trees in animated babbles and Henry VIII and Elizabeth I hunted here. Today it remains a royal park, open to the public by the Queen's good graces rather than by government fiat.

In addition to the lake, the park's 40 or so square miles of rolling landscape embrace farms, woodlands, gardens, a deer park, a vast polo field (where you can often see Prince Charles playing on Saturday afternoons between April and August), and many of the gifts the Queen lugs home from her world tours, like a totem pole from British Columbia and rare trees from all over. Apart from an occasional idyllic cluster of weatherboarded cottages (the homes of park workers), much of the landscape has remained unchanged for centuries. Even now, particularly on an early spring morning, it is easy to imagine Elizabeth I and her retinue galloping out of the mists in pursuit of a panicked stag. There's hardly anyplace that doesn't present an outlook of calm perfection. Miles of paved roads (for pedestrians only; the occasional cars belong to estate employees), bridleways, and footpaths lace the whole.

The simplest way into the park is via the aptly named Long Walk, a straight, broad, three-mile-long avenue lined with plane and chestnut trees and running from the base of Windsor Castle to a massive statue of George III (mounted on a horse and dressed incongruously as a Roman emperor) at the summit of Snow's Hill in the park itself. It's a trudge, but if you can resist the temptation to look back, you'll be confronted at the top with one of the most breathstopping views I know of. At the far end of the Long Walk, sprawled majestically across its hill, is Windsor Castle, the largest inhabited residence in the world and quite possibly the handsomest. This spot (on which, incidentally, Henry VIII once stood to hear the sounds of distant cannons announcing the execution of Anne Boleyn) provides almost the only view from ground level that shows the massive scale of the castle in its fullness. Spread out at its feet, and dwarfed by comparison, are the spires and rooftops of the twin towns of Windsor and Eton. Across the broad, green plain of the Thames Valley lie the distant Chiltern Hills. Just to the right of center is the green roof of Frogmore, the mausoleum housing the tombs of Queen Victoria and Prince Albert (open to the public only two days a year). Farther off to the right in the middle distance, planes silently descend and take off from Heathrow Airport like bees at a hive, and beyond them, just visible on a clear day, are the distant landmarks of London—the Post Office Tower and Battersea Power Station—some 30 miles away. It's a wonderful, inspiring view, and with any luck you may have it all to yourself.

To avoid retracing your steps, you can follow the road at the base of the statue to bus stops at either side of the park. The left (as you face the castle) will take you to the park's one village, where there are White Bus services to Windsor and Ascot. Following it to the right will lead you to the gates of the Royal Lodge, the residence of the Queen Mother and childhood home of Queen Elizabeth and Princess Margaret. (Not open to the public.) Take the exit there (called Bishopsgate), out past the Fox and Hounds pub, and it's a pleasant, level walk of about a mile to the village of Englefield Green, where Green Line buses run back to Windsor.

Details: Windsor is about 30 miles west of London and can be reached from London by train from Waterloo or Paddington stations or by bus from Victoria. If you're going to explore the Great Park, it's worth investing a pound in *The Story of Windsor Great Park*, a booklet available at any of the local bookshops, which not only describes the park's attractions, but also provides a rough but useful map of its layout. The bus services mentioned earlier can be a bit patchy, especially the White Buses through the park's village. It's worth making inquiries at the main train station in Windsor (opposite the castle) before setting out.

The World's Most Unusual Barn, Buckinghamshire

In 1620, as every American schoolchild knows, 104 brave and determined souls sailed from Plymouth, England, in the *Mayflower* to start a new life in a New World. Conditions were difficult and only 53 of the pilgrims—barely half—survived the first winter, but those 53 became the ancestors of nearly one million Americans today. Both Plymouth in England and Plymouth Rock in America are shrines to that momentous voyage. But what of the *Mayflower* itself?

Today it stands in the village of Jordans in Buckinghamshire, about 20 miles from London, but you are unlikely to recognize it. In 1624, just four years after her historic sailing of the Atlantic, the *Mayflower* was sold to an English farmer named Russell, who unceremoniously broke it up and converted it into a barn. Almost in its shadow—and entirely by coincidence—is the grave of William Penn, another of America's great founding fathers. There is every reason to believe that Penn, when he chose his burial spot, had no idea that the barn standing so near was once the ship carrying the settlers to the land he himself had done so much to promote.

Both Penn's grave and the *Mayflower* barn are in the care of the English Society of Friends, or Quakers, who have built on the land a hostel-retreat for people seeking solitude and inspiration. Visitors are welcome to look around so long as they don't disturb others' peace. The grounds also contain a simply furnished but carefully preserved seventeenth-century Quaker meeting house, one of the oldest in Britain, and a small museum chronicling the history of the Quaker movement. Today the barn stands empty ten months a year, but each July and August a series of public concerts by area orchestras are held in it. The acoustics are surprisingly good.

Details: Jordans, which is the name of both the Quaker estate and the village just outside it, is 21 miles northwest of London on the A413 road, midway between Chalfont St. Giles and Chalfont St.

Peter. Trains run frequently from Marylebone Station in London to Seer Green Station, from which Jordans is an easy walk of about three-quarters of a mile. (But taxis are also available at the station.) Although the Jordans estate was designed principally for Quakers, it is open to people of any denomination. Rooms in the hostel are simply furnished but very clean and also very reasonable at about $16 for a single and $25 for a double. Visitors are also welcome to eat in the Refrectory, or communal dining hall, where the food is hearty and costs only about $5 for lunch and just a bit more for a three-course dinner. There is no charge for the *Mayflower* barn or museum. For details or reservations, write to The Warden, Old Jordans, near Beaconsfield, Buckinghamshire, HP9 25W, or phone Chalfont St. Giles 4586.

Walking the Ridgeway Path

The Ridgeway Path, which runs for about 100 miles through some of the most glorious countryside in southern England, is the oldest roadway in Britain. For at least 3,000 years, and possibly a great deal more, it provided the only real passage for travelers across the southern part of the country. Today, obviously, hundreds of alternative routes exist, but none is more rewarding than this wide, unpaved trackway. From its start at Ivinghoe Beacon in Buckinghamshire, just north of London, the Ridgeway plunges off across the high ridge of the Chiltern Hills and North Wessex Downs, meandering in and out of five counties, before depositing you at East Kennett, Wiltshire, almost on the perimeter of the Avebury stone circles (see page 104). Along the way you pass a dozen or more prehistoric tombs and fortifications, scenic landmarks with splendidly evocative names like Dragon Hill and the White Horse of Uffington, and even amble right through the grounds of Chequers, the official country retreat of Britain's Prime Ministers (equivalent to Camp David but without the walkie-talkies and helicopters). Wander off the path and you'll find inviting country pubs with names like the Shepherd's Rest and the Shoulder of Mutton and villages whose redolent names—Ogbourne St. George, Letcombe Basset, Owlswick—manage to capture in a word or two their tranquil ambience.

It takes about five days to walk the path from end to end, but if pressed for time you could join it at, say, Letcombe Bassett (just south of Wantage) for a two-day hike to Avebury. Some of the hills may make you puff, but the views across the dreamy, unspoiled, and gently undulating countryside to the distant Cotswolds are a reward worth suffering for. This stretch of the route takes you past the famous White Horse—a magnificent, centuries old chalk horse, 365 feet wide and 130 feet high, carved into a sweeping hillside—and Barbury Castle, one of the largest and most important Anglo-Saxon hill forts in Britain. For anyone with a few spare days, sufficient stamina, and a bit of luck with the weather (the path can become a muddy morass in prolonged rain), I can think of no more appealing introduction to the lush glories of rural England.

Details: Anyone considering a serious assault on the Ridgeway should get hold of the excellent and highly detailed Ordnance Survey maps (numbers 165 and 173–75 cover the whole of the Ridgeway), available in most British bookshops. The Countryside Commission (52 Minster Street, Reading, Berkshire) provides a free leaflet on the Ridgeway and other long-distance footpaths in its care. Better still is the booklet *Discovering the Ridgeway*, price 60 pence, available from the Thames and Chiltern Tourist Board, 8 The Market Place, Abingdon, Oxfordshire.

Kettle's Yard, Cambridge

Tucked away in a quaint cottage close by St. Peter's Church in Cambridge is one of the most extraordinary small museums in Britain, Kettle's Yard. Step inside and you find yourself, a bit disconcertingly, in someone's home—a light, airy place with plain white walls and thick bare floorboards casually strewn with Persian rugs. The simple furniture looks like (and indeed is) the lifetime's accumulation of a discerning beachcomber and devotee of junk shops: an old barrel serves as a bedside table, seashells, pebbles, and other found objects are clustered here and there, and the chairs and chests are mostly other people's castoffs that have been patiently stripped and restored. Everywhere works of art abound, inexplicably fine for their surroundings, tucked away in corners and distributed with almost casual abandon. A Miró painting—thought to be one of the best examples of his work in Britain—hangs on one wall, half hidden by an old wooden cider press; a priceless piece of sculpture by Gaudier-Brzeska sits practically unnoticed on a cupboard in the bathroom.

This was the house of H. S. Ede, who started his professional life in the 1920s as an assistant at the Tate Gallery in London. There, struggling along on a salary of just £250 a year, he began collecting works of art by little-known artists, seldom paying more than a couple of pounds for any one piece. His tastes were eclectic and stunningly prescient. By 1957, when he and his wife, Helen, moved to Cambridge and knocked four tiny, derelict cottages into the present Kettle's Yard, they had assembled one of the finest private modern art collections in Britain, with works by Ben Nicholson, Henry Moore, Christopher Wood, David Jones, Brancusi, Miró, and Max Ernst, among many others. In 1966, the Edes donated the house and all its contents—not only works of art, but also their books and furniture and even their bedspreads and potted plants—to Cambridge University, and then quietly moved on to Edinburgh.

The result today must rank as the world's most intimate and informal art museum. Chairs are meant to be sat on, books browsed through, seashells and other objects picked up and held to the light. Nowhere that I know of has a museum where you can to this extent quite literally poke around. Only the feeling that Ede himself might pop through the door at any moment to offer you a cup of tea and ask about your journey keeps you from looking through his drawers and stretching out on his bed.

Upstairs in the attic is the heart of the Edes' collection and the one room in the house set out like a traditional museum. It contains the work of the French sculptor Henri Gaudier-Brzeska, who was killed in World War I aged just 24. Ede snapped up virtually the whole of the sculptor's work when no one else would buy it. Much later, when Gaudier-Brzeska's brilliance was at last recognized, Ede gave some pieces to the Museum of Modern Art in Paris, which thought enough of them to display them in a room of their own. But almost every other work he executed is here.

If, like me, you've never been crazy about modern art, this may be because you've always seen it in the cold and formal setting of a gallery. Here you'll view it as the artists intended it—simply as part of the decorations of a home. Your taste could be transformed.

Details: Kettle's Yard is just off Northampton Street in Cambridge and is open daily from 2 to 4 P.M. In an extension to the building added in 1970, there are separate revolving exhibitions and occasional concerts.

The Most Haunted Village in Britain, Kent

There are, at a conservative estimate, some 6,000 ghosts in Britain. They range from the phantom bus driver of Holland Park in London, who is still said to cause occasional consternation late at night by driving a red double-decker bus through walls and other solid objects, to the invisible but affectionate soul at the Black Horse pub in Windsor, who confines himself to caressing ladies' bottoms. Ghosts are so common, in fact, that some 10 percent of all Britons—about five million people—claim to have seen one.

If you'd like to join the ranks, there is no better place to start looking than in the quiet and unassuming village of Pluckley in Kent, about 30 miles southeast of London. A small gathering of homes and shops clustered around a thirteenth-century church and village green, Pluckley is, with 12 ghosts to call its own, the most haunted place in Britain, if not the world. Its specters include: the Red Lady, who can be seen frantically searching the local graveyard for her lost child; the Screaming Man, who shrieks for help from the local clay pit into which he long ago fell to his death; the Highwayman, who stumbles around looking wretched, a sword thrust through his midriff; the Schoolmaster, who hanged himself; the Monk, an amiable middle-aged cleric who, it is said, occasionally stops to chat to passersby; and the Mistress of Rose Court, who sometimes accompanies the monk. Why ghosts find Pluckley such a congenial spot no one knows, but on a good moonlit night, according to more than one townsperson, you can scarcely move for the damn things. Make light of it if you will, but the parish vicar was concerned enough to perform two exorcisms in the local churchyard and not long ago the local postman, afer being confronted at dawn by a "shadowy, white figure—neither man nor woman," announced that he had had enough and promptly quit his job.

Details: Pluckley is on the B2077 road, just off the main London-Folkestone highway, and is linked to the outside world by both buses and trains. Canterbury, with its famous cathedral, is 12 miles to the northeast. Although no one can guarantee that you'll see a ghost, your chances are said to rise appreciably if you choose a suitably spooky night—one with a full moon and a rising wind. Your best bet is to take up a position outside the St. Nicholas Church graveyard

or Black Horse Inn in the center of town and hope for the best—
or worst.

Potter's Museum of Curiosity, Arundel, West Sussex

This little museum is quite simply one of the most remarkable places
you could ever hope to spend a rainy afternoon. Walter Potter, who
started it in 1862, was a taxidermist of considerable—but wildly
eccentric—talent. Where other taxidermists were content to stuff
an owl or squirrel and stick it under a glass dome, Potter dressed
his animals up in costumes and presented them in elaborate tableaux.
There is, for instance, a kittens' tea party, in which 37 kittens dressed
in the fashionable clothes of the day play croquet and take tea on
the lawn of a country house. The Rabbits' School has 20 young
rabbits sitting at school desks earnestly doing their sums and learning
to read. The Death of Cock Robin, on the other hand, is a splendidly
mawkish but fastidiously accurate rendering of the old children's
tale. Potter was also an avid collector of animal abnormalities, mostly
contributed by farmers in the area. Saved for posterity at the museum
are a two-headed lamb, a goat with six legs, and a number of other
anatomical aberrations. All the exhibits are packed into a dark and
musty room, so the effect is rather like wandering through some
demented man's attic. A pure delight.

Details: Potter's Museum of Curiosity is at 6 High Street in Arundel
(Tel. Arundel 882420) and is open from April 1 to September 30 on
Monday-Friday from 10:30 to 1 and from 2:15 to 5:30, and on
Saturday and Sunday from 11 to 1 and 2:15 to 5:30. Admission is
50 pence for adults and 25 pence for children. Nearby in the High
Street, at No. 23, is the interesting Arundel Toy and Military Museum. Arundel (pop. 3,400) is an attractive town about 60 miles
southwest of London. It is the seat of Arundel Castle, the ancestral
home of the Dukes of Norfolk. Built in the eleventh century, though
extensively remodeled since then, it is open to the public and noted
for its collections of china and tapestries and for its expansive views
over the town and surrounding countryside. Altogether, a good day
out.

Horseback Riding in the New Forest, Hampshire

In 1079, when kings were kings and people were mere impediments, William the Conqueror plowed under 26 Saxon villages and usurped several thousand acres of land to create the vast hunting preserve still known as the New Forest. He informed the startled locals that they would be blinded if they so much as disturbed his deer and executed if they were really naughty, but by way of compensation offered them the right to graze their herds on what until then had been their land anyway. This may have been small comfort to the inhabitants, but it accounts today for the animals that still roam freely over the forest's 146 square miles (the largest open space in the south of England). The most famous animals are 2,000 wild ponies. Particularly around the villages of Brockenhurst and Burley you can find herds of them spread out across the broad meadows or serenely tearing up clumps of grass along the villages' streets. It's a fantastically charming sight.

The main town and administrative center of the forest is Lynd-hurst, an attractive place that would be lovelier still were it not for the heavy traffic rumbling through its narrow streets and a certain zeal to capitalize on it with a surfeit of filling stations. About a mile outside town is the exceptionally pleasant Parkhill Hotel, once a boarding school where T. S. Eliot taught, and nearby are the Decoy Pond Stables. For the horseback riding enthusiast the combination is well nigh unbeatable. All around for miles and miles is a tranquil landscape of wooded glades and little streams, where you can ride for hours without seeing another soul. This is almost the only place in southern England that shows what the countryside looked like before humans tidied it up with hedgerows, fences, and farmsteads, and a wonderful sight it is. From spring to early fall there are organized pub rides every Friday evening leaving at 6:30 P.M. If you can't stand horses, it's equally a great area for walking, particularly in the autumn when the leaves are turning color and the air takes on that strangely invigorating dampness peculiar to England. Few experiences are more gratifying than to go for a bracing tramp through the open air and return to that greatest of England's glories, a cream tea, in the warm, welcoming atmosphere of a country house hotel.

Details: The Parkhill Hotel is on the Beaulieu (pronounced *Bewley*) Road. It's set in nine acres of grounds with a pool and sauna, and a bar, dining room, writing room, and library. Rates for room and breakfast range from about £18-£35. The telephone is 042128 2944. The Decoy Pond Stables (Tel. 042129 2652) charge £7.50 for a two-hour ride.

Buckler's Hard Maritime Museum, Hampshire

Although it has never been anything more than a village, in the eighteenth century Buckler's Hard was perhaps the most important shipbuilding center on earth. At a time when Britain was the greatest naval power the world had ever seen, here, in a one-street village on the edge of the New Forest, the nation's fleet was built.

Buckler's Hard remains today a living community, but selected houses and a pub have been restored and refurnished to show what life was like in its heyday. What sets this apart from other such museums is that by drawing on historical records the curators have been able to freeze a moment in time—a late afternoon in 1793. The effect is captivating. In each cottage are life-sized (and very convincing) wax likenesses of the people who actually lived there, engaged in their daily activities. The master builder, Henry Adams, sits at his desk amid a clutter of charts and drawings discussing plans with a Navy Board overseer. A few doors away a village shipwright, just home from work, prepares for an evening's relaxation while his children play boisterously on the settle and his wife fixes supper. The house, with its spare furnishings and single shared bedroom, looks exceptionally frugal, but wait until you move on to the tiny laborer's cottage next door to the restored inn, where the six members of the Bound family lived in just two cramped rooms. If their look of contentment seems unlikely, remember that they and all the other families at Buckler's Hard enjoyed a life of considerable prosperity compared with their contemporaries elsewhere in Britain. Throughout the restored houses such care has been taken with the historical details that you feel almost like a traveler in time.

A separate exhibition hall contains several first-rate models, including one of the whole site as it was in the 1790s. A fascinating cutaway model of the famous ship *HMS Illustrious*, launched from here in 1789, depicts what it was like inside an eighteenth-century man-of-war. Such ships were surprisingly large—up to 2,000 trees went into the construction of each—yet, as another model shows, they were built by fewer than a dozen men.

At the foot of the village's single, very wide street is an appealing hotel, The Master Builder's House Hotel, where the eighteenth-century atmosphere has been preserved in the restaurant, bar, and bedrooms, and just beyond it is the start of an exceptionally relaxing two-mile riverside walk to the village of Beaulieu, home of a famous abbey and the National Motor Museum, with one of the largest collections of vintage cars in Europe.

Details: Buckler's Hard is about 10 miles southwest of Southampton, just off the B3054 road to Lymington. The Maritime Museum is open every day but Christmas from 10 A.M. to 9 P.M. from May 1 to September 30 and from 10 A.M. to dusk the rest of the year.

World's Best Sandcastles, Dorset

Nobody can build sandcastles like Fred Darrington. From May to September for more than half a century he has been constructing elaborate monuments on Weymouth beach in Dorset, often laboring from seven in the morning until nearly midnight. Using only a knife, a brush, some powdered paints, and his own bare hands, he may, as the mood takes him, build a gothic cathedral, a scene from Snow White and the Seven Dwarfs, a detailed depiction of a mounted St. George slaying a fire-breathing dragon—or even, sometimes, a castle. The more ambitious projects may be five feet high and up to ten feet wide and take about eight days to complete. If the weather is good, they last up to three weeks.

Sand sculptures were once a regular feature at British coastal resorts, but Darrington is now the last of the sand men. His skills—all self-taught—are incomparable, but he insists he would be lost without the special limestone sand found only at Weymouth. The uniqueness of the sand, in fact, has kept Darrington's skills from being more widely known. In 1974, he was invited to tour Australia, but the deal fell through when the organizer discovered that Darrington wouldn't go unless he could take 800 bags of Weymouth sand with him.

Details: Fred Darrington's sandcastles can be seen any day (weather permitting) from early May to late September on the beach directly opposite the Alexandra Gardens in Weymouth. It is free, though a small box is discreetly in evidence for those who wish to subsidize this dying art form. Weymouth (pop. 41,000) is a small resort on the edge of some of Britain's most beautiful countryside. Direct train links run from Waterloo Station in London 131 miles to the north-east. It is also one of the two principal ports for ferries to the Channel Islands (see page 121). Also in Weymouth is the Mariner's Museum, a Tudor cottage preserved just as it was when it served as the home of a sixteenth-century sea captain.

St. Michael's Mount, Cornwall

Most travelers are familiar with Mont St. Michel in France. A steep granite isle off the Normandy coast, surmounted by an ancient Benedictine priory, it is one of the most romantic sights in Europe—and one of the most overrun by tourists. Happily, if a bit inexplicably, far fewer travelers appear to be aware that England possesses a sacred mount of its own that is a mirror image both in name and appearance of its French counterpart.

St. Michael's Mount, which presides from its rugged offshore summit over the majestic sweep of Mount's Bay on the westernmost tip of England, is every bit as commanding and memorable as its more famous namesake across the Channel, but infinitely less commercialized. For about 350 years, from the late eleventh to early fifteenth centuries, it was a sort of branch priory for Mont St. Michel. Eventually it fell into the hands of the St. Aubyn family, whose members have owned it continuously for 300 years, though since 1954 its commercial interests have been looked after by the National Trust. We can thank this noble charity for the fact that the Mount has none of the insistent street hawkers and kitschy souvenir shops that mar the atmosphere of Mont St. Michel.

The Mount is a circular island about a mile in circumference and lying about a quarter of a mile offshore. At low tide it can be approached on foot along a causeway. At high tide you must take a bobbing boat from the village of Marazion. In either case, you are greeted by a sheltered harbor and a charming cluster of whitewashed fishermen's cottages. A tearoom and two small shops are the only commercial intrusions. The tour of the island begins with a brief film providing a helpful perspective of the island's history and legends. Then it's a long walk up a steep, cobbled path to the manor house 300 feet above. The interiors have the look of a medieval castle, with beamed ceilings, arched doorways, and thick stone walls. But there is also a certain unexpected coziness about them. The explanation is quite simple: most of the present structure was built only a century ago by a gifted architect member of the family, Piers St. Aubyn, who ingeniously grafted a vast extension onto the twelfth-century core in what Nigel Nicolson has called one of "the greatest achievements in nineteenth century domestic architecture." The furnishings and craftsmanship throughout are handsome and beguiling, but you are likely everywhere to find yourself being drawn to the mullioned windows for the stunning and generally precipitous views down to the sea far below. Don't overlook the display case containing a remarkable model of the Mount made entirely of discarded champagne corks by one loyal and patient servant. Outside on the broad terraces are panoramic views out to sea and along the coast from Prussia Cove to Penzance and the splendidly named village of Mousehole (pronounced *Mowzzle*). Well worth a detour.

Details: St. Michael's Mount is off the coast at Marazion, which can be reached by bus from Penzance. The most memorable approach to it, however, is along the road from St. Ives, a small, attractive fishing town and artists' haunt with narrow streets and many good art galleries. If your itinerary allows, I'd suggest spending the night there and traveling on to the Mount in the morning. The view of it in the bay as you come over the hills behind Penzance is one that will stay with you for a long time.

Isles of Scilly, Cornwall

Someone once said that there was nothing wrong with Britain that couldn't be rectified by taking the whole country and towing it 500 miles south. Anyone looking at a map could be excused for wondering if the Scilly Isles hadn't taken him at his word. Strung out in the Atlantic Ocean off the coast of Cornwall, they give every appearance of trying to slip off from the mainland in search of balmier climes. Remarkably, they seem to have achieved it. Although a scant 26 miles from mainland Britain, the Scillies enjoy a climate that is, thanks to a freak trough of the Gulf Stream, decidedly un-British, with average wintertime temperatures warmer even than those of the French Riviera. Daffodils bloom in December and the islanders enjoy several weeks of private spring while the rest of Europe huddles in overcoats.

More than 100 islands constitute the Scillies chain, but only five of them are inhabited, and most of those only just. St. Mary's is the largest, and its modest capital, Hugh Town, is the chain's principal port and community with 1,700 of the islands' 2,000 inhabitants. The Scillies' compactness (all together they take up less than 4,500 acres of space) and almost complete absence of traffic make them a walker's paradise. In fact, apart from taking boat excursions to the "off islands," as they are known locally, or going out for a bit of sea fishing (sharks a specialty), there's little to do but ramble along through the hedgerows of the islands' narrow lanes and footpaths or seek out a secluded beach—never a dfficult task.

Nightlife is to be found mostly in pint glasses in the islands' many pubs or hotel bars—at Hugh Town's Star Castle Hotel, a former Elizabethan fort, you can drink in what were once the dungeons— or by wandering down to watch the fiery sunsets over Samson Island.

For those who seek a slower pace still—if that's possible—the neighboring, privately owned and slightly smaller island Tresco offers it. With just one hotel and one guesthouse, accommodations can be difficult if you don't book ahead, but there's a fascinating little museum called Valhalla where you can see more than 70 restored ships' figureheads salvaged from shipwrecks off the islands, plus other maritime artifacts, and the unique Abbey Gardens, which contain an astonishing abundance of palm trees and other plants not normally grown outside the tropics—some 5,000 species from all over the world, many of them brought home by Scillonian seamen.

Spring and fall are the best times for a trip to the islands, yet even in the height of summer they rarely get really crowded, thanks to the limited accommodations. For the same reason, however, I wouldn't suggest making the crossing in July or August without securing a reservation first. The Scillies are not for those who like to keep busy, but for anyone seeking a few days of peace and relaxation and that rarest of all things in Britain, decent weather, they can't be beat.

Details: There are three ways to the Scillies—by ferry (2½ hours) or helicopter (20 minutes) from Penzance or by airplane from Plymouth, Newquay, or Exeter on Brymon Airways. The islands' tourist office (Town Hall, St. Mary's, Isles of Scilly, Cornwall) can provide a list of guesthouses and hotels. Rates for bed and breakfast range from about £6 for a simple guesthouse in low season to about £25 in the top-class Bell Rock Hotel in high season.

Home of Has-Beens, Somerset

For anyone who has wondered what Madame Tussaud's, the famous London waxworks museum, does with its models once they cease to be in the public eye, the answer can be found 125 miles away at the Wookey Hole Caves in Somerset. There the heads of the no longer famous are unceremoniously plunked onto shelves in the world's most impressive display of has-beens. These shelves reach almost 20 feet from the floor to ceiling, and younger versions of Queen Elizabeth II and her family sit literally cheek by jowl with the likes of Fay Wray and Tyrone Power, Dwight Eisenhower and Idi Amin.

In addition to the waxwork heads and the caves themselves, there are two other attractions at the Wookey Hole complex: one of the world's finest collections of old fairground equipment, consisting of organs, calliopes, and gleaming wooden merry-go-round animals from the days when such mechanical contrivances were both a marvel and a work of art, and also a restored Victorian paper mill where you can watch paper being made by hand just as it was a century ago. Taken together, the four attractions make a fascinating, if somewhat discordant, day out.

Details: The Wookey Hole complex is two miles northwest of Wells, the historic cathedral city in Somerset, and is open daily from 9:30 to 5:30 from March to October and from 10:30 to 4:30 the rest of the year.

World's Most Challenging Maze, Wiltshire

Since 1978, the Marquess of Bath, by all accounts a kind and decent man, has been reducing grown men and women to a state of quiet despair by allowing them to become hopelessly lost in the world's largest and most baffling maze, on the grounds of his ancestral home at Longleat in Wiltshire. A masochist's delight, the maze sprawls over 1½ acres, contains almost two miles of deviously convoluted pathways, can take hours to get out of, and is regarded with awe by all those who have trodden its dark alleys. Mazes have been a common feature of Europe's stately homes ever since the first was erected at Hampton Court, near London, in 1680. Although the one at

Longleat is less than a decade old (and only now are its 1,600 yew trees reaching their full height of about seven feet), what it lacks in history it makes up for in size and sophistication. It is the brainchild of a young professional mazemaker named Greg Bright, who has written two books on the subject and regards Europe's older and more famous mazes with thinly veiled disdain. "They were all designed by gardeners," he says dismissively, making it clear that such projects are better left to people of vision and science. Bright certainly has taken a more cerebral approach, employing a complex "multicursal" (many-pathed) layout, with 60 junctions, four resting spots (each cunningly designed to convince you that you have been there already) and, of course, dozens of maddeningly circuitous byways that really do take you back to the spot from which you so confidently set out 20 minutes before. The maze is so difficult, in fact, that Bright agreed to install four "cheating boxes" at strategic points giving directions for the way out. Even so, few people manage to escape in less than an hour and the average time is 90 minutes. Fortunately, the design also incorporates a much simpler, 30-minute path for those who are less daring or more sensible, depending on how you look at it.

Details: Longleat is about three miles from Warminster on the A362 road to Frome. Built in 1568, it is one of Britain's stateliest homes, approached along a 2½-mile private drive. There are interesting guided tours of the house. Outside, the attractions include gardens by Capability Brown, a 40-acre wildlife park—an open-air zoo in which lions, cheetahs, giraffes, and the like roam freely—and a boating lake. All are open to the public every day but Christmas, from 10 to 6 from Easter to the end of September and from 10 to 4 the rest of the year.

Avebury Rings, Wiltshire

Everyone's heard of Stonehenge, that mysterious circle of stones on the Salisbury Plain in southwest England. But far fewer people are aware that an infinitely more ambitious, and no less mysterious, stone age project is just 20 miles away, the rings at Avebury. These rings, or circles 'of stones, may have less immediacy than those at Stonehenge, but that's largely because they are spread over a much greater area—some 28 acres in all, covering a space 12 times the size of Stonehenge and encircling almost the entire village of Avebury. This is, in fact, the largest prehistoric monument in Europe.

The 100 or so ragged monoliths that mark Avebury's boundary were heaved into place 4,500 years ago by men using primitive implements fashioned from deer antlers. In 1938 when a toppled stone was re-erected, it took 12 men usings hoists and cranes five days to reposition it. That stone weighed just eight tons. Others at Avebury weigh up to 60 tons—and come from as far as 50 miles away. How primitive men were able—and why they were willing—to spend generations building such a vast and elaborate monument remains one of the most compelling and elusive questions of modern archeology. One authority has called Avebury "one of the six most mysterious spots on earth." Certainly for more than 1,000 years it was one of the most sacred. Today, particularly on a misty morning, a timeless hush continues to hang over the hulking stones that dot its sweeping perimeter. The existence of a village in its midst adds a dimension of incongruity: huge stone sarsens stand in a number of backyards and are posted like sentinels around the Red Lion pub. For those who like to ponder the achievements of ancient man, it provides a tranquil alternative to the ceaseless hordes of tourists just down the road at Stonehenge.

Details: Avebury is on the A361 Swindon-Devizes road and can be reached by bus from either. Near the parish church there is a small museum containing an assortment of prehistoric relics and providing a useful introduction to the history of the site. Less than a mile from Avebury—and almost certainly connected with it historically—is another enduring mystery: Silbury Hill, a vast, manmade mound some 130 feet high and covering five acres. The largest such mound in Europe, it looks like nothing so much as a huge overturned bowl, but its appearance belies the enormous engineering skills (and an estimated 18 million hours of labor) that went into its construction. For years it was assumed to be a prehistoric burial mound, but in 1967 scientists and archeologists discovered that there was not and never had been anyone or anything buried there. What its purpose was is, like Avebury, a question that probably will never be answered. Also nearby is the start of the long-distance Ridgeway Path (see page 92).

Castle Combe, Wiltshire

Castle Combe is one of those almost too perfect places. As with the better known villages of Broadway and Upper and Lower Slaughter in the Cotswolds, you cannot walk around without suspecting that it is a quaint but bogus creation of the English Tourist Board. Tucked into a green hollow in the gentle Wiltshire hills, it offers everything you would expect of a picture postcard village: mellow stone cottages with sharply sloping slate roofs, a babbling river crossed by an old stone bridge, an ancient church spire poking out from the trees. But apart from the occasional invasion of film crews looking for a photogenic backdrop (as when the village was transformed into a seaport for the movie *Dr. Doolittle*) Castle Combe remains a somnolent but entirely genuine community.

In addition to savoring its gentle beauty, there are two very good reasons for coming to Castle Combe. One is to drink in the White Hart pub, which offers all those things you hope to find in a country pub but all too often don't—a roaring fire, mullioned windows, flagstone floors, a good range of beers, and a welcoming ambience. With pubs all over Britain increasingly falling victim to Space Invaders machines and disco-inspired decor, places like the White Horse are to be sought out and cherished. The other attraction, for those who can afford a bit of a splashout, is to stay the night at the Manor House Hotel, a lovely old country house full of oak panelling, deep armchairs, open fires, and four-poster beds. The manor, which dates mostly from the seventeenth and eighteenth centuries, was once the home of Sir John Fastolf on whom Shakespeare may have modeled his Falstaff. There's a dining room of repute and 26 acres of partridge- and pheasant-infested gardens and parkland for post-prandial strolling.

Castle Combe also makes an excellent base for exploring nearby attractions. One not to be missed is Lacock, about eight miles to the south, another relentlessly attractive village (preserved by the National Trust), with a beautiful abbey and a museum commemorating the work of the pioneering photographer Henry Fox Talbot. About 18 miles to the east is Avebury and the start of the Ridgeway Path (see pages 92 and 104). Bath is just 10 miles to the southwest and the Cotswolds about 30 miles to the north. It is no exaggeration to say that you could easily and profitably spend two or three weeks of active sightseeing without traveling farther than 30 miles from Castle Combe.

Details: Castle Combe is six miles from Chippenham, just off the M4 motorway. The Manor House Hotel (Tel. 0249 782206) charges about £30 a night for a single, breakfast not included. Reservations advisable.

Snowshill Manor, Gloucestershire

Charles P. Wade (1883–1956) was a man of many facets: scholar, architect, artist. But, like any good English gentleman, he was above all an eccentric. And, thanks to his family's business interests in the West Indies, he had both the wealth and time to make eccentricity a full-time pursuit. In 1919, Wade bought Snowshill Manor in Gloucestershire, once the home of Catherine Parr, wife of Henry VIII, but by then in a sad state of neglect. He immediately began restoring the house and then filling it with—well, junk. Wade would buy almost anything—old musical instruments, spinning machines and weaving looms, toys, clocks, bicycles, ships' models, tools, baby carriages, Persian lamps, a camel harness, a miniature windmill—anything, in short, that no one else wanted. All these things he arrayed in a splendid jumble throughout the many rooms of his seventeenth-century mansion. The result today is a house of infinite surprise, containing what one writer has affectionately called "the least coherent collection in the country." The contents are all very fine of their type, but entirely random. Toys jostle for space with wine presses and music boxes vie for your attention with penny farthings. In one room—a bit startling if you're not prepared—a Japanese war council sits in full session. Arranged around the room are life-sized models of fierce-looking Samurai warriors, resplendent in their armor and crouched with their swords across their laps. Scattered haphazardly are the rest of their weapons, plus an eclectic assortment of other Oriental objects covering several centuries.

In 1951 when Wade made a gift of his house to the presumably astonished National Trust, the directors had the presence of mind to realize that there was a certain bizarre genius in its contents and very prudently decided to leave the house just as it was. In its time it must have been just about the most unlivable house in the world— in addition to all the clutter Wade never allowed any modern conveniences like electric lighting or heating in his domain—but today it stands as perhaps the most extraordinary and unlikely residence in Britain.

Details: Snowshill Manor is in the Cotswold village of Snowshill, about three miles south of Broadway. It is open from May to September on Sundays from 2 to 6 and from Wednesday to Saturday from 11 to 1 and 2 to 6. In April and October it's open only on weekends. Even without its remarkable manor, the village of Snowshill would invite a visit for its unspoiled appearance and lovely setting overlooking a Cotswold valley. The nearby village of Broadway, though well known and perhaps a little touristy for some tastes, is also incredibly beautiful and shouldn't be missed. The Lygon Arms Hotel in the middle of the main street is one of the best provincial hotels in the country, though not cheap.

Bodnant Garden, North Wales

An American tourist once asked a gardener at an English stately home how he managed to keep the lawns so green and perfect. "Oh, it's really quite simple," came the reply. "You just cut and rake the grass once a week, and feed and fork it once a year. Repeat that for 500 years and eventually you should get a pretty fair lawn." There's a good deal in what he said. Even at one of Britain's youngest public gardens, Bodnant in north Wales, patience and continuity have played an essential part in making it what it is. Bodnant was started in only 1875—a mere eyeblink in gardening terms—but it has been in the control of one family, the Lords Aberconway, throughout that time and, perhaps even more important, since 1920 the role of head gardener has been passed down from father to son through three generations of the Puddle family. The result of their commitment and effort is one of the most rewarding bits of landscape anywhere.

Bodnant's greatness is due in part to its incomparable setting overlooking the lush Vale of Conway. And partly it can be attributed to its sheer size: the garden sprawls across 120 acres, 70 of which are open to the public. But mostly it is the result of hard work and careful planning. The first Lord Aberconway envisioned it as a place of "calculated informality" and he succeeded magnificently. Every turning presents an enchanting prospect of oaks and yews and flowerbeds, or great masses of rhododendrons (for which Bodnant is famed), which yield to unforgettable views across the valley to the misty, distant slopes of Snowdonia. It all appears so natural and settled that it's inconceivable that only 80 years ago most of what you see today was scrubby farmland and pasturage. One of the focal points of the upper garden, the early eighteenth-century Pin Mill, standing serenely above its reflection in a long, shallow pool, was transferred stone by stone from Gloucestershire as recently as 1939.

The upper terraces lead down to a woodland area called The Dell, where an old mill and stone bridge stand over the rushing water of the little River Hiraethlyn, framed by a dense backdrop of flowering magnolia and cherry trees. With its trilling water and birdsong, and its lush canopy of green, this must be one of the most tranquil spots anywhere.

Britain has about 3,000 public gardens—an incredible number for a country of its size—and I would be committing the purest folly to try ranking them. But by anyone's standards Bodnant must stand among the top half dozen—don't miss it if you can help it.

Details: Bodnant is eight miles south of the coastal resort of Llandudno on the A470 road; the entrance is a half-mile along the Eglwysbach road. It is open daily from March 19 to October 30 from 10 A.M. to 5 P.M.

Portmeirion, North Wales

There is only one word for the little Welsh village of Portmeirion: fantastic. A piece of Italy set down on the wooded slopes overlooking Cardigan Bay in north Wales, it is the work and vision of one man, the architect Sir Clough Williams-Ellis, who as a youth had long nurtured the dream of building his own utopia—a place of, in his words, "serenity, kindness and architectural good manners." Williams-Ellis spent several years fruitlessly scouring Britain for a suitable site and was on the point of giving up when an uncle asked him to find a buyer for a piece of property just four miles from the family home near Porthmadog. At first sight, Williams-Ellis knew he had found exactly what he had been looking for. He bought the land and in 1926 began turning it into a village modeled roughly on Portofino—a place of pastel-colored cottages and buildings clustered around a series of gardens and terraces overlooking the sea.

Because he was perpetually strapped for funds, Williams-Ellis needed flexibility as much as vision. He became an architectural magpie, collecting colonnades, porticoes, windows, staircases, a vast clock from an old brewery, and anything else he could lay his hands on from stately homes and other buildings facing demolition. He ingeniously incorporated all of these into the fabric of Portmeirion. A gothic fireplace became part of the domed Italianate campanile, which towers over the rest of the village. A seventeenth-century town hall was rebuilt stone by stone on the site. Somehow, unbelievably, they blend into a harmonious whole that evokes the sunshine and sleepiness of the Mediterranean on the damp, green coast of Wales. Everywhere you turn are what Williams-Elllis called his "eye traps"— gazebos, resting places, and other architectural follies designed for no other purpose than to delight the eye and to make use of some unexpected delivery of architectural oddments.

Below the village, on the seashore, is a rambling Victorian hotel, where, among other things, Noel Coward wrote *Blithe Spirit*. The hotel was shut by fire in 1981 and, at the time of writing, its reopening date was still uncertain. But there is a wide range of holiday accommodations, from single rooms to cottages and apartments, in the village's other buildings. For day visitors and longer-staying guests, the facilities include antique and souvenir shops and a restaurant, a children's playground, uncrowded beaches, and miles of tranquil footpaths for exploring. If it all looks faintly familiar, it may be because the 1960s cult television series *The Prisoner*, starring Patrick McGoohan, was filmed here.

Details: Portmeirion is one mile off the A487 Dolgellau-to-Porthmadog road at the village of Penrhyndeudraeth in Gwynedd, North Wales, and is open daily from April to November from 9:30 to 5:30. Rates for a double room with bath and color TV start at about £25 a night; cottages and apartments start at about £80 a week.

Hardwick Hall, Derbyshire

Every year tens of thousands of people trek to Derbyshire to astonish themselves with the vastness and undisputed beauty of Chatsworth House, little realizing that just a few miles away is another stately pile a bit less grand and a good deal less famous, but possibly—just possibly—even more memorable. In fact, Nigel Nicolson has called Hardwick Hall "one of the most beautiful buildings ever created." Once you've seen it I think you'll find it difficult to disagree with him.

Hardwick, like Chatsworth, owes its existence to the daughter of an obscure country squire named Elizabeth Shrewsbury, better known as Bess of Hardwick, who had a knack for marrying wealthy men who were not long for this world as well as a bit of a passion for housebuilding. Hardwick Hall, begun in 1587 when Bess was 70, was the culmination of her efforts—and, indeed, the culmination of late Elizabethan architecture. With its vast mullioned windows, unusually large for the time, it is a magnificent place, sober and noble yet utterly captivating. A lot of stately houses look like Grand Central Station removed to the countryside, and are about as homey. Hardwick manages to be impressive without being intimidating. Six turrets neatly punctuate the facade, and take on an added poignancy when you realize that until fairly recent times they served as servants' quarters even though the only access to them was a drafty sprint across the roof.

The interiors are no less masterly or splendid. For a house of the period, there is an unusual and refreshing subtlety inside—many floors are bare or covered in simple rush matting, and many ceilings are free of cornices and other intrusions—neatly setting off the heavy oak and mahogany furniture and the incomparable tapestries and embroidery for which the house is famed. The most memorable room is the great chamber, which Sacheverrel Sitwell has called the most beautiful room in Europe (the place, you'll note, tends to attract superlatives rather than tourists). A large painted frieze runs around the room, surmounting a vast plasterwork fireplace and a fabulous array of tapestries. These last so perfectly fit the walls that you suspect they were made specifically for this room; in fact, it was the other way around.

Were Bess to return today she would find the house almost exactly as she left it. Her descendants, like today's tourists, turned their energies to nearby Chatsworth, treating Hardwick as a place of secondary importance. We should be grateful to them.

Details: Hardwick Hall is near Glapwell, just south of Chesterfield, on the A617 road in Derbyshire. The M1 motorway runs nearby and in fact is visible from the house. The grounds are open all year, but the house only from April 1 to October 31 on Wednesdays, Thursdays, Saturdays, Sundays and Bank Holiday Mondays from 1 to 5:30.

Britain's Oldest Pub, Nottingham

There are 77,000 pubs (or, more properly, public houses) in Great Britain, far more than anyone could possibly visit in a single lifetime, though you could happily die trying. Even if you faithfully visited a new one every day, it would take you 210 years to see them all. So recommending one out of the thousands of first-rate pubs in Britain is an insanely impetuous exercise. But having said that, Ye Olde Trip to Jerusalem in the heart of Nottingham does rather neatly contain all the ingredients of a good pub: history, conviviality, coziness, and decent beer. It is also—albeit arguably—the oldest in Britain. Although several others claim that title, the Jerusalem has been the site of an alehouse since 1189, on which basis it is indisputably the oldest in the country. The present building dates from 1760, making it a relative infant, but the foundations and cellar are the originals. The name, incidentally, comes from the fact that the inn was a gathering spot for Crusaders en route to the Middle East in the twelfth century. Nestled up against the walls of Nottingham Castle, the Jerusalem consists of nine small, atmospheric rooms on two floors, all filled with dark, ancient furniture and dusty curios (watch out for the clock that runs backwards). There is a prodigious range of hand-pumped beers and an attractive assortment of cheap and filling sandwiches at lunchtime. The castle behind, built by William the Conqueror in 1068, is worth dragging yourself away from the pub for. It is now the city's museum and art gallery and contains, among other things, one of the world's finest collections of lace, for which Nottingham is famous.

Details: Ye Olde Trip to Jerusalem is at 2 Castle Road, Nottingham. In common with other English pubs, the Jerusalem is open only from 11 A.M. to 2:30 P.M. and from 6 P.M. to 10:30 P.M. (till 11 P.M. on Fridays and Saturdays). The opening hours, which vary slightly from region to region and even sometimes from pub to pub, were introduced during World War I to keep factory workers from drinking away their afternoons and are now, like much else in Britain, a pointless but cherished anachronism. Nottingham (pop. 271,000), one of England's principal industrial cities, is 128 miles north of London.

Forest of Bowland, Lancashire and Yorkshire

One of the great glories of the English countryside is the names of the villages and towns. What person, however pressed for time, could resist the temptation to turn off the main highway and take at least a fleeting look at Chew Magna or Nether Wallop, Sixpenny Handley or Budleigh Salterton? Almost wherever you go in the country you will encounter place names that mix charm and absurdity in roughly equal measure. One of the richest of the hunting grounds lies in the north, near Lancaster. Here clustered together you'll find Giggleswick and Wigglesworth, Horton in Ribblesdale and the practically unbeatable Goosnargh. It must be dispiriting to have to go through life admitting to people that you are a son of Goosnargh or a Giggleswickian born and bred. But by way of compensation there is the realization that just outside your door stretches one of the loveliest and most unsung corners of England, the Forest of Bowland.

Its name is a little misleading. The word *forest* originally meant only an area set aside for hunting, whether of woodlands or open countryside. Bowland is mostly the latter, a roughly circular area of high, rolling hills and tranquil dales dotted with farms, stone-built villages, and gentle streams—broadly similar to the Yorkshire Dales and parts of the Lake District, but without the crowds.

This is ideal territory for random exploration, either on foot or by car. Particularly along its eastern edge, where the counties of Yorkshire and Lancashire run together, there is a succession of charming villages, among them Giggleswick (a ravishing little place of mostly seventeenth- and eighteenth-century cottages whose residents appear almost without exception to have a passion for gardening), Hornby, Inglewhite, Abbeystead, and Chipping (where you'll find the largest bluebell wood in Britain; very pretty in springtime). Almost every valley harbors a welcoming old inn and there are a couple of surprisingly good restaurants for such a backwater. For a drink, try the ancient Hark to Bounty Inn at Slaidburn and for food the Water Wheel Restaurant at Chipping in a converted mill. Lancaster, on the western perimeter, is a comfortable old university town. For anyone traveling between southern England and the north or Scotland, the whole Forest of Bowland makes an ideal place to break the journey.

In Search of the Beatles, Liverpool

Every day of the year one or two people will stop in front of a modest and unremarkable house at 251 Menlove Avenue in Liverpool and just stare. Most take pictures. A few look around for a small memento—a broken twig or a leaf from the privet hedge. One, to the annoyance of the present owners, went into the front yard and began filling a large plastic bag with dirt. No. 251 Menlove Avenue is the house where John Lennon grew up, raised by his Aunt Mimi (now long since departed).

At three other modest houses, a number of pubs, and even a parking lot the same quiet ritual is played out daily: reverent people of various ages and nationalities arrive, stare, take pictures, and depart. Until quite recently Liverpool officials showed an almost haughty disdain for the city's most famous native sons, most ignominiously in 1974 when the City Council allowed the Cavern Club, the most revered Beatle landmark of all, to be torn down and replaced with a parking lot. Finally in the spring of 1984, a local radio station, with financial help from the city, opened Beatles City, a $3 million museum in Seel Street tracing the rise of the Beatles and containing over 800 items.

Despite this belated recognition of the city's debt to the group, you can still find the Beatles' childhood homes and old haunts preserved much as they were 25 years ago when Beatlemania seized the world. Standing outside No. 10 Admiral Grove, the tiny, white-painted row house where Ringo Starr grew up (and now the home of a plumber), it is almost impossible to imagine that 10,000 shrieking young girls once filled the street hoping for a glimpse of the terrified young man cowering inside. Paul McCartney grew up at 20 Forthlin Road and George Harrison at 12 Arnold Grove.

The local tourist authority arranges three-hour bus tours of the homes and other famous Beatles sites, but anyone armed with a city map can as easily make a freelance exploration. Wandering around the old neighborhoods will also throw up a number of surprising discoveries. Who would have guessed, for instance, that the bucolic-sounding Penny Lane is really a major thoroughfare (don't look for street signs, by the way; they're always stolen as fast as the city can put them up) or that Strawberry Fields, just around the corner from Lennon's old house, is the name of a Salvation Army orphanage?

Details: The Merseyside County Council publishes an indispensable book called *In the Footsteps of the Beatles*, which describes about 100 Beatles landmarks and includes 50 photographs and three helpful maps. It's available for £1.50 from the city tourist office at 29 Lime Street (Tel. 709 8681) or at most bookstores. The tourist office can also provide tickets for the Beatles bus tours, which run every Sunday from early May to late September, departing at 10 A.M. from St. John's Lane in the city center. Tickets, which cost £1.95 for adults and £1.25 for children, can also be acquired on the bus if there are any spare seats. On Saturdays from March to the end of September 90-minute walking tours begin outside the Everyman Theatre on Hope Street at 3 P.M.. Tickets cost 80 pence for adults and 40 pence for children.

Durham Cathedral and Town, County Durham

Durham Cathedral is everything an ecclesiastical structure should be: massive, inspiring, and ancient, with three soaring towers that dominate the town at its feet and the countryside for miles around. It is the finest Norman building in the world and one of the glories of Western civilization. Yet it attracts a smaller number of foreign visitors than almost any other cathedral in Britain. When you consider that Durham itself is a handsome university town with a network of winding lanes and streets, a wealth of medieval architecture, and a couple of superb museums, its neglect by travelers becomes more curious still.

The cathedral, which was built in just 40 years (1093–1133), stands high up on what is effectively an island (now mostly traffic free) created by a broad loop in the River Wear. Facing it across a broad sweep of lawn called Palace Green is the castle, built at about the same time and now part of the university, though still open to the public. All around them wind ancient, narrow streets full of inviting shops and restaurants.

The cathedral is massive, measuring 500 feet in length and 200 in width, roughly the size of two American football fields. On the front door hangs a replica of the famous sanctuary knocker, which guaranteed safety to any medieval thief or murderer who grasped it (an option happily exercised by 283 murderers between 1464 and 1525). Inside, you'll find a vast perspective of stout, intricately carved stone pillars leading the eye up to a soaring vaulted ceiling, which was a marvel in its day and still capable of bringing a gasp to the lips of the modern stone mason. An aura of sanctity hangs as profoundly in the air as it must have eight centuries ago. The church's treasures include an ornate, gilded bishop's throne—the highest in the world—and the tombs of two of medieval England's most famous clerics: St. Cuthbert, for whom the church was built (and effectively the patron saint of northern England), and the Venerable Bede, the great scholar and historian who died in 735. The Treasury contains the original sanctuary knocker, manuscripts from the time of Bede and even earlier, bibles, ornaments, silver plate, and much more. There is a library of 40,000 volumes, of which 23,000 date from 1700 or earlier, and, more unusually but refreshingly, what must be the best restaurant in any British museum or monument—good enough for a listing in England's respected *Good Food Guide*.

Across the River Wear, reached by a lovely stone bridge dating from 1772, is the Durham University Oriental Museum (formerly the Gulbenkian Museum), containing one of the world's finest collections of objects from India, the Middle East, and the Orient, some dating from the twentieth century B.C. Also interesting is the Burlison Art Gallery in the Town Hall.

Details: Durham Cathedral is open daily from 7:30 A.M. to 8 P.M. in the summer and until 5 P.M. the rest of the year. The Oriental Museum is open throughout the year, except for two weeks at Christmas, from 9:30 to 1 and from 2:15 to 5 on weekdays. From Easter to Christmas it is also open at weekends from 9:30 to 12 and from 2:15 to 5.

Hunterian Art Gallery, Glasgow

In a relatively short time in the late eighteenth century, William Hunter, a leading obstetrician, assembled one of the finest private art collections in Europe. How he did it has always been something of a mystery. Although Hunter's finds included some undisputed bargains—he bought a Rembrandt for just 12 guineas—his income as a doctor cannot begin to explain how he was able to acquire 60 works by such artists as Rubens, Tintoretto, and Chardin, while simultaneously putting together one of his century's most superb collections of rare coins, antiquarian books, and archeological treasures.

By whatever machinations the collection was acquired, it forms the core of the Hunterian Art Gallery at Glasgow University, one of the most outstanding small museums in Britain and one of the two world-class but little known art collections in the city (for the other, see next entry). In addition to the old masters and an interesting collection of paintings by twentieth-century Scottish artists, the museum possesses the most complete assemblage of the works of James McNeill Whistler anywhere in the world apart from the Freer Gallery in Washington, D.C. There are 180 paintings and pastels, hundreds of prints and drawings, and a wealth of letters, furniture, and other personal effects. As with the Toulouse-Lautrec museum at Albi in France, this provides a rare opportunity to survey a great artist's work from his first faltering efforts to his final undertakings—in this case up to 1903 when Whistler died at age 69.

In addition, cunningly grafted onto the modern museum building is a faithful replica of the Glasgow townhouse of Charles Rennie Mackintosh, an early-twentieth-century pioneering architect and designer. If you are unfamiliar with the name, it may be because he was years ahead of his time. His work anticipated by half a century the spare, clean lines of modern design—and as a consequence met with only mixed success in his own lifetime. The entire interior of the replica house—furniture, ceramics, and more than 600 drawings and watercolors—was the work of Mackintosh himself. It's a fascinating place and as you walk through it you'll marvel that it was designed and built more than 60 years ago.

Details: The Hunterian Art Gallery (not to be confused with the Hunterian Museum, which houses William Hunter's archeological collection) is on Hillhead Street, just around the corner from University Avenue, and is open Monday to Friday from 10 A.M. to 5 P.M. and on Saturdays from 9:30 to 1. If your curiosity about Charles Rennie Mackintosh is piqued by the museum, you may be interested to know that the Glasgow District Council (offices in George Square) produces a free leaflet called "Mackintosh Buildings in and Around Glasgow," which provides walking tours and a historical background to Mackintosh's principal structures in the city.

The Burrell Collection, Glasgow

In 1944, two interesting events occurred in Glasgow: Sir William Burrell, a wealthy shipowner, gave his art collection and a large sum of money to the city, and the town fathers set in motion what was to become possibly the most sustained and exasperating episode of dithering and indecisiveness in the history of local government. It was 28 years before the city council could agree on the architectural plans for a museum to house the treasures and a further 11 years before the building was actually erected. Finally, in late 1983 after Burrell's treasures had spent almost four decades locked away from public view, a museum was opened. The wait, I'm happy to say, was worth it.

The Burrell Collection is quite simply one of the most handsome and appealing museums in Europe. Spread across a woodland setting in the city's Pollok Park, it employs long banks of windows to suffuse the galleries with soft natural light and provide a lush backdrop of greenery against which to view the treasures within. And what treasures they are. For over half a century, Burrell spent an average of £20,000 a year on his art—a fair sum of money, though a pittance when put alongside the outlays of the Hearsts and Mellons. But, thanks to an unerring eye and Celtic shrewdness, Burrell's collection is the match of any assembled in this century. Its breadth is staggering. The paintings, covering the period from the fifteenth to the early twentieth centuries, include works by Corbet, Corot, Delacroix, Cezanne, and Manet. There is a wonderful little painting by Daumier called *The Collector* and a self-portrait by Rembrandt painted when the artist was 26. The collection of stained glass is probably the finest in the world (and certainly the most appealingly displayed) and the tapestries must rank in the top three or four collections anywhere. And there's more—furniture, ceramics, armor, bronzes and silver, sculptures in wood and stone from fourteenth- to seventeenth-century Europe; jades, bronzes, and ceramics from ancient China; and antiquities from Egypt, Greece, the Middle East, and Italy. Many architectural oddments—doorways, lintels, and the like—have been skillfully incorporated into the structure of the building itself. In the middle of the museum, the hall, dining room, and drawing room from Burrell's home, Hutton Castle, have been reconstructed just as they were in his lifetime. This is not the random assemblage of some robber baron with bottomless pockets, but the careful gleanings of one who had to choose his acquisitions with discernment and not a little love. If you're within 500 miles of Glasgow and don't see it, you'll be sorry.

Details: The Burrell Collection is at 2060 Pollokshaws Road in Pollok Park, about three miles from downtown Glasgow. From the city center it can be reached on buses 21, 23, 45, 48A, and 57. The museum is open from Monday to Saturday from 10 to 5 and on Sunday from 2 to 5. Admission is free.

Craigievar Castle, Scotland

Craigievar Castle is one of the most beautiful but most unusual-looking buildings in Britain. Little wider than a normal house, it soars up seven stories, its smooth beige walls erupting at the top in a profusion of lofty crenellations and conical turrets—rather as if the architect had been instructed to build a fairy-tale castle on a blanket. Why its proportions are so unusual is not entirely clear, unless its builder—himself an unusual man—simply had more vision and enthusiasm than funds.

The man in question was William Forbes, better known to his contemporaries as Danzig Willie because of his repeated business coups in the Baltic. In 1626 he built Craigievar on a wooded setting amid 100 acres of parkland. With its smooth walls and small, lofty windows it appears designed to withstand sieges, but throughout its three and a half centuries it has escaped the attentions of invading armies and, no less mercifully, most tourists. That accounts in large part for its remarkable state of preservation. Forbes' descendants were blessedly disinclined to knock the place about or embellish it with new wings, so it has come down to us almost precisely as Forbes himself last saw it.

Inside, it is every inch a man's house, baronial in its scale and conception, yet with a coziness and informality unusual in such a residence. You could imagine yourself actually living here, and as you proceed through the rooms with their dark panelling, comfortable-looking old chairs and beds, thick rugs, and small windows giving superb views over the Grampian foothills, you're likely to find admiration giving way to covetousness. The focal point of the house is the great hall with its heavy furniture upholstered in plaid, vast fireplace surmounted by a magnificent coat of arms, and carved minstrels' gallery. But the master stroke here, as throughout the house, is the vaulted ceiling with its deep-relief molded plasterwork. Created by anonymous craftsmen, it is the best preserved plasterwork in Britain and provides a dramatic contrast to the delicate, cake-icing embellishments common to most ceilings of the period. Here the plasterwork contains deep, imaginative patterns, rich and sumptuous without being excessive. They really are magnificent. Craigievar is one of the most remarkable houses in Europe, yet it attracts only about 20,000 visitors a year—an astounding oversight, and one you should hasten to take advantage of if you're in Scotland.

Details: Craigievar Castle is on the A980 road, six miles south of Alford and 26 miles west of Aberdeen. It is open from May 1 to September 30 from 2 to 6 P.M.. Closed Fridays. The grounds, which include an interesting nature trail, are open all year from 9:30 A.M. to sunset. The property is owned by the National Trust for Scotland.

The Landmark Trust

Any vacation organization so successful it has never had to advertise is unusual. One that has achieved this success by offering its clients accommodation in a disused arsenic mine, or a Victorian railway station, or a house shaped like a pineapple, has got to be unique—and could only be British. Such an enterprise is the Landmark Trust. It was formed as a charity in 1964 by a conservation-minded banker and politician named John Smith, who was disturbed at the number of distinctive British buildings falling into disrepair. He decided to save at least some by turning them into vacation homes.

The trust now looks after more than 100 properties throughout Britain, including three castles, a Gothic temple, a disused lighthouse, several mines and mills, an island off the coast of Wales called Lundy, and an entire village in Cornwall. There are also a number of more conventional farmhouses and cottages, though all are either very old or historically and architecturally significant. Each of the properties has been restored with heroic care—during European Architectural Heritage Year the trust won 11 awards, more than any other British recipient—and furnished with period pieces, but given modern conveniences like central heating and decent plumbing. A particularly nice touch is that each house is provided with a shelf of books—fiction, nonfiction, and poetry—relating to the area. The whole idea, as the trust itself engagingly puts it in its splendid catalogue, is to provide the visitor with a holiday of "a mildly elevating kind." It succeeds enormously.

Renovating long-neglected properties is not cheap—a medieval manor house in Devon, for instance, cost only $20,000 to buy but almost $500,000 to restore—but even so Landmark manages to keep its rates quite reasonable. You could, for example, rent a restored nineteenth-century chapel in a glorious setting in Devon for as little as $50 a week. Something a bit more ambitious, like a seventeenth-century townhouse in the heart of Bath across the square from the abbey, will cost about $180–$280 a week depending on the time of year. When you compare that with hotel prices in Britain, it's exceptionally reasonable for a place capable of sleeping four people in unique surroundings while offering the additional satisfaction of helping to preserve a piece of Britain's heritage. (It's also possible, particularly in the off season, to rent many trust properties for only a day or two.)

The one drawback with the Landmark Trust is that it can accommodate only about 10,000 visitors a year and it's very popular. So it can prove difficult to get the particular property you want at the particular time you'd like. But for anyone with perseverance and a degree of flexibility, it provides a wonderful and uniquely rewarding holiday option in Britain.

Details: Arranging a stay in a Landmark property requires some diligence, and, unless you are coming in the depths of winter, you will almost certainly have to make reservations long before you leave home. Space constraints here don't allow a detailed description of the trust's properties, but its illustrated, 164-page catalogue gives a thorough, and refreshingly honest, description of them all. It's available for $3 from the Landmark Trust, Shottesbrooke, Maidenhead, Berkshire. This find can't be recommended highly enough.

Herm, Channel Islands

Any group of people who get their language, culture, and television services from Britain, but their food and weather from France can be fairly said to have gotten their priorities right. Such are the inhabitants of the Channel Islands. These five verdant isles—Jersey, Guernsey, Sark, Alderney, and Herm—lie just off the coast of France, but have been more closely associated with Britain for seven centuries. Thanks to a pact signed with King John in the thirteenth century, the islands have enjoyed most of the privileges of being British while retaining almost complete autonomy over their own affairs. They have their own courts, parliaments, postage stamps and coins, set their own income taxes (at a comparatively miserly 20 per cent), and have absolutely no sales taxes—which helps make their prices for cigarettes, liquor, and most other goods among the cheapest in Europe.

All the Channel Islands are eminently visitable, but Herm is probably the least known and most appealing. Only a tiny place (half a mile wide by one and a half miles long), it is the domain of one couple, Peter and Jenny Wood, who took out a lease from the neighboring island of Guernsey in 1954 and have been turning Herm into a paradise ever since. When the Woods first came to the island, it was so overgrown that they spent three days just finding the manor house in which they now live. Since then, however, the Woods have restored the island's chapel, opened a pub, a restaurant, and three small shops, converted a low stone house into a quiet and captivating hotel called the White House, and turned a dozen or so cottages into holiday homes.

Although visitors often outnumber the island's 40 residents by more than ten to one, even at the height of the season the island manages to preserve a feeling of remoteness and serenity. There are caves and woods for exploring, glorious views to be had from the island's cliffs, and an abundance of coves that offer more or less private swimming. Particularly notable is Shell Bay, where the beach consists entirely of tiny sea shells, many of them unique to Europe and some carried by tides from as far away as the Gulf of Mexico. The White House Hotel is usually booked well in advance, but if you get a chance to stay there, take it. You may never come away.

Details: Rates at the White House range from £25 per person in winter to £32.50 in high season, but include breakfast and dinner. For reservations simply write to Peter Wood, The Manor House, Herm, Channel Islands, UK. Herm is a 20-minute ride in an open boat from the harbor of St. Peter Port on Guernsey, which in turn can be reached by air from 17 British airports (it's a 45-minute flight from Heathrow) or by sea from Weymouth and Portsmouth. There are also sailings from St. Peter Port to St. Malo in France.

Guernsey itself invites a stay. Apart from its quiet beaches and good restaurants, it has a number of small, intriguing museums— including a museum of telephones and one of tomatoes. The house in which the writer Victor Hugo lived from 1856 to 1871 is another must-see. A gothic monstrosity full of exotic and elaborate furnishings, many built by Hugo himself, it's in the heart of St. Peter Port. Also marvelous is the tiny chapel of St. Andrew's, a faithful copy of the cathedral at Lourdes, but big enough for only six people. One devoted monk spent 15 years building it by hand, but had to tear it down and start all over again when it was discovered that the bishop who had come to consecrate it was too fat to get through the doorway.

GREECE

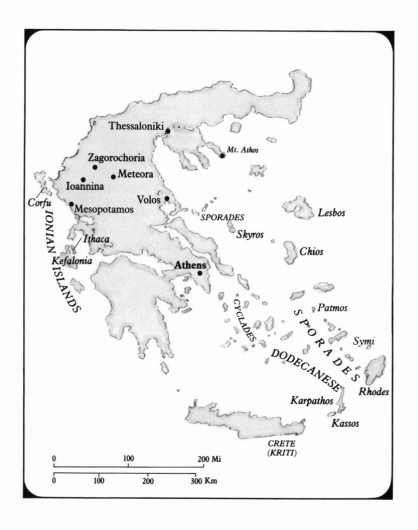

Thessaloniki
Mt. Athos
Zagorochoria
Meteora
Ioannina
Corfu
IONIAN ISLANDS
Mesopotamos
Volos
SPORADES
Lesbos
Skyros
Chios
Ithaca
Kefalonia
Athens
Patmos
CYCLADES
S P O R A D E S
Symi
DODECANESE
Rhodes
Karpathos
Kassos
CRETE
(KRITI)

0   100   200 Mi

0   100   200   300 Km

Kefalonia, Ionian Islands

It didn't attract much attention at the time, but about 20 years ago Corfu, that celebrated Greek isle, quietly disappeared. Those who noticed assumed it had died—killed off by an acute overdose of package holidaymakers, tacky souvenir shops, and sprawling resort hotels—but I'm happy to report that in fact Corfu simply moved a few miles south. It's now going by the name of Kefalonia. That at least is my theory.

Kefalonia (sometimes spelled Cephalonia) is in any case a gem. Lush, fragrant, and fertile, it is part of the same chain of islands as Corfu, the Ionians, and offers everything its more northerly sister once did, including relative solitude. In a corner of the world that we normally associate with barren and arid landscapes, Kefalonia is like one large garden, with geranium bushes up to ten feet high and hibiscus, bougainvillea, phillyrea, and salvia growing in every cottage yard and sprouting in profusion along the sunny roadsides. The fertility of the olive and citrus groves and the existence of the best natural harbor in Greece have given Kefalonia the sort of prosperity that leads to a contented, unhurried life-style and an abiding interest in good food and drink.

An earthquake in 1953 devastated Kefalonia and several other nearby islands and as a result the capital of Argostoli and main port of Sami were rebuilt almost from scratch. Today they enjoy striking settings but little else. To make the most of the island, you'll need to head north to Assos or Fiskardo (stopping en route, if time allows, at the Milissani Grotto, a ravishingly beautiful underground lake where the waters fairly glow with every shade of blue from the palest clair de lune to the deepest aquamarine). Fiskardo, a fishing village, was the only community on the island to escape the ravages of the 1953 earthquake, so its Venetian architecture is intact. Tiny, elegant, and unspoiled, it stands over a good harbor, backed by hills and waving cypresses. There's a fine restaurant and taverna and a beach of soft, white sand—in short, all the elements for a tranquil break. Even more striking, at least in its location, is Assos, a few miles south on the west coast. Your first, memorable view of it is from the road hundreds of feet above. Below you a small fishing village snuggles up against a sheltering headland in the shadow of a Venetian fort, overlooking a dazzling expanse of the purest blue sea. Descending to the village, you are again confronted with unspoiled perfection, excellent beaches, and a welcoming atmosphere. But hurry: property developers are said to have their eye on Assos and its days as a secluded idyll are no doubt numbered.

For anyone wanting to savor Greek island life but without the time to seek out one of the more scattered eastern isles, Kefalonia is probably the ideal choice. Although overlooked by most tourists, it is easily reached from several places *on* the beaten track, including Athens and Brindisi in Italy, and the island's bus services are, by Greek standards, not bad.

Details: To Kefalonia there are daily flights from Athens and ferry services from Piraeus, Patras, and the other Ionian islands of Ithaca, Zakynthos (itself largely unspoiled), and Corfu. In the summer there are sailings to and from Brindisi on alternate days.

Monasteries of Meteora

On the western edge of the green plain of Thessaly, a series of massive gray rocks, breathtaking in their grandeur, soar up abruptly from the ground like a forest of stone. This is nature at its most dramatic. Teetering impossibly on the summit of these stark, sheer-walled crags are a number of medieval monasteries. This is man at his.

These ancient rock outcroppings, some up to 2,000 feet high, have been a sacred retreat since the eleventh century when early hermits sought refuge in the caves that pock their surfaces. In the fourteenth century, monks from Mt. Athos (see page 131) founded the first monasteries. The name they gave, Monasteries of Meteora, or "monasteries hanging in the sky," describes them to perfection. At Meteora's zenith in the sixteenth century there were 13 large monasteries and 20 small ones, and these lofty retreats served as a center not only of religion, but also of scholarship and Byzantine art. They must be among the most dramatically sited structures on earth and, until fairly recent times, the most inaccessible. Up to the 1920s, the only way to the summits was to be winched up in a net— a lurching, swinging journey made all the more harrowing by the knowledge that the monks traditionally changed the ropes only when one broke. How the first monks themselves got up the sheer walls, much less built their formidable retreats, is an achievement that has defied all explanation.

Today, rough steps hewn from the rock allow you to make the ascent with comparative ease. The view from the top simply surpasses description. Words like *breathtaking* and *amazing* and *unforgettable* become mere babbles when confronted with the awesome sight of these ecclesiastical fortresses perched on their sheer towers high above the sweeping plain. Only four monasteries remain occupied. The largest and most important is the Great Meteoron, perched 1,700 feet up on its pinnacle of rock, with a particularly beautiful domed chapel and a refectory that is now a museum containing a very good collection of carved wooden crosses. In summer only, the monastery also offers a hostel and restaurant. Also nearby are the monasteries of Barlaam (or Varlaam), filled with exquisite frescoes, and Roussano, built on the edge of a sheer precipice, making it perhaps the most dramatically sited of the three. Roussano is now closed, but you can get as far as the front door by crossing a bridge from a neighboring pinnacle.

Because of the relatively recent addition of a paved road, the area around Grand Meteoron can sometimes become packed with tour buses. But farther on, a walk of about two or three hours, are two monasteries that are much more secluded, though no less majestic. The first, Agia Trias (or Ayia Triada), commands what may be the most spectacular setting of all, practically tumbling over the sides of a dramatic outcropping at the head of a lovely green valley. It is now a convent and orphanage (how the nuns keep their young charges from falling off into the void is itself something of a small daily miracle) and possesses the oldest chapel in the Meteora, dating from 1476. Farther on is Agious Stephanou (Ayios Stafanous), which offers a very good restaurant and the chance to examine monastic life relatively unsullied by the intrusions of tourism.

The whole is spectacular and unique. If you plan to spend any time on the Greek mainland at all, don't miss Meteora. But do read the details below carefully first, and see the map on page 140.

Details: Meteora lies in northwestern Thessaly between Ioannina and Larisa and just north of Trikala. From the neighboring town of Kalambaka there are rail connections to Trikala and Volos, from which there are further connections to Thessaloniki, Athens, and beyond. Although there is an erratic bus service along the road linking the various monasteries, you can make a circuit of the area in a day on foot. In several places footpaths (not usually very well marked) provide shortcuts. Grand Meteoron is open every day but Tuesdays from 9–1:30 and 3:30–5:30; Barlaam every day but Fridays from 9–1:30 and 3:30–6; Agia Triada daily from 8–12 and 3–6; and Agia Stephanous every day but Mondays from 8–12 and 3–5. Since it can be a long hike between sites, be sure to check with the tourist police (on the road out of Kalambaka en route to Kastraki) that the hours haven't changed since the time of writing. You will be expected to pay a small admission charge at each of the monasteries. Finally—and most important—note that all women should wear skirts and all men and women must cover their arms (e.g., with a jacket or sweater). Failure to do so is likely to result in exclusion from the monasteries.

The Zagorochoria and Vikos Gorge

Head west out of Ioannina, take a right off the main highway onto the little road to Zitsa, and suddenly you find yourself in another world. This is the edge of the Zagorochoria, a slumbering arcadia of lush pastures and pure mountain streams, where a series of country lanes leads you over graceful stone bridges and through a succession of utterly captivating villages—46 in all—strung out along the steep slopes and lush valleys of the Zagoria Mountains. This was once an area of considerable prosperity, as evidenced by the unexpectedly large and numerous churches and once-graceful mansions (now mostly rundown) that dot the landscape. Today, however, it is breathtakingly unspoiled and virtually forgotten.

Zitsa, a flower-filled mountain village of cobbled streets and charming stone houses, is the best stepping off place for a tour of the area. Byron called it "the prettiest place in Greece" and celebrated the local monastery, St. Elias, in his poem "Childe Harold." About ten miles beyond it to the northeast is Monodendri and the monastery of Agia Paraskevi, perched spectacularly high on a rocky platform whose edges end in a sheer plunge to the floor of the Vikos Gorge 3,000 feet below. To stand on this dizzying outcrop is an unforgettable experience, more like wing-walking than sightseeing. The gorge itself is a small-scale Grand Canyon, but intensely lush, with trees growing out of the most impossible crannies, as if able to find sustenance in the rockface itself. There's nothing else like it in Greece and few sights anywhere in the world to rival it.

This is not a particularly easy area to explore, especially for those without a car, nor does it offer much in the way of creature comforts. There are no hotels; accommodation is in small tavernas and tends to be spartan, though spotless. But for those willing to forgo for a day or two the certainty of a hot bath and to do a fair bit of hiking, the scenic rewards are immeasurable.

Details: The first essential for a tour of the Zagorochoria is a good map. Probably the best is "The Tourist's Map of the Epiros," published by J. Rekos & Co. of Athens. From Ioannina (pop. 40,000) bus services link many of the villages. The tourist police at Kaloudi 10 in Ioannina can advise you. A more ambitious option is offered by an English company called Sherpa Expeditions (131a Heston Road, Hounslow, Middlesex, England), which organizes friendly and not very strenuous hiking tours that take in not only the Zagorochoria, but also the monasteries of Meteora and still leave you with a couple of days on the beach at Parga. The advantage is that it spares you all the headaches concerning food, accommodation, routes, and the Greek language, and, best of all, your luggage is ferried ahead to your next overnight stop. Against all this convenience, of course, must be balanced the fact that it is cheaper to do it on your own.

Skyros, Sporades

Sporades means "the scattered isles," and Skyros is about as scattered as you can get in the western Aegean. Thanks in large part to its relative isolation from—and poor ferry links to—the other islands of the chain, it is largely overlooked by tourists. As a result there isn't much on offer in the way of booming discotheques or raucous nightlife. But if you're looking for good beaches, appealing villages, and relief from the madding throngs, this is the place to deposit yourself. When you consider that it's a scant four hours from Athens by bus and boat, its obscurity is nothing short of astounding.

Skyros (or Skiros) is 22 miles long and about five miles wide on average and lies 25 nautical miles from the port of Kimi (a two-hour ferry crossing). Almost all the island's inhabitants live in one of two towns, the port of Linaria (pop. 500) and the capital of Skyros Town (pop. 2,500 and generally called Horio by the locals), about six miles away on the east coast.

Skyros Town is particularly attractive. Its geometric, white-washed houses—more reminiscent of the architecture in the Cyclades—sprawl across a vast natural amphitheater under the shadow of a Venetian castle. Peep into almost any interior, even the most humble cottage, and you will almost certainly see a trove of family heirlooms—rich embroidery, carved wooden furniture, copperware, and decorative plates—for which the island is famed. If you fail to catch a glimpse into any of the houses, you can see examples of local handiwork in the town's museum—and however dreary that may sound, it's actually quite an interesting place—or indeed find it for sale in many of the local shops.

For swimming and sunbathing, the island is just about unbeatable, dotted as it is with sandy bays, secluded inlets, and beachside tavernas, which sometimes seem to have been put there for your exclusive convenience. There can't be many experiences more deeply satisfying than spending a day frolicking in the surf and then retiring, scrubbed clean with saltwater and sunshine, to the dappled shade of an open-aired taverna to sit with a cold Fix Hellas in your fist against a backdrop of deep blue skies and a glittering sea. There are at least two of these demi-paradises on Skyros. One is just around the bay from Linaria, reached by an unpaved road, where you will find a broad sandy beach and lone taverna. Similarly, from Skyros Town you can head for Atsistsa, where again you'll discover a secluded beach fringed by fragrant pines and blessed with a single vine-clad taverna. Wonderful.

Details: The most direct route to Skyros from Athens is by bus to Kimi and then by ferry to Linaria. More circuitously and expensively, but worth considering if you want to do some island hopping, you can reach Skyros from the ports of Agios Konstandinos or Volos via the islands of Skiathos, Skopelos, and Alonissos. On the island itself are bus services between Linaria and Skyros Town. You can also rent motorbikes in Skyros Town. I hesitate to mention it because so many people get wrecked on them every year, but if you are inclined to take to two wheels, it is an ideal way to get to the more secluded beaches and Skyros is one of the safer islands. But do be careful of ruts in the dirt tracks and, above all else, check your travel insurance to see if there are any exclusion clauses for motorbike accidents. (There often are.)

Mount Athos

I don't know anyplace in the world that does more than Mount Athos to discourage casual visitors, except perhaps Albania—and even Albania doesn't discriminate against women. To visit this monastic community you must be a male at least 18 years old (there was a time when you had to be bearded as well); you must be prepared to sleep in spartan quarters and eat a fairly grim and mostly vegetarian diet; you must forswear tobacco and indecorous behavior for the duration of your stay; you must do a fair bit of shuttling around to secure the necessary documentation to be allowed in to the monastic complex (see details below); and you must be a bit lucky since only ten non-Greeks are allowed into the compound each day. You must, in short, really want to go there.

But having said that, there are some compelling reasons for really wanting to go. For a start, Mount Athos is very old, very peaceful, and very, very beautiful. It is also unique. For just over 1,000 years this self-governing monastic republic has stood as a male-only bastion on the Chalcidice peninsula, a narrow finger of land 40 miles long and four wide, boxed in by the deep blue waters of the Aegean and towered over by the imposing and (usually) snow-capped peak of Mount Athos. Often called the most beautiful stretch of landscape in Greece, it certainly is among the lushest.

At its peak in the Middle Ages there were 40,000 monks in 40 great monasteries here, plus countless hermits living in caves in the mountainside. Today there are something like 1,500 monks and 20 monasteries, plus an assortment of smaller monastic houses and *skitis*, or hamlets, inhabited by devout but nonmonastic members of the Greek Orthodox Church. All the monasteries are prepared to feed and shelter visitors, often with considerable warmth, particularly for those who show a genuine interest in the monks' singular way of life. The oldest and most important monastery is Megistis Lavras, or Great Lavra, about eight miles south of Karyes, the "capital" of Mount Athos, where all visitors must begin their trips. It's a good six-hour hike to Lavra, though it can also generally be reached by boat or bus. The monastery dates from 963 and contains 15 chapels inside its vast and heavily fortified walls. The excellent frescoes alone make the trip worthwhile. From Lavra, the road leading on around the promontory takes you past the peninsula's most rewarding scenery and some of its most impressive monasteries—Pavlou, Dionysiu, Grigoriou, and Simonos Petras. All are spectacularly sited, often Meteora-fashion on precipitous crags and outcrops. Of the four, Dionysiu enjoys perhaps the most dramatic setting, but Grigoriou has the finest treasures. These include what is said to be the preserved hand of John the Baptist, a splinter from Christ's cross, and a wealth of Byzantine icons.

Mount Athos obviously is not for everyone. But if you are a male aged at least 18 with an interest in monastic life, or simply in scenery and seclusion, there's no place on earth like it.

Details: Mount Athos is 150 miles east of Thessaloniki (Salonica) in northern Greece. To secure entry you must first acquire a letter of recommendation from your consulate in Thessaloniki (for Americans it's at Vass Konstandinou 59)—a simple formality—that you then take to the Ministry of Northern Greece at Plateia Diki-tiriou. The officials there will give you a permit to visit Mount Athos. Then, finally, you must go to the Aliens Police at No. 41 Polytekh-niou, where you will be given a date on which you may begin your visit to Athos. When all this business is completed—and it is gen-erally fairly straightforward—you must catch a bus to Ouranoupolis and from there a boat to Daphne on the Athos peninsula. A waiting bus will take you to Karyes, where you must visit the Aliens Police and the Government Offices to exchange your documentation for a pass to the monasteries, good for four days. You will have to pay for this—at the time of writing it was about $10, slightly less for students—but your food and lodging for the next four days will be provided for free. The groundwork obviously is all very tiresome, and the rewards very spartan, but there can't be many better travel deals in the world.

Karpathos, Dodecanese

Karpathos is another Greek island that has amazingly managed to escape the attention of all but the most discriminating travelers, partly because it's rather more remote than many other islands— there are no direct boat or air services from any mainland port or airport—and partly because it already enjoys the prosperity that allows it to regard tourism as more of an agreeable sideline than a serious business. Even so, given its ravishing beauty, relaxed at-mosphere, and above all its clean, uncrowded beaches, it is aston-ishing that more people don't seek it out. The inconvenience of having to travel first to Crete or Rhodes—if indeed a visit to either island can ever be thought inconvenient—to catch an onward boat or plane is an exceedingly small price to pay for a few days, or weeks, on Karpathos.

As to the facts: Karpathos is a sliver of an island some 30 miles long but only about three miles wide. It is part of the Dodecanese chain and lies roughly midway between Crete and Rhodes. It is effectively two places. The southern half is dense with forests and rushing streams, interspersed with occasional lemon groves, leading down to magnificently empty beaches. The northern half is rough, rocky, and almost completely undeveloped—primitive even. The women there still generally dress in traditional peasant costumes. The capital of the island, Pigadia (pop. 1,200 and generally called Karpathos by the locals), is in the more prosperous southern half and is an exceptionally pleasant place with good hotels and restaurants, a sweeping beach running along its wide bay, and almost all the island's social life, such as it is. For those seeking absolute tranquility, a number of attractive villages lie south of town, beyond Ammopi, where you can generally count on finding a deserted beach and a clean bed in a welcoming taverna. Alternatively, you can take a boat from Karpathos Town to the northern village of Diafani, where there is more good swimming and gratifyingly cheap accommodation. Near Diafani, and worth seeking out, is the mountain village of Olimbos (or Olimpos), above which are spread 40 derelict windmills. This is probably the cheapest, friendliest, and most unspoiled place on the whole island and the view from its lofty summit down the sheer precipice of the island's western side erases the memory of the long hike uphill from Diafani. If you're looking for a quiet retreat in Greece, especially if your itinerary already includes Crete or Rhodes, Karpathos is well worth considering.

Details: To Karpathos, there are two or three ferries a week from Rhodes (seven hours) and Crete (six hours) and several plane flights daily from Rhodes (less than an hour, but more expensive).

Symi, Dodecanese

Symi, like many other Greek islands, has known better days. Quiet, extremely rugged, and hauntingly beautiful, it is a small place (just 22 square miles in area) snuggled up close to the Turkish coast. Its capital and port, known also as Symi, presents an unforgettable sight to anyone chugging into the harbor aboard a ferry: a large and apparently prosperous town sprawling up and over a semicircular hill, its white and honey-colored houses glinting seductively above the calm waters of a strikingly beautiful bay. If you are struck by the thought that such a large community seems unlikely on such a barren piece of rock, you're right. Symi, you see, is something of an illusion.

The island was once heavily forested. But its trees were cleared for boatbuilding, an industry from which Symi derived both its fame and its prosperity for centuries. Richer and more populous than Rhodes until as recently as a hundred years ago, it began a slow descent toward poverty when deforestation and overfishing of the nearby sponge beds forced a huge part of its population to emigrate. In more recent times, tourism has helped halt the slide, but a chronic lack of fresh water means that Symi can never hope to have the sprawling resort hotels that bring wealth—and crowds—to other Greek islands.

Most of Symi's life is to be found in the tavernas and restaurants that cluster invitingly around the harbor. Daytrippers from Rhodes can sometimes make this part of town (called Yialos) quite busy. But wander up the hillside to the upper town (called Chorio), and you'll find a startling contrast. Those noble mansions that looked so impressive from below are, you will discover, mostly derelict and roofless, with gaping windows and, sometimes, trees growing through their rotting floors. An intricate network of steep side streets, more like extended staircases than roadways, lures you into random exploration. Although some of the houses are still inhabited and others have been converted into holiday villas, the effect nonetheless is of wandering through a ghost town—at once melancholy and even slightly eerie, yet tranquil and captivating. There's a stillness here, enhanced by the almost total absence of motor vehicles on Symi, that is quite incredible. Only the most occasional sound—voices from an open window, the phut-phut of a caïque in the bay far below—remind you that you're not entirely alone.

Symi's main value is that it offers an appealing mix of solitude and sociability, much quieter than Rhodes but livelier than the nearby islands of Tilos and Astipalea. Around the harbor are two very good restaurants, Katerinetes and Kyriakos, a few interesting shops (hand-painted icons and vividly colored weavings are the island's specialties), and, on the water's edge, a friendly, partly open-air discotheque called the Coco Club. But amble for an hour or so along almost any of the paths that lead out of the town and you will stumble on a beach or inlet where you are more or less assured of a day's swimming and lazing in private. Although busy during the daytime, the area around the harbor becomes blissfully sedate when the last ferries carry off the daytrippers at about 6 o'clock.

Details: Several ferries run daily to Symi from Rhodes, a two-hour trip. The island has only two small hotels, but it is usually not difficult to find a room in a private home. Two local travel agencies, Syme Tours and Symean Holidays, can both help if you are unable to find anything yourself. Apart from swimming, eating, drinking, and ambling, Symi's only diversions are a small historical museum in the lower town (open 9–2:30 every day but Monday; admission free) and a large monastery called Panormitis on the far side of the island. Both, however, are for enthusiasts only.

Chios, Northern Aegean

Whereas Symi was once very wealthy but now is not, Chios is rich and always has been. The explanation is quite simple: by a remarkable coincidence, almost every family in the Greek shipowning aristocracy comes from the island. A notable exception is the Onassis clan and even they once lived here. The quite phenomenal wealth of the island's dozen or so richest families not only lends Chios an air of sophistication and classiness (enhanced by the splendid yachts that bob in its harbors throughout most of the summer), but also allows the Chians to take a more relaxed attitude to tourism. Although they are happy to share their island with you, they don't mind in the least that it remains little known to the world at large.

Like Symi farther to the south, Chios is hard up against the coast of Turkey, separated by a channel just five miles across. Shaped like a kidney bean, it is one of the larger Greek islands (325 square miles) and most populous, with slightly over 52,000 inhabitants. Apart from the scenic beauty, charming villages, good restaurants, and expansive beaches that you have by now no doubt come to regard as your due in Greece, Chios also possesses more unusual diversions, interesting architecture, and cultural outlets than most other Greek islands. Uniquely, for instance, it offers concerts, ballets, and plays at the impressive Homeric Center, built by one of the island's wealthiest families and dedicated to its most famous native son, Homer. Chios is also notably greener than most other islands in the northern Aegean and produces perhaps the most delectable sweets in the whole of Greece.

Nearly half the island's population lives in the capital and port, Chios Town (often called Hora), but it's a largely unappealing place and, apart from two very good archeological museums, is principally notable as a point of departure to remoter parts of the island. Probably the most interesting village on the island—certainly the most unusual—is Pyrgi (or Pirgi), where the houses and churches are decorated in very striking gray and white floral and geometrical patterns called *sgraffito*. The effect is hectic, but memorable—and more than a little mysterious since no one knows quite how the custom arose. Nearby is the medieval fortress village of Mesta, also very attractive, with narrow lanes and shadowy, arch-covered alleys in a glorious mountain setting. Many houses follow the traditional arrangement of a windowless ground floor for the domestic animals with the family quarters above. But several houses have been converted by the national tourist organization into holiday residences. If you don't mind the relative remoteness, they are quite appealing and extraordinarily cheap (about $15 a day for a small house sleeping five). Also not to be missed if time allows is the monastery of Nea Moni, one of the most impressive and important Byzantine structures in Greece, nestled in the mountains about eight miles from Chios Town. Wonderful views lead down onto the town and to the sea beyond, and the monastery has some of the finest medieval mosaics. There are good beaches all around the island, but particularly notable are those at Nago, Marmaro, and Emborio.

If you're looking for a place largely unspoiled by foreigners, but are afraid you might find some of the smaller islands a bit dull or claustrophobic, Chios is probably your best bet.

Details: Chios can be reached by daily plane flights from Athens or boats from Piraeus (Athens' port; about ten hours) and Lesbos (four hours). There are also weekly sailings to and from Thessaloniki and islands in the Sporades and Dodecanese. There are also services to Turkey (port of Cesme), which makes Chios a handy stepping-stone for anyone traveling between the two countries.

Patmos

Like so many places in Greece, religion is at the heart of Patmos. For more than 700 years, beginning in 1088, this little island in the eastern Aegean was effectively an independent monastic republic, run by and for monks, much like the more famous republic of Mt. Athos (see page 131). But its greatest moment of glory came almost a millennium earlier, in about A.D. 95, with the arrival of St. John. In a cave high on a hill, he lived here for a year with his faithful disciple Prochoros and found the inspiration to write the Book of Revelation.

Although the island's monks long ago relinquished active political control of Patmos, they continue to exert a benign influence—strong enough to keep the island free of the worst excesses of tourism, but not to make it oppressive. There's an aura of sanctity and tranquility that's almost palpable, and very refreshing for anyone who's just arrived from the livelier pleasures of, say, Kos or Rhodes or Athens. That may not be quite so evident in the relatively busy, and very pretty, little port of Skala, a community of typically pink and white-washed brilliance built around a large central square. But wander uphill to the little town of Hora (a short bus ride or an extremely pleasant 30-minute walk through pine woods) and you'll begin to appreciate the role religion has played in the history of Patmos.

More than 40 churches and monasteries are scattered about in Hora. But dominating them all—indeed, dominating the whole of the island—is the large monastery of St. John the Divine, looking more like a Norman fortress than a place of worship. Although the monastery dates from the eleventh century, most of the present structure is from the fifteenth. Its treasures, which include a wealth of jewels, chalices, icons, crosses, rare embroidery, and paintings (including three attributed to St. Luke), are said to be the finest in Greece apart from those at Athos and really are quite breathtaking. But the most precious of all are found in the monastery's library— 33 leaves of the Gospel of St. Mark from the famous fifth-century *Codex Porphyrius*, written in silver on purple vellum. Here also you'll find an eighth-century manuscript of the Book of Job, plus almost 900 other ancient manuscripts and 2,000 books.

Roughly halfway down the hill between Hora and Skala, just beyond the theological college, is the Monastery of the Apocalypse, built around the cave where St. John was said to have lived. Here you can see the rock where Prochoros knelt to take dictation and another that the saint reputedly used as his pillow. Even if you are entirely unmoved by history or religion, the walk is its own reward, with marvelous views down onto the gleaming, cube-like houses of Skala and the glittering waters of the Aegean and neighboring islands of Samos and Ikaria.

Patmos is a tiny place—just 13 square miles in area with a population of only 2,500—and there's little in the way of nightlife. But good beaches are abundant, particularly on the northern side of the island around Kambos. In fact, if you're looking for a perfect blend

of excellent swimming, rugged beauty, historic diversions, and bliss-
ful quietude, it's just about unbeatable.

Details: Patmos is the northernmost of the Dodecanese Islands in
the eastern Aegean, about 106 miles from Rhodes. It can be reached
by boat from there or from Piraeus, Leros, Kos, or Kalymnos.

Oracle of the Dead, Mesopotamos

The Nekromanteion, or Oracle of the Dead, just outside Mesopotamos in Epirus, is one of the most impressive and historic archeological sites in western Greece; Homer describes it at length in the
Odyssey. But it is also, perhaps more interestingly, a monument to
one of the most elaborate cons in ancient history. Until the second
century B.C., and for no one knows how many centuries before that,
gullible Greeks would come here to communicate with the dead in
the cult of Persephone. She was the mythological daughter of Zeus
and Demeter who was abducted by Hades and carried off to the
Underworld. The Nekromanteion, quite simply, was the entrance.

Standing amid the ruins today you might have difficulty seeing
them as anything more than a rather impressive archeological curiosity. But if you can manage to suspend your disbelief and imagine
yourself as an ancient Greek surrounded by the mighty walls and
gloomy corridors of this sinister edifice, you may just begin to appreciate what a quietly terrifying ordeal a pilgrimage to the
Nekromanteion must have been.

The priests who devised it had an unerring sense of basic human
psychology. First, the whole was deeply rooted in secrecy—visitors
were told that if they revealed the tiniest detail of what they saw the
gods would punish them with instant death—so new arrivals had
no idea of what was to confront them. Pilgrims were first taken to
one of a series of waiting rooms, where they were relieved of their
gifts to the gods and made to sit for an indeterminate period, possibly
lasting several days, listening to the deathly and unsettling howls of
the priests from nearby rooms. Eventually, they would be instructed
to stumble and grope their way down a dark, labyrinthine corridor
to a room where they would be bathed and purified, fed hallucinogenic substances, and then made to perform an animal sacrifice.
Finally, they would be led to a vast and presumably very spooky
central chamber, where the main part of the procedure would be

played out. So great was the secrecy surrounding these rituals that we don't know what exactly went on here. We do know, however, that the priests devised elaborate pulleys, which must have helped them in appearing to conjure up dead spirits as if from nowhere. There were also probably secret passages (now vanished) behind the walls, allowing the priests to move around unseen. This must have been an absolutely unforgettable experience to anyone sufficiently impressionable to have believed it.

In 167 B.C., a Roman army razed the site. But the walls, up to 11 feet thick, remain to give the modern visitor an unusually clear idea of the site's scale and layout. You can also see the storage chambers for wheat, barley, honey, and other votive offerings, as well as a more modern church incongruously plunked on the site at a much later date.

Details: The Nekromanteion is open weekdays from 9 to 3:30 and Sundays from 10 to 4:30. It's 32 miles from Igoumenitsa and 15 from Parga, one of the main ports for the Ionian islands. The nearest bus stop is at Kastri, about three miles from the site.

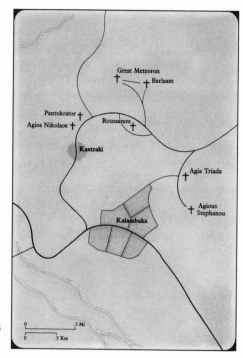

Monasteries of Meteora
(see page 127)

IRELAND

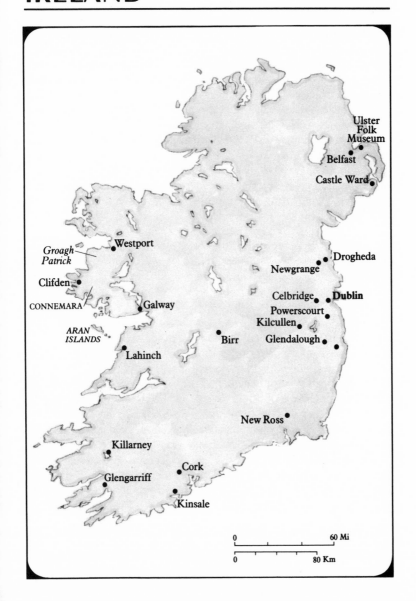

Ulster
Folk
Museum

Belfast

Castle Ward

*Groagh
Patrick*

Westport

Drogheda

Newgrange

Clifden

Celbridge

Dublin

CONNEMARA

Powerscourt

Galway

Kilcullen

*ARAN
ISLANDS*

Birr

Glendalough

Lahinch

New Ross

Killarney

Cork

Glengarriff

Kinsale

0		60 Mi
0		80 Km

Powerscourt Gardens, Co. Wicklow

In 1974, Powerscourt House, one of Ireland's stateliest homes, was devastated by fire. At the risk of sounding undiplomatic, the loss was more the Irish nation's than the modern traveler's. Powerscourt House had never been open to the public. The appeal here was, and always has been, the huge garden, which remains one of the most glorious in Europe.

Like Bodnant in Wales, the grounds of Powerscourt enjoy every natural advantage: a hillside setting, natural lake, and a sweeping view across an undulating green landscape to the hazy blue Wicklow hills and Sugar Loaf Mountain. With so much to work with, the man who designed it all need not have exerted himself much—and in fact he didn't. Named Daniel Robertson, he was a chronic sufferer of gout, brought on by an even more chronic affection for alcohol, and he spent his days sprawled in a wheelbarrow, a bottle of port on his lap, laconically supervising the work as an apprentice wheeled him around the site. Another apprentice was posted to keep a lookout for debt collectors, whose appearance would produce in Robertson an uncharacteristic agility and send him scampering off to hide in one of the cellars or outbuildings. Once even he had to be helped down from the roof.

Despite these distractions and drawbacks, Robertson evidently retained a spark of genius because the gardens at Powerscourt are one of the most assured and masterly creations of the nineteenth century. Laid out in a series of vast formal terraces, up to 800 feet wide, they lead down to the little lake—once called Juggy's Pond, but hastily rechristened the Triton Pool. Overlooking it is the focal point of the garden, the *perron*—an elevated viewing platform enclosed with a delicate wrought-iron balustrade and paved in bold geometrical patterns with white and gray pebbles from a nearby beach. Here and throughout the garden, carefully scattered among the trees and formal flowerbeds, is a wealth of fountains and statuary, sundials and giant urns, some of them up to eight feet high. The whole effect suggests the elegant formality of a French garden, but wonderfully softened by the gentle, unsubdued countryside at its feet. This is, in short, one of the great gardens of the world—and the last in Europe to be built in the grand style.

Details: Powerscourt is just outside the very pretty village of Enniskerry, about 12 miles south of Dublin and connected by bus services. The estate—which covers 14,000 acres and contains a 400-foot-high waterfall, the highest in the British Isles—and garden are open every day from 10 A.M. to 5:30 P.M. between Easter and October 31.

Glendalough, Co. Wicklow

Glendalough, "the valley of the two lakes," is intensely beautiful. The steeply wooded slopes of the Wicklow Hills rise up above the slate black waters of its two lakes, remnants of the Ice Age, to provide one of the most striking and memorable settings in Ireland. In 545 the hermit St. Kevin came to the valley, attracted by its remoteness and mellow grandeur, to meditate in peace. His seclusion didn't last long. Word of his extreme devotion—it was said he could pray with such intensity that birds would perch on his outstretched arms—soon attracted followers. Before long an entire monastic city had sprung up where more than 1,000 monks quietly toiled. Its historical significance, both to Irish culture and to Western civilization, cannot be overemphasized. At a time when the Roman empire was crumbling and the Dark Ages were spreading a shadow over Europe, Glendalough remained a seat of learning and scholarship, preserving a heritage the Romans themselves were helpless to save. Today all that remains of this celestial city are three clusters of ruins spread out along the valley. The most important is the middle group, between the Lower Lake and river bridge, where you can see the large arched gateway that once marked the entrance to Kevin's city, and a tower 110 feet high and 52 feet around. It looks relatively new, but is in fact more than 1,000 years old.

Because it's only 30 miles from Dublin, Glendalough tends to be a magnet for tour buses. But you can escape the crowds, and capture the most memorable views of the valley, by hiking to the Upper Lake and beyond to the pass through the mountains called the Wicklow Gap, where streams tumble over the rocks on their way to the lakes below. The view back along the valley is simply magnificent. The pass leads on through some wild and desolate landscape to the village of Hollywood. Half a mile south of it, and a delight to explore, is the "hanging valley" of Hollywood Glen, which few tourists penetrate. About halfway down the three-mile-long valley are the remains of St. Kevin's Church, thought to mark the spot of Kevin's first hermitage before he moved on to Glendalough.

Details: Glendalough is about 30 miles south of Dublin and can be easily reached from there on the "St. Kevin" bus.

Dan Donnelly's Arm, Co. Kildare

This isn't one I'd suggest you travel halfway around the earth for, but if you happen to be in the general neighborhood of Kilcullen and crave a life-sustaining pint of Guinness and a bit of grisly diversion, then read on. The story begins on a chilly December afternoon in 1815 when thousands of shouting people gathered around a grassy hollow (now marked by a stone obelisk) just outside Kilcullen to watch two large, bare-chested men try to beat the bejesus out of each other. The men were Dan Donnelly, the all-Ireland boxing champion, and George Cooper, England's top pugilist. For two hours the two pummelled each other with bare fists until at last the bloodied Cooper threw in the towel. Donnelly was carried off to lasting fame and an eventual knighthood. Today, even among his countrymen, he is largely forgotten. But his arm lives on—after a fashion—in the Hideout Pub, just down the road in Kilcullen. There, reverently preserved in a glass case, lies the great boxer's right arm— black and grizzled, but intact from shoulder blade to fingertips— pointing a bit disturbingly at the food counter. It is a big arm: supposedly Donnelly could scratch his shins without bending over. But how it became detached from his body and ended up enshrined in a drinking parlor is a mystery to which there is—happily, I think—no answer. The Hideout is a big, friendly pub spread over several rooms, with glowing fireplaces and an eclectic assortment of stuffed animals and fish and historical odds and ends. If you're looking for a genuine country pub, or even just something to write home about, this is the place.

Details: Kilcullen is on the River Liffey, four miles south of Droichead Nua and about 30 miles from Dublin. Unlike English pubs, Irish pubs are open all day except for what is jocularly known as the "holy hour" (from 2:30 to 3:30 P.M.). They close at 10 P.M. on Sundays and at 11:30 P.M. the rest of the time.

Galley Cruising Restaurants, Co. Wexford

You couldn't really blame the proprietors of this cruising restaurant if all they served you was a slab of gnarled roast beef, a couple of lukewarm roast potatoes, and a bit of indistinguishable foliage masquerading as asparagus. After all, the tiny kitchen of a river cruiser is hardly the environment for producing haute cuisine. And in any case the real attraction of a dinner cruise is the passing scenery along the riverbanks, isn't it?

Fortunately, in this case the answer is no. Somehow, amazingly, the Galley's cramped cooking quarters bring forth quite exceptional meals (smoked ham and cheese soup followed by roast guinea fowl and topped off with chocolate profiteroles in double cream, for example) twice a day for up to 70 passengers—meals of a quality rarely encountered even on dry land in the British Isles and good enough to merit the praise of such worthies as Michelin and Egon Ronay. The food alone guarantees you a memorable experience. The gentle passing scenery simply makes it sublime.

Galley's dinner cruises depart from New Ross every Tuesday to Saturday from April to September for a three-hour, 20-mile cruise up the Barrow or Nore River. Meals are generally served after the boat turns around to begin the unhurried homeward journey, allowing you to enjoy the first half of the trip sitting on the open top deck, drink in hand, watching the villages, farms, and densely wooded countryside slip off into that most enchanted time of a summer's day, twilight. Dusk, particularly in June, lingers for hours in this part of the world and there can't be any more magical way of experiencing it than from the prow of a churning boat.

There are also daily two-hour luncheon cruises and, for those who cannot afford either the calories or the cost of a full meal, two-hour tea cruises departing at 3 P.M.. Alternatively—or even in addition—the Galley has a separate river cruiser a few miles south in Waterford, which offers two-hour tea cruises and two-hour high tea (i.e. supper) excursions. It is also possible to go for the cruise alone, subject to space availability.

Details: From New Ross, luncheon cruises depart at 12:30 P.M. from April 1 to early October and cost £9 (£4.50 for children); tea cruises depart from June to August at 3 P.M. and cost £4; dinner cruises start at 7 P.M. from April 1 to August 31 and at 6 P.M. in

September and cost £12–£16. On most Mondays there are no cruises. From Waterford, tea cruises depart at 3 P.M. and cost £4; high tea cruises depart at 5:10 P.M and cost £8. Both are available from June to August only and both are closed on Sundays and Mondays. Cruises only from both New Ross and Waterford cost £3–£6. Reservations are recommended. Write to Galley Cruising Restaurants, New Ross, Co. Wexford, Eire, or telephone (051) 21723.

Kinsale, Co. Cork

Kinsale is a charming, attractive, slightly raffish waterfront town of mostly Georgian houses lining narrow hilly streets. An important naval center in the eighteenth century (the hapless Andrew Selkirk sailed off from here to an unwelcome shipwreck, providing the inspiration for Robinson Crusoe), it is now a fishing port and yachting haven. This is one of those curious places that act as a magnet for upscale dropouts—refugees from city life who come for a visit and end up staying for years—which, with the yachting fraternity, gives it an air of nonchalant worldliness out of all proportion to its size. An agreeable side effect is that many of the interlopers open restaurants. There are 18 in Kinsale for a resident population of less than 1,800. Most are very good and a few—Man Friday, The Bistro, Gino's, and the Circle—are outstanding. In line with the general tone of relaxed amiability, the restaurateurs work out a rota of opening hours among themselves so that competition doesn't become too fierce.

Kinsale also has two friendly and atmospheric pubs—the Bullman on the quayside, filled with fishermen and yachting people in bulky sweaters, and, high on a hill overlooking the town, the Spaniard, with chairs outside so you can watch the sun setting over the Bandon River estuary and sea beyond—a perfect place to pass a summer's evening. There are good walks near the town, in particular to Summer Cove and Charles Fort (a large and impressive star-shaped battlement dating from the late seventeenth century and still in use until as recently as 1922). But if the weather is fine, consider a more ambitious trek to the promontory known as the Head of Kinsale, with magnificent cliffs and views across the sea. Somewhere out there, about ten miles offshore, lies the wreck of the *Lusitania*, which went down with 1,500 people after being torpedoed by a German submarine just off the headland in 1915. A bit farther on are the very pretty resorts of Garrettstown and Courtmacsherry, both offering good beaches and splendid settings. Finally, if you are still somehow at a loose end, there's some of the best sea fishing in Ireland, boat trips up the Bandon River to Innishannon, and a surprisingly good little municipal museum in the town's Courthouse with model ships and relics celebrating Kinsale's days of greatness as a seafaring community.

Like Glengarriff a bit farther along the coast (see next entry), Kinsale is an appealing place to wind down for a couple of days. But be careful—you could end up staying for years.

Details: Kinsale is 18 miles south of Cork and can be reached by frequent buses from there.

Glengarriff, Co. Cork

This little resort, tucked away in a beautiful glen on Bantry Bay, is quite simply a jewel. The Gulf Stream, which keeps the weather in this part of Ireland surprisingly mild, has been especially kind to Glengarriff, allowing subtropical vegetation to flourish here as almost nowhere else in northern Europe. Here you can hole up for a couple of days in one of the several comfortable hotels and guesthouses scattered about the village, and indulge yourself with unhurried walks around the bay—to Lady Bantry's Lookout and the Eagle's Nest beyond, for instance—or just laze in the mild, warm sunshine on the beach at Biddy's Cove. One must for every visitor is a trip to the remarkable gardens at Ilnaculin, or Garinish Island, which were constructed about 50 years ago by John Annan Bryce. When you see the exotic vegetation growing in fabulous luxuriance here—fuschias up to 25 feet high, for example, and plants and shrubs from as far away as the Himalayas, Amazonia, and Asia—you'll never believe that every speck of dirt on this once-barren island had to be imported from the mainland. There are Japanese and alpine gardens, an Italian garden clustered around a rectangular lily pool massed with flowers, and a Greek temple, all framing magnificent views of the bay; a lookout tower stands at the summit of the island. Among the island's eminent visitors was George Bernard Shaw, who wrote part of *Saint Joan* here.

Farther afield, but easily reached from Glengarriff, is the Beara Peninsula, as beautiful as the famous Ring of Kerry nearby, but much quieter. A circular signposted tour takes you around the mountainous, 30-mile-long peninsula and through the stunning Healy Pass.

Near Castletownbere is the ruined Dunboy Castle—the last strong-hold of the Irish rebellion of 1602—and there are excellent beaches near here and farther down the peninsula at Ballydonegan. All in all, a perfect way to spend a couple of days.

Details: Glengarriff (pop. 250) is 68 miles west of Cork and can be reached by bus from there. Garinish Island, reached by ferry from the town, is open from March 1 to October 31 from 9:45 to 5:30 Monday through Saturday and from 12:45 to 6 on Sunday.

Golfing in Ireland

Every year tens of thousands of people make a pilgrimage to Scotland to hack their way around such famous golf courses as St. Andrews, Turnberry, and Gleneagles. But only the tiniest portion of them take the trouble to cross the Irish Sea to try their hand on the courses of Eire. It's an unfortunate oversight. Golfing in Ireland is a splendid experience. The courses may not be as historic as in Scotland, but the better ones are every bit as beautiful and challenging—and oc-casionally even more so. They also tend to be less crowded and almost always are cheaper, especially when you consider that green fees in Ireland are per day rather than per round.

Ireland has 180 courses, compared with Scotland's 400. Two in particular, Lahinch and Killarney, are notable, partly because they are very beautiful as well as challenging and partly because their settings offer a number of alternative attractions for any nongolfers in your party.

Lahinch, lying along the Atlantic coast in County Clare, is an old course with an easygoing air—a fact that becomes evident as soon as you try to consult the barometer hanging just inside the clubhouse door. Where the hands should be is instead a simple note saying: "See Goats"—a reference to the small herd cropping the grass just outside. If the goats are standing on the hilltop you can count on fine weather, if they are clustered near the clubhouse, expect rain. The Old Course, founded in 1892 by the members of a Scottish army regiment, is a links course—that is, one built on a sandy plain along the sea, where the fairways can be nearly as rough as a North Amer-ican rough and the roughs are simply unspeakable. To call it a challenging course would be putting it mildly. Playing here is an experience that wavers between the exhilarating and the intimidating with long periods of deep confusion in between. The ocean provides not only scenic grandeur, but also whipping winds that can carry the truest of drives halfway to Limerick, and the cliffs are a constant invitation to suicide, especially when you encounter such challenges as the 156-yard, par 3 hole with a completely blind green. Take along a club to break or confine your activities to the shorter, easier New Course.

For a complete contrast, there's the Killarney Golf and Fishing Club, on the outskirts of the town of Killarney. It has two championship courses, Mahony's Point and the slightly longer Killeen. Although both are formidable, you may feel on more equal terms with them since both are park courses, more similar in layout to those of America. The real appeal here is that they are two of the most spectacularly beautiful courses in the world. Both spread out amid woodlands along the banks of Lough Leane with a verdant backdrop of mountains. The biggest challenge is to maintain your concentration amid such awesome scenery.

Details: Green fees in Ireland range from about £4–£8 a day and clubs rent for about £5. Most courses are fairly easy to get on (weekends excepted), but it's worth checking to be sure that there aren't any tournaments or events that would keep you from getting a starting time. The Irish Tourist Board produces a very useful *Visitors' Guide to Irish Golf Courses*.

Birr, Co. Offaly

Birr is a thriving and attractive little market town of about 3,600 people in the very center of Ireland, with a large market square and a wealth of good Georgian architecture. It's a splendid place for strolling, but especially so if you direct your ambling up Emmet Street, off the main square, and then along the handsome, tree-lined Oxmantown Mall to the grounds of Birr Castle. The castle, home of the Earl and Countess of Rosse, is a striking edifice, a mostly nineteenth-century gothic building whose large and rather stern exterior is softened by creeping vines. The castle is not open to the public, but don't lose heart. The grounds are, and their 100 acres of trees, shrubs, and flowers are nothing short of wonderful. More than a thousand species of trees and shrubs flourish here, including the two tallest box hedges in the world, more than 30 feet high and a century old. There's also an arboretum, a lake and landscaped park, a river garden with two waterfalls, and one of the first suspension bridges in the world across the little river.

This last is a relic of the period in the nineteenth century when the Rosses had a brief flowering of their own as scientists. The third earl was an astronomer of international repute, as was one of his sons. Another son invented the steam turbine. In 1843, Lord Rosse built on the grounds the largest telescope in the world—so large, in fact, that it would be almost 80 years before anyone built a larger one. The telescope's working mechanisms are long since gone, but the 56-foot-long walls and cylinder that housed it remain, along with a display of drawings, photographs, and other astronomical odds and ends. There's an interesting working scale model of the original telescope and a brief taped commentary on its history and significance.

Spring is the best time to visit the gardens when the countless magnolia and cherry trees are in bloom, but the abundance of variegated foliage everywhere and handsome landscaping make it a winner throughout most of the year.

Details: The grounds of Birr Castle are open year round from 9 A.M. to 1 P.M. and from 2 to 6 P.M. (dusk if earlier). Admission is £2 for adults, £1.50 for children.

Aran Islands

Someone once observed that the world's historians owe the Irish a great debt for building an independent civilization and preserving it almost intact into modern times. Nowhere perhaps is that truer than on the Aran Islands. Although a bit of tourism and television have brought the twentieth century creeping in, these three hunks of rock stuck 30 miles out in the steely gray waters of the Atlantic off the coast of Galway remain very much of another time, one of the last outposts of the real Irish culture. Gaelic, for instance, remains the first—and for many islanders the only—language.

The three islands—Inishmore, Inisheer, and Inishmaan—are home to about 2,000 people, though they have little more than 18 square miles of area between them. For scholars they are notable for their prehistoric monuments—the great stone complex of Dun Aengus on Inishmore is perhaps the finest prehistoric fort in Europe—but for many others the appeal lies in their bleak and elementary beauty. Few landscapes can have offered a more forbidding prospect to their early settlers or been more painstakingly conquered. The early Christian hermits who were the islands' first inhabitants found a terrain not only treeless but soilless. The earth that today nurtures the islands' animals and crops is entirely manmade, compounded of alternating layers of sand and seaweed and sustained by generations of patience. The only thing the Arans possess in abundance is rocks, which are everywhere piled in a dense network of sheltering, waist-high, dry stone walls, making the islands look from every vantage point like outsized jigsaw puzzles.

Of the three islands, only Inishmore has a harbor that can accommodate ferries. To reach the other two islands, the ferry heaves to as near the shore as it can and the islanders come out in curraghs—frail-looking canvas-covered boats—to bring ashore passengers and provisions. For anyone really trying to get away from it all, the two smaller islands are perhaps the more rewarding—not only for the excitement of coming ashore in one of the featherweight curraghs but also because there are fewer visitors. On the other hand, Inishmore has better attractions—and comforts.

No hotels exist on any of the islands, but Inishmore has a number of pleasant guesthouses, mostly clustered around the little harbor at Kilronan. There are also three pubs, a restaurant, a tearoom/fish and chip shop, and, inevitably, a few souvenir shops, some of them selling some quite good island handicrafts. You can be taken around the island on a pony and trap or you can rent bicycles for only about £2.50 a day at the harbor. Inishmore is a cyclist's paradise thanks to the almost complete absence of traffic, the island's surprisingly mild climate, compact size, and wealth of dramatic vistas. The stone fort of Dun Aengus, perched on a sheer cliff 265 feet above the sea, provides a memorable destination, but wherever you go a gratifying prospect of hardy thatched cottages, abundant wildflowers, and steep descents to a crashing sea will confront you.

Details: There are daily air services throughout the year to all three Aran Islands (it's about a 20-minute flight from Galway), but most people cross by ferry from Galway. There are two ferries a day and the trip takes about three hours.

Croagh Patrick and Connemara, Co. Galway

Croagh Patrick is the holiest spot in Ireland and one of the loveliest. St. Patrick retreated to this pyramid-shaped mountain for 40 days and nights in A.D. 441 and from here drove the snakes out of Ireland—not to mention moles, toads, and about a dozen other species of animals curiously absent in Ireland. There's a famous chapel on the windswept summit, site of a vast annual pilgrimage, but the long, long trudge to the top is rewarded (in good weather at least) with fabulous views over Clew Bay, speckled with islands, and across great stretches of that most beautiful and neglected corner of Ireland—Connemara.

This area of Galway is so unremittingly lovely that you can scarcely put a foot wrong; whatever route you follow will almost certainly reveal panoramas of unspoiled grandeur. It's a rough landscape of dark mountains and broad bogs, where Gaelic-speaking farmers must literally scratch a living from soil too rocky for plows.

Croagh Patrick is easily reached from Westport, a well-preserved Georgian town with a notable mansion, Westport House, and good transportation links to the rest of the country. Even if you don't stop at the holy mountain, the road from Westport along Clew Bay and onward to Clifden is magnificent—the Irish writer James Plunkett has called it "surely the most beautiful in Ireland." This route takes you through the pleasant town of Louisburgh and then past the incredible Kylemore Castle, a vast and elaborate Victorian graystone mansion that was once one of the grandest houses in Ireland (even though one bathroom served every thirty guests), but since 1920 has been a convent, though still open to the public. Again, even if you don't stop, it's worth the trip just to glimpse this remarkable, sprawling mansion in its incomparable setting. Beyond Kylemore is the Connemara National Park, set in 4,000 acres of countryside under the shadow of a range of mountains known as the Twelve Bens. The park's visitors' center is housed in converted farm buildings with exhibitions of traditional Irish furnishings and, more important, an audio-visual presentation explaining the unique history and geography of the area. Very useful for those who regard travel as a learning experience.

From Clifden, an agreeable coastal town about five miles to the south, the road runs on for about 50 miles to Galway, where train and bus connections link up with the rest of the country. But if time allows, consider continuing south along the winding coastal roads, which take you through some lovely little resorts of whitewashed cottages like Kielkieran and Roundstone. All along this coast are countless rocky coves and deserted beaches of fine white sand, with views across to the Aran Islands and the commanding Cliffs of Moher beyond. It's a more circuitous means of reaching Galway and could add at least a day to your traveling time—perhaps more if you're hitching—but it's also one of the best detours in Ireland.

Newgrange Burial Chamber, Co. Meath

Newgrange, a vast prehistoric burial chamber high on a ridge overlooking the River Boyne, is the sort of place that would set Erich Van Daniken's heart racing. Apart from the bare facts of its dimensions, almost everything about it is a deep mystery. It is assumed that foreigners built it some 4,000 years ago, since the Irish of the time lacked the necessary skills to make it themselves, and it is known that it took a great effort of will to construct (an estimated 180,000 tons of stones were hauled to the site). But no one knows whose death was important enough to justify such an expenditure of resources and labor, nor why the builders (thought to have come from Brittany) ventured so far from home to build it.

Today what remains is the best preserved, most important, and far and away the most enigmatic burial chamber in Europe. The chamber encompasses about an acre of ground with a dome 44 feet high and 280 feet across. Once, it is thought, it was entirely covered in brilliant white pebbles. Scattered around it are twelve large sculptured stones. You enter the chamber along a passage three feet wide and 62 feet long to emerge at the end in a central chamber, a room about ten feet wide and with a vaulted ceiling 19 feet high. Off it are three recesses that may once have been used for sacrifices. Everywhere the stonework is intriguingly decorated with carved squiggles and zigzags, which in terms of sophistication and craftsmanship were centuries ahead of anything else in Europe. And to add to the mystery, a hole in the ceiling allows a shaft of light to pierce the chamber for precisely 17 minutes at sunrise every year on December 21, the shortest day of the year.

Also at the site is a small but interesting museum explaining the historical significance of the chamber—insofar as it is explicable. Newgrange is just part of a vast stone age complex spread over three square miles and known collectively as Brugh na Boinne. Nearby are similar chambers at Dowth and Knowth. The latter is said to be even more impressive than Newgrange, but is not open to the public.

Details: The Newgrange Burial Chamber is between Slane and Drogheda, about 20 miles north of Dublin. It is open daily from

June 15 to September 30 from 9 to 7, and the rest of the year on Tuesday through Saturday from 10 to 1 and 2–5 and on Sundays from 2–5.

Castle Ward, Co. Down

Castle Ward, one of the great houses of Ulster, is the result of a remarkable compromise in the eighteenth century between a certain Lord and Lady Bangor. He wanted a traditional house in the conservative classical style. She wanted the racier "Gothick" style made fashionable by Alexander Pope at Strawberry Hill in Twickenham. Unable to agree, they built (between 1760 and 1780) a house with a classical Palladian face on one side and a vigorously Gothic facade on the other. This battle of styles continued inside, where the staircase, dining room, and music room are in the classical tradition, while the sitting and withdrawing rooms are in the style favored by Lady Bangor. The result satisfied no one, least of all Lord and Lady Bangor, who stopped talking and eventually split up.

Apart from its remarkable interiors, Castle Ward offers a beautiful setting overlooking Stranford Lough plus 700 acres of gardens and woodland walks to stroll through. There's an unusual Victorian laundry, a temple, and a tower house, a crafts center and a shop and tearoom. If you're in Northern Ireland, it really shouldn't be missed.

Details: Castle Ward is at Strangford on the A75 road south of Belfast. The house is open from April 1 to September 30 every day but Fridays from 2 to 6. The grounds are open from dawn to sunset throughout the year. In addition, there are vestiges of St. Patrick throughout this area. Saul, about three miles west of Castle Ward, is where Patrick landed in Ireland in A.D. 432 and two miles farther west at Downpatrick, in the graveyard at the Church of Ireland Cathedral, stands a granite boulder reputed to mark his burial place.

Castletown, near Celbridge, Co. Kildare

Castletown, a Palladian-style mansion 13 miles from Dublin, is something of a rarity in Ireland—a historic house you can actually enter. In a country where so many great houses are still in private hands or crumbled into dereliction, Castletown is not only gloriously preserved, but also wonderfully public. Since 1967 it has been cared for, and lovingly restored, by the Irish Georgian Society, whose directors have made it their headquarters. They chose well.

Built in 1722 for a social climbing Speaker of the Irish House of Commons, William Connolly, it is quite simply one of the finest Georgian residences anywhere. Castletown is also the largest house ever built in Ireland, with a sweeping frontage that runs and runs for more than 400 feet. Curving colonades connect the outer wings to an imposing central block some 60 feet high.

The interiors relentlessly continue Connolly's taste for grandeur. He imported the finest workmen from all over Europe and it shows, particularly in the elegant and delicate plasterwork that graces every ceiling. The tone throughout is Italianate, not too surprising since the architect was the great Alessandro Galilei. Focal points of the house are the print room—the only one of its kind in Ireland—and the Long Gallery, a vast and lavishly overdecorated salon that somehow manages to preserve an air of homeyness. If you are at all interested in architecture or Irish social history, Castletown is your perfect textbook. A not inconsiderable side benefit is that it's very easy to get to: from central Dublin a No. 67 bus will deposit you right at the gates. But do beware: opening hours are patchy.

Details: Castletown is at Celbridge, just off the main Dublin-Galway highway. It is open from April 1 to September 30 on Saturdays, Sundays, and Wednesdays from 2 to 6 pm, and from January 1 to March 31 on Sundays only from 2 to 6. Closed October, November, and December.

Ulster Folk and Transport Museum, Co. Antrim

Anyone tempted to groan at the inclusion of yet another open-air museum in this book has my complete sympathy. However, open-air museums are something the Europeans do supremely well and nowhere better than at the Ulster Folk and Transport Museum near Belfast. Spread over 170 acres on the grounds of an old manor house on the shores of Belfast Lough, it carefully and convincingly recreates life as it was in Ireland up to about the turn of the century. There are some two dozen structures scattered around the grounds—cottages, mills, workshops, a church, and school—each brought from elsewhere in Ireland and re-erected stone by stone. So sympathetically are they blended into the landscape that it's impossible to believe they haven't been there forever.

Great care has been taken to evoke the sights and smells of the past: chickens scratch in the grass outside tiny white cottages, turf burns in open fireplaces (no one in Ireland calls it peat, incidentally), bread bakes in ovens, giving the houses a lived-in aura that makes you feel like a secret intruder. Unusually, and most laudably, each building has a resident warden who is only too happy to explain how things work and what life was like for the residents. Separate buildings contain a wide and surprisingly fascinating assortment of tractors, airplanes, ships, and cars (including the ill-fated De Lorean, built near here), brought from the old Belfast Transport Museum when the two merged in 1967. The museum is rapidly expanding— by the time you read this there should be an entire hamlet spread out around an old church from County Down—but even so it is already good enough to have been named Britain's Museum of the Year in 1983. The title was well deserved.

Details: The Ulster Folk and Transport Museum is on the A2 Belfast to Bangor road (there are buses from either), about two miles east of Holywood and seven miles from Belfast. It is open daily from May to September from 11 A.M. to 6 P.M. (on Sundays from 2 to 6 only) and until 5 P.M. the rest of the year.

ITALY

LAKE ORTA

LAKE GARDA

Venice

Collodi

Lucca

Florence

Urbino

Livorno

Todi

Bomarzo

Rome

Monte St. Angelo

Naples

Ravello

SARDINIA

AEOLIAN ISLANDS

Cefalu

SICILY

| 0 | 100 | 200 Mi |
| 0 | 100 | 200 | 300 Km |

Gabriele D'Annunzio's Villa, Lake Garda

Gabriele D'Annunzio was a man of many parts, most of them private. Although short, scrawny, bald as a pebble, and with only one eye after the other was shot out in World War I, he was irresistible to women. At a conservative estimate, he slept with 1,000 in his life, ranging from peasants to countesses, and treated most like dirt. In between he found time to be a poet and author, fascist, spendthrift, war hero, adventurer, bon vivant, and brute. His whole life was a succession of flamboyant outbursts. Outraged by the settlement terms of the war, for instance, he organized a private army and captured the Yugoslavian town of Fiume, which he ruled dictatorially for a year. Such activities brought him to the attention of the ascendant Benito Mussolini, who made D'Annunzio a prince and gave him a villa (confiscated from a hapless German professor) on the banks of Lake Garda and the wherewithal to decorate it.

This house, called Vittoriale, is open to the public and has to be one of the most incredible residences in the world. As flamboyant as its owner, it is absolutely packed with objects—books, letters, weaponry, army tunics, pieces of statuary (some of them decked out in little velvet jackets and sporting necklaces), oriental boxes, photographs, stained-glass windows, a huge globe of the world, masks, ancient friezes, and innumerable clutter. An airplane—a real one— hangs from a ceiling; an Austrian machine gun graces a desk. There are stairs that lead nowhere, doors too small to walk through without stooping, columns that give no support to the ceilings.

Every room is a masterpiece of excess, but the summit of D'Annunzio's decorative achievements is the Music Room, which is done up like a cross between a sultan's harem and an opium den, and filled with Persian rugs, piles of cushions, ornate furniture, and vaguely Oriental objects. Here D'Annunzio, dressed in a monk's robe, would receive visitors or show movies (*The Bengal Lancers* was a perennial favorite). On nights when music was to be played, he would hang the room with red or black silk to suit his mood.

Outside the extravagance continues. Among the pools, waterfalls, statuary, and quite attractive flowerbeds, you'll find a bridge decorated with artillery shells, a World War I field gun, and—a classic touch—a full-sized ocean cruiser from the Italian navy, the *Puglia*, half buried in a hillside.

Details: Vittoriale is near Brescia, from which there are frequent buses. It is open daily except Monday mornings from 8:30 to 12 and from 2 to 6.

Lake Orta

Of all the Italian lakes, Orta is perhaps the most beautiful; certainly it is the bluest, most peaceful, and least touristed. Just eight miles long by about 1½ miles wide, it enjoys a memorable setting, cradled deep amid wooded hills and in the shadow of Mt. Mottarone. Sumptuous villas line its banks and an inviting road marks its perimeter, running at shore level on the eastern side and climbing high up the mountainside on the other. The principal lakeside town, Orta San Giulio, is a miraculously tranquil place with its old houses set out around a shady square against a backdrop of trees and hills and water.

In the lake, accessible by boat from the town, is the little island of San Giulio (Saint Julius). Just 350 yards long by about 200 yards wide, it is a jumble of ancient buildings that run down to the water's edge and in some cases jut out over it. Both the island's name and its buildings are the legacy of a priest named Giulio, who was struck by the beauty of its setting and founded a religious sanctuary there—after first, according to local tradition, ridding the lake of a dragon and other assorted serpents. The island's Romanesque basilica dates from the fourth century A.D. and its interiors include some interesting frescoes and a black marble pulpit decorated with the mythical beasts Julius was said to have driven away.

There are two interesting side trips from Orta. One is up the steep slopes on the western side of the lake to Sacro Monte, a sort of religious community where 20 chapels were built between 1591 and 1770. The views alone are worth the effort of getting there. Alternatively—or, better still, additionally—you can set out in the opposite direction to Mottarone, whose summit offers spectacular views across the other Italian lakes—Maggiore, Lugano, and Como—and beyond to the Alps and Po plain. Near here is the Giardoni Alpinia, or Alpine Garden, with a collection of over 2,000 Alpine plants and more stunning panoramas.

Apart from rambling around the lakeside, drinking in the views and tranquility, or sitting on Orta's shady square with a beer or cup of coffee, there's precious little else to do here—but that is, of course, its charm. If you're looking for a spot to spend a day or two away from the throngs, you'll find it here.

Villa Nazionale, Venetia

All along the Brenta Canal, between Venice and Padua, stand an extraordinary collection of summer villas. Here, starting in about the eighteenth century, the wealthy citizens of those two cities would retire each summer. A few still do. Today many villas are crumbling or have been put to unfortunate uses (the Villa Foscarina at Mira, for example, is now a post office) or, worse still, cower in the shadow of belching factories. But the grandest of them all, the Villa Nazionale (formerly the Villa Pisani), built in about 1730 for a Venetian doge named Alvise Pisani, stands as proudly now as ever.

If you were to stumble on it unexpectedly, you might be drawn simply by its immense size. On the other hand, seeing its rather dull and by now conventional facade—a central block of Corinthian columns flanked by symmetrical wings—you would be inclined to dismiss it as just one more stately pile. That would be unfortunate because, apart from anything else, it would mean missing the world's most lavish and incredible stables.

The original plans for the house were drawn up by Girolamo Frigimelica, but when he died suddenly, the commission went to Francesco Maria Preti, who submitted his own designs. The Pisanis, not being the sort to let good plans go to waste, decided to use Frigimelica's designs in the outbuildings. From the main house your view is carried along a shallow rectangular pool, a quarter of a mile long, to what appears to be another great villa, as substantial as any other along the Brenta Canal. In fact, however, this is the stable block. A certain logic lurks behind this lavishness. Apart from providing a focal point for the garden, the stable block also had the virtue of cutting off the view from a road at the foot of the garden. It is something of a deceit—up close you discover it is only a few feet deep, almost like one of those false-fronted buildings on film lots—but even so its grandeur and architectural detail are absolutely incomparable.

Further modest deceits exist inside the main house. Most rooms are predictably vast and sumptuous, interesting but unmemorable. But then you come to the ballroom. Here is one of Europe's great rooms—one, in Nigel Nicolson's words, "worth crossing continents for." Vast and high windowed, it rises to a gallery set off by an ornate and delicately carved wooden railing and beyond that to a high ceiling and a magnificent painting by Tiepelo—his last work in Italy and, in many people's view, his finest. The immediate impression is of dazzling grandeur, but on closer inspection you begin to see how each tiny detail enhances the whole. On closer inspection still, you discover that much of the admirably crafted architectural detail—ceiling cornices and the like—is in fact trompe l'oeil, skillfully painted to give the effect of three dimensions. Saying any more here would spoil the surprise, but see how long it takes you to work out which parts are real and which are clever fakes. You'll be amazed.

Details: The Villa Nazionale is seven miles east of Padua and is open every day but Monday from 9 to 12:30 and 3 to 4:30 (Sundays from 9 to 12:30 only). The best way to see the villa is on a boat from Padua to Venice, which meanders down the canal past the old villas and stops at the Nazionale. Even if you have no interest in the villa itself, the boat trip is an infinitely better way to enter Venice than by train. For tickets apply in Padua to the CIT, 12 Via Matteotti (Tel. 25349) or in Venice to the CIT at the Piazza San Marco (Tel. 85480).

Lucca, Tuscany

It's hard not to feel smug in Lucca. Here you are in an enchanting small city literally a few hundred yards off the main road between two of Europe's most tourist-infested cities, Pisa and Florence, and you are almost the only foreigner around. Lucca, like Todi and Urbino, is one of those Italian miracles—an ancient jewel that has somehow escaped outside notice. It may not have the architectural glories of Todi or the art and history of Urbino in quite the same profusion, but what it does have is charm and elegance and an air of cozy containment.

To arrive in Lucca is more like entering a fortress than a community. The town is contained within vast sixteenth-century ramparts, broad enough for a road and trees and running for almost three miles around the town's dense and narrow streets. Four massive gates are the only ways in to the little city of 50,000 people. The tops of the wall not only carry traffic, but also serve as a local park and promenade and provide a succession of viewing spots over Lucca on the inside and the Tuscan plain on the outside.

Although Lucca possesses some noble architecture—most notably in the twelfth-century duomo, or cathedral, whose Romanesque surface hides a darkly gothic interior—its main appeal is simply as a place to wander. Narrow streets and alleys, often lined with alluring boutiques and shops, give way to frequent piazzas graced with al fresco cafes or to such surprises as the site of a Roman amphitheater. The amphitheater itself is long gone, but its shape is preserved by an oval of tall, narrow houses overlooking what is now a busy marketplace. Where gladiators once fought, you can pick over peaches or haggle over leather goods.

Details: Lucca is 12 miles from Pisa and can be reached by frequent trains from there (30 minutes) or Florence (90 minutes). Buses link it to most other parts of Tuscany. There are also trains to the coastal resort of Viareggio, just 20 minutes away.

The Church of Near Misses, Tuscany

In November 1871, little Laira Angiolini, aged 12, tumbled out of a third-floor window in Livorno (or Leghorn), but was miraculously saved from death by a strategically placed clothesline "and the help of the Most Sacred Virgin of Montenero." In 1840, Cesare Tocchini suffered the alarming ignominy of being attacked with a knife in the street by his brother and sister-in-law, but managed to pull through "with the grace of the Most Sacred Madonna." On April 26, 1893, Santi Martelli was run over by a wagon and left for dead, but recovered in a month "by the Grace of the Madonna."

Our Lady of Montenero, you'll gather, is something of a busy woman around Livorno. For nearly two centuries she has been snatching its citizens from the jaws of death, and they in turn have been tramping up the hill to her shrine of Montenero to render it into a sort of museum of near misses and lucky scrapes. No one knows quite how the tradition started, but for almost 200 years local amateur artists have made a cottage industry of putting down on canvas the townspeople's lucky escapes. Some 9,000 paintings are packed onto the church's walls showing in graphic detail people tumbling out of windows or into machinery, being gorged by bulls, attacked by knife-wielding strangers or jilted lovers, disappearing into holes, or laid low by some other unreasonable misfortune. Most paintings are marvelously amateurish and lacking in perspective and scale. Unable to convey certain details like facial expression, the artists have portrayed both victims and witnesses with strangely impassive visages, relying instead on a profusion of blood from the victims and upraised arms among the onlookers to indicate the horror and gravity of the situation. A great number of the works bear simple written accounts of the miracles and many also carry passport-style photos of the recovered victims. Some provide documentary evidence as well. The painting of little Laira Angiolini's dramatic fall is accompanied by the clothesline that saved her life; Alvaro Ceccarini's deeply blood-stained T-shirt hangs as macabre testimony to his goring by a bull. In more recent years photographers have gotten in on the act by staging elaborate recreations of the near-fatal moments. One laboriously hand-tinted picture, for instance, shows a bicycle mangled beneath the wheels of a car on a mountain road and young Mario Martelloni sprawled melodramatically alongside.

The collection is simultaneously awesome, touching, and hilarious. That the people of Livorno could have suffered such a super abundance of misfortune in 200 years is remarkable; that so many of them could have survived is simply incredible.

Details: Our Lady of Montenero Church is just outside Livorno at Montenero and can be reached by bus. Livorno (pop. 178,000), 13 miles from Pisa, is a largely unattractive city, but there are two exceptionally nice and little known coastal resorts nearby, Quercianella and Castiglioncello.

Urbino, Marches

The five hundredth anniversary of the birth of Raphael in 1983 briefly—and a bit worryingly—focused attention on his hometown of Urbino. Happily, the crisis passed and Urbino quickly reverted to its long status as one of the most overlooked places in Europe. A Renaissance gem, it is a small walled city (pop. 17,000) commandingly situated on a hilltop in the Italian Marches. It's a wonderful town for wandering through, with a wealth of Renaissance architecture to add character and a small university to give it life. Once it rivalled Florence and even today it is more visibly dedicated to art than that Tuscan city, with an abundance of furniture makers, picture restorers, and other craftsmen working from shadowy workshops along its back streets. The views across the Marches plain are marvelous, particularly from the aptly named Strada Panoramica, off the Piazza Roma.

The one sight in town not to be missed is the great Ducal Palace, which Kenneth Clark called "one of the most beautiful pieces of architecture in the world." Its vast and forbidding exterior, built originally as a fortress, contains 200 rooms and art of incalculable greatness. These rooms are, to quote Lord Clark again, "so perfectly proportioned that it exhilarates one to walk through them: in fact it's the only palace in the world I can go round without feeling oppressed and exhausted." For all this we can thank Federigo de Montefeltro, first Duke of Urbino, who combined in one remarkable character all the attributes of a ruthless soldier of fortune with those of a scholar and man of taste. A famous portrait of the duke by Justus of Ghent can be seen in the palace, along with rare tapestries and furniture and paintings by, among many others, Titian, Piero della Francesca, and Andrea Verrocchio. But the real attraction is the palace itself with its vast fireplaces, decorated doorways, and other superb, but sparing, architectural touches. Federigo's study contains what must surely be the most detailed and exquisite inlaid woodwork in the world.

Although Raphael's father was court painter to Montefeltro, not a single important work by Raphael is in the palace or in any of the other galleries in Urbino. In fact, strangely, there is not a single painting in town that can be attributed to Raphael with any certainty. You can, however, see the house where he spent the first 14 years of his life. Furnished as it might have been during the artist's lifetime, it contains a fresco on a bedroom wall that might just have been done by the artist.

Not to be missed if you can possibly help it.

Details: Urbino lies in central Italy near the east coast. A branch rail line from Pesaro connects it to the main east coast line running from Milan and Bologna in the north to Brindisi in the south. The Ducal Palace in Urbino is open Tuesday through Saturday from 9 A.M. to 2 P.M. and on Sundays from 9 to 1. Raphael's house, on Via Raffaello, is open every day but Monday from 9 A.M. to 1 P.M.

The Garden of Monsters, Bomarzo

This is easily the weirdest garden in the world. Set on a steeply sloping site of about half an acre overlooking the Tiber valley, it offers the visitor not the usual serene blend of fountains and flowers, but instead a ragged landscape of scrubby trees and overgrown grass punctuated by an assortment of grotesque and unearthly statues, all of them vast and most of them brutal. A 20-foot-high stone elephant, a castle on its back, is frozen in the act of trampling a Roman soldier; a colossal Hercules is shown tearing a victim to pieces; cut into a hillside is a vast, unhuman head, 20 feet high, its eyes two empty sockets, its mouth a gaping hole large enough to accommodate three grown people. Elsewhere, scattered entirely at random, are dragons, lions, snarling dogs, bears, a bare-breasted mermaid with a pot of flowers plonked incongruously on her head, a whale, a house with a more severe tilt than the leaning tower of Pisa, winged nymphs, a statue of Neptune, and a chapel decorated with symbols of death. All are arranged without pattern. The effect is like a schizophrenic's visions given material form. Many of the bizarre pieces were carved in the huge volcanic boulders, called *peperino*, that are strewn across the site. Their vastness and mossy, lichen-encrusted surfaces lend them an air of permanence, as if they had grown from the rock rather than been formed by the hand of man. Most unsettling.

Little is known about the history of the gardens or of the vast Palazzo Orsini standing on the hilltop above them other than that they were built in 1572 by a Renaissance prince and dilettante named Pier Francesco Orsini. Whether they were designed as an outsized prank or because Orsini loathed the world isn't known. For well over a century they were apparently lost and forgotten—at least no nineteenth-century guidebook mentions them—but today they have been restored to their former glory, if that's the word for it. Whatever you make of them, you certainly won't see anything stranger in Europe.

Details: The Bomarzo Gardens are about 60 miles north of Rome, just off the Autostrada del Sole, and are open daily from 9 A.M. to dusk. The Palazzo Orsini is open from 9 A.M. to 1 P.M. only. Bomarzo can be reached by bus from Viterbo, 10 miles to the west, a handsome medieval town famed for its fountains, winding streets, and, I'm assured, its beautiful women.

Todi, Umbria

Todi completes our triumvirate of secret and unspoiled Italian towns— Lucca and Urbino are the others—and in many ways it's the most perfect. This is due in part to its superb setting on a hill overlooking Umbria, and partly because it has so successfully managed to evade the attentions of tourists. But mostly it is the sublimity of its main square, the Piazza del Popolo (officially the Piazza Vittorio Emanuele II, though no one calls it that), around which is grouped an unblemished collection of medieval buildings: the austere duomo, or cathedral, with its single tower, and three palaces, the Palazzo del Popola, the Palazzo dei Priori, and the Palazzo del Capitano, all dating from the thirteenth century. There's an interesting museum of Etruscan artifacts upstairs in the Palazzo del Popola, including coins, sculptures, and pottery, and an astonishing wealth of other ancient buildings in the nearby streets and squares, most notably the Church of San Fortunato on Via Mazzini, which, like the duomo at Lucca, is an arresting blend of Romanesque on the outside and gothic inside. At the very least pop in for a quick look at the Madonna by Masolino.

From the church a path leads past the ruins of La Rocca, a medieval castle, to a park, the Parco della Rocca, which is cut through with a sharply zigzagging walkway. Follow it to the end and there, outside one of the ancient town walls, is what I think is Todi's most supreme glory, the Church of Santa Maria della Consolazione. Built between 1508 and 1607, it was the work of several architects, but based on the inspired vision of Bramante. Shaped like a very compact cross, it is made of luminous white stone and capped by five exquisitely graceful domes. With its setting high above the green and hazy Umbrian plain and with an almost invariable backdrop of blue sky and towering white clouds, the church is quite simply one of the most beautiful visions in the world and worth traveling a very long way to see. Don't miss it.

Details: Because Todi (pop. 17,000) is fairly small and little visited, there's not a great deal of choice for hotels, so do try to secure a room early if you are planning to stay. Public transportation can also be a little frustrating. Although it's linked by trains to Perugia and beyond, the station is a two-mile walk or taxi ride from the town center. Todi can also be reached by bus from Rome.

The Bone Crypt, Rome

Of all the 480 churches in Rome, that of Santa Maria della Concezione might well rank as the least impressive. Thousands of people pass it every day without giving it a glance—many, indeed, without even noticing that it's a church. Although it contains one very fine treasure—a painting of St. Francis of Assisi by Caravaggio—a single painting is not exactly a magnet for passing tour buses and most guidebooks mention it not at all. But descend to the cellars and you will find one of the most macabre collections in the whole of Italy— five chapels filled with human bones and laid out in a quite staggering array. The bones came from 4,000 Capuchin monks, plus a judicious assortment of aristocrats, who died between 1530 and 1870. Four thousand may not seem all that large a number, but reflect for a moment on what your basement would look like if you had to make room in it for 4,000 bodies and you may get some idea of the breathtaking assemblage the monks have put together. Actually, taken apart would be the more apt description because most of the bones have been carefully separated and arranged around the chapels in fastidious patterns. Vertebrae drift across walls like butterflies; pelvises are clustered together like faded bushes; little shrines are set off by tidy, symmetrical stacks of skulls. The arrangements are indisputably harmonious—artistic even—and rather moving. As an additional macabre touch, standing here and there are complete skeletons, dressed in hooded monk's cassocks.

No one knows quite why or by whom these curious bone designs were made, but the inescapable impression you are left with is that the Capuchins at some time in the past harbored in their midst a half-mad monk with time on his hands and a certain passion for tidiness. However unlikely an explanation that may seem, this branch of the Capuchins has a reputation for possessing eccentric talents. In the nineteenth century, for instance, a certain Friar Pacifico developed such an unfailing knack for forecasting the winning numbers in the national lottery—which he shared with his parishioners— that the Pope was compelled to banish him to the countryside lest the whole system be irremediably undermined.

I wouldn't skip the Colosseum to see this one, but if you're in the neighborhood of the Via Veneto—as you are bound to be at some point during any visit to Rome—it's worth peeking in on.

Details: The Church of Santa Maria della Concezione is on the Via Veneto in central Rome (nearest subway station: Barberini) and is closed every day from noon to 4 P.M., but is generally open during other daylight hours.

Capodimonte Palace, Naples

Naples is everything—brash, dirty, boisterous, friendly, noisy, exasperating, and, at least in parts, lovely. There's hardly an adjective that can't be attached to it. And much can be said against the city: the poor part of town, the Vicaria, has possibly the highest population density in the world, with a dozen or more people frequently living together in tenements called *bassi*—fetid one-roomed apartments without windows or running water. Thousands of children scarcely ever go to school, but instead spend their days selling cigarettes on street corners or working in back-alley sweatshops. There are, at a conservative estimate, twice as many rats as people. No one would call it paradise. The city has, moreover, a justified reputation as a haven for *scippatori*—gangs of purse snatchers on Vespas. All of this has helped kill Naples as a tourist center. But those prudent travelers who give it a wide berth miss also its friendliness, generosity, vibrancy, and all the other things that go to make it one of the most endlessly fascinating cities in the world. Above all else, they miss Capodimonte—but then, sadly, so do all too many of those who actually visit the city.

The palace of Capodimonte was built in 1738 by Charles III of Bourbon on a heartstopping setting on Naples' highest hill with a sweeping view across the city and bay. Charles married a German princess whose dowry included craftsmen from Meissen who brought to Italy the closely guarded secret of making fine porcelain. At the palace today are five rooms full of porcelain pieces—some of the finest in the world—but the most memorable is a room that is itself made of porcelain. All four walls and the ceiling gleam with white porcelain, all heavily embossed with brightly colored and relentlessly vivid rococo enbellishments—garlands, baskets of fruit, frolicking monkeys, birds, Chinese figures, bits of foliage, butterflies, and much else. This room is *intense*, but compelling for all that. Much of the rest of the palace is furnished as it was in Charles' day, but upstairs is one of the finest and least known picture galleries in Italy. The works include paintings by Botticelli, Bellini, Mantegna, Van Dyck, Goya, El Greco, Velazquez, Breughel, and Caravaggio. There's a drawing by Michelangelo and a whole room of Titians.

But at least as rewarding as all of the palace's collections is the panorama from the terraces across Naples and its bay. This view is one of the most famous and memorable in the world and there's no better place to see it from.

Details: Capodimonte is open Tuesday through Saturday from 9 A.M. to 2 P.M., and on Sundays from 9 to 1. It can be reached by buses No. 110 or 127 from the central station in Naples.

Underground Church of Monte St. Angelo, Gargano Peninsula

Monte St. Angelo is one of those towns where the centuries fall away. Remote more by inclination than by geography (Rome is only 300 kilometers to the west and the main road and rail lines to Brindisi pass nearby), it is a mountain community of brilliant whitewashed houses and shady alleyways, where you can still find men riding sidesaddle on donkeys and old women dressed entirely in black. Goats wander freely in the streets.

The town is built high up on a ridge overlooking the Adriatic and pocked with caves. In many shops and restaurants you'll find the walls and ceilings are roughly hacked out of the rock. But nowhere in town—or anywhere else in the world for that matter—have the caves been put to more dramatic use than in the underground church of St. Michael. Here the Archangel Michael was said to have left his red cloak with a group of presumably startled shepherds, though in fact the cave has been a sacred site since long before Christianity. It's approached through a gothic courtyard (lined with the inevitable stalls selling religious trinkets) and then down a long, gloomy flight of 86 steps—more like entering a dungeon than a place of worship. At the bottom are the doors to the church, which the writer H. V. Morton called "among the most beautiful antiquities in Italy." Made in 1076, they are masterpieces of Byzantine art, heavily worked with bronze and silver and depicting biblical scenes. Pass through the doors and you encounter a vast, dank cavern, warmed by the glow of candles and echoing with the occasional plink of dripping water. Slowly, as your eyes adjust to the darkness, the interior begins to take shape in all its cathedral-like majesty and you are able to pick out the high altar, the life-sized winged statue of St. Michael made of alabaster, the bishop's chair of ornately carved marble with two lions as its base. All the glitter and richness of a church is here, but set within the vast sloping dome of a very damp and rather oppressive cave. An awesome yet eerie effect.

Monte St. Angelo is on the Gargano peninsula, one of the least visited parts of Italy. Although much of the landscape is harsh, there are pockets of intense lushness—most notably in the nearby Forresta d'Umbra, or Shady Forest, a vast and unlikely spread of beech and oak trees, which is a favorite Sunday picnic spot for locals and a blessed refuge from the summer's heat. The coastline along the promontory between Punta Rossa in the south and Bellariva in the north—a stretch of about 60 miles—is one of fabulous and unspoiled grandeur, where precipitous cliffs give way to some of the best and cleanest beaches in southern Europe. For anyone in this part of the country—traveling on to Greece via Brindisi, say—it offers a peaceful few days' detour.

Details: The nearest rail link to the Gargano peninsula is at Foggia, but there are buses throughout the area. If you're making for the coast and beaches, two of the most appealing of the promontory's several attractive fishing villages are Peschici and Vieste.

Ravello, Campania

The coast road along the Sorrentine peninsula, south of Naples, is quite possibly the most breathtaking in the whole world. Running for just over 40 miles on a cliff-hugging road between Sorrento and Salerno, it offers a dizzying succession of unforgettable views, precipitous plunges, and more than 1,000 hairpin turns, around which crazed Italian drivers bounce their cars like pinballs. For visiting drivers it's a nightmare, but even if you're a passenger (in a bus, say) it provides a disconcerting combination of exhilaration and quiet terror. If you can imagine having a heart attack and enjoying it, you will have some idea of the contradictory emotions this experience arouses.

All along the coast villages climb up the hills like stairsteps. A few of them are a bit touristy and overrun—Amalfi and Positano, for instance—but even the worst are infinitely quieter and cheaper than almost any resort on the French Riviera. The best of all, I think, is Ravello, floating high on a hill overlooking the village of Aerani and the sea beyond. Because it lies slightly inland and can be reached only by a spur road, Ravello has managed to keep its charms largely to itself. It houses a number of excellent small hotels, including two of the best little ones in Italy: the Hotel Caruso Belvedere, where you can dine on a terrace with incomparable views, and the slightly more upscale Palumbo, an eleventh-century manor house whose guests have included Greta Garbo, Gore Vidal, Humphrey Bogart, and John and Jackie Kennedy. Despite its charm and fame, it is exceptionally good value at about $50 a day full board.

Ravello's attractions include the handsome cathedral of San Pantaleone, which contains a wealth of fine sculpture and carving, and two great houses, the Villa Cimbrone and Villa Rufolo, both famed for their gardens and views. Rufolo, which dates from the eleventh century, is the more historic, having been in its time the residence of the composer Wagner, several popes, and Charles of Anjou (Wagner and at least one of the popes, Adrian IV, are said to haunt it still), but neither house should be missed.

From Ravello are literally dozens of captivating excursions, starting with the Dragon Valley (Valle del Dragone), the lush but torturous depression connecting the town to the sea. A mile or so beyond, Amalfi offers a striped cathedral, handsome promenade, and steamers to Capri, Naples, and Salerno. Positano and Sorrento are both busy, but inexpressably beautiful. There are excellent beaches everywhere and the famous Grotto di Smeraldo (Emerald Grotto)—that rare thing, a water cave that's really worth the effort of going to—is only a mile or so beyond Amalfi. Slightly farther afield, but well within striking distance, are the incomparable ruins of Pompeii, Herculaneum, and Paestum.

It's not exaggerating to say that you could happily spend a couple of months here. Try at least to make it a few days.

Details: Reservations are recommended at both the Hotel Caruso Belvedere (at 52 Via Toro, Tel. 089 85-71-11) and Hotel Palumbo (Tel. 089 87-23-38), at least in high season. The Villa Cimbrone is open daily from 9 A.M. to 7 P.M. The Villa Rufolo is open from 9:30 to 1:30 and from 3 to 7:30; closed Thursdays.

Cefalu, Sicily

How Cefalu manages to retain its relative obscurity on an island as popular as Sicily is a perennial mystery. A seaside town of pastel-colored fishermen's cottages strung out along a tranquil harbor, it offers almost everything you could ask of a seaside resort—quaintness, charm, excellent swimming, great food, and endless sunshine. Moreover, it's not in the least bit remote, lying as it does on the main rail line between Palermo (an hour to the west) and Messina. Yet somehow it has managed to escape the notice of all but a small—though rapidly expanding—number of travelers.

Part of the reason is the Cefalu makes few concessions to overseas visitors. There aren't many hotels, so rooms can be difficult to find, particularly in August. More important, the bars, shops, and restaurants are almost without exception determinedly geared for the local clientele. Don't expect to see a convenient English translation on the back of your restaurant menu. But for anyone looking for the real Sicily, this is one of the few places to find it without sacrificing the coast and plunging miles inland. The town has a beautiful Norman cathedral, built in just 15 years in the twelfth century, with a soaring ceiling covered in fabulous mosaics. There's also a surprisingly good museum for a town of this size, the Museo Madrilisca, with an impressive collection of old coins and pottery. If you're feeling especially vigorous, you can climb up the Rocca, the Gibraltar-like outcrop that towers over the town, for one of the island's most memorable panoramas. As a small bonus, there's a motley assortment of ruins, mostly medieval, to clamber over when you get there.

But the real attraction in Cefalu is just wandering around the narrow, stepped streets, gorging yourself on the invariably excellent seafood and pasta, and soaking up the tranquility. Sit for an hour by the waterside and your peace is unlikely to be broken by anything more disturbing than the distant sound of a motorboat and the gentle knocking of water on stone. Club Med has built a big holiday village just half a mile outside town and others can't be far behind, so I wouldn't leave this one too long.

Details: If you have difficulty finding a room in Cefalu, the tourist information office at Corso Ruggera 114 should be able to help.

Aeolian Islands

This small cluster of islands off the northern coast of Sicily has long been very popular with the Italians—which means it can be a risky place to drop in unannounced at the height of summer if you want a bed to call your own—but only recently has word of its charms begun to leak out to the wider world. Sometimes called the Lipari

Islands, the chain consists of seven inhabited islands, all volcanic in origin and all exceptionally beautiful, plus countless rocky islets. Most present a vivid contrast of whitewashed houses, black volcanic beaches, deep blue waters, and bottle green verdure. Everywhere geraniums bloom and bougainvillea flower. As Mark Twain once said, "You go to heaven, I'm staying here."

The largest of the islands is Lipari, though with an area of just 14 square miles, such a description is decidedly relative. Its principal town, also called Lipari, is an attractive place flanked by two splendid beaches and overshadowed by an unusual complex consisting of a Spanish citadel dating from 1544, a Norman cathedral, an excellent archeological museum in a former bishop's palace, four other churches, and a very good youth hostel. The island is criss-crossed with footpaths and mule tracks that are sometimes a bit arduous but almost always emerge at some sunny and secluded cove. Swimming everywhere is wonderful and the waters are full of unusual creatures—sea horses, turtles, flying fish, and the like.

The most visually impressive of the islands are Vulcano and Stromboli, both of whose histories and ever-uncertain futures are dominated by volcanoes. Vulcano, the legendary home of Aeolus, the king of the winds, from which the islands take their name, has three volcanic peaks. The mightiest, Gran Cratere, can be reached in an hour up a twisting path from the village of Porto Levante. The views are superb. It last exploded in 1888 and, on its record, is overdue for another. Today the air is still hung with the smell of sulphur, sometimes unpleasant and always ominous, but by way of compensation there are numerous excellent beaches whose waters are warmed by *fumaroles*—underwater fissures through which the volcanic heat transpires.

Stromboli, called the Lighthouse of the Mediterranean, is more dramatic still, with a single dark volcanic cone rising steeply from the sea. It too is said to be harmless, though its deep rumblings and fiery belchings may leave you unconvinced. The walk to the 3,000-foot summit is a demanding slog of about five hours and is supposed to be undertaken only in the company of a guide (a rule widely ignored). At the top is a more or less never-ending display of bubbling lava and periodic explosions that spew molten rock into a channel called the Sciara del Fuoco (Pit of Fire) down which it flows to flop into the sea with a steaming hiss. It's very dramatic, particularly at night.

Details: The Aeolian Islands can be reached by frequent boats and hydrofoils from several Sicilian and mainland Italian ports — principally Messina, Naples, Milazzo, Cefalu (see page 171), Palermo, and Reggio di Calabria. There are also frequent boats between the islands themselves.

LIECHTENSTEIN

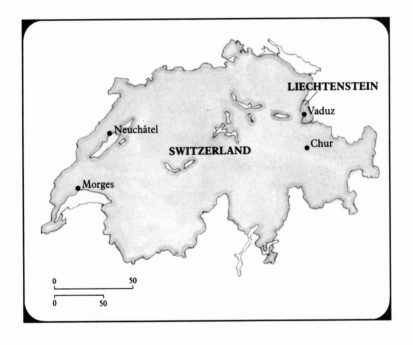

Endearing is the word for Liechtenstein. Almost everything about this tiny Alpine principality (just one-twentieth the size of Rhode Island) is touchingly absurd. So obscure that its ruling family did not even bother to come and see it for almost 150 years after they took control, it is a country without an airport or army (its eight soldiers were sent home in 1868 when it was realized that they could defeat no one), and its modest capital of Vaduz (pop. 5,000) has no rail services. Its three political parties are named after colors (the Reds, the Greens, and the Blacks) and have so few ideological differences that they even share the same motto: "Faith in God, Prince and Fatherland."

A tax haven, Liechtenstein is the only country in the world with more registered companies than people (30,000 versus 26,000). It is Europe's largest producer of false teeth and sausage skins and the only country on the continent that does not allow its women to vote. Its monarch—his full title is Prince Franz Josef II Maria Aloys Alfred Karl Johanes Heinrich Michael George Ignatius Benediktus Gerhardus Majella von unde zu Liechtenstein, Duke of Troppau and Jaegerndorf, Count of Rietberg—walks around town without bodyguards and does not make official state visits to foreign countries on the logical argument that he is far too unimportant. You can find him listed in the telephone book under Furst—the German word for prince.

Liechtenstein is, in short, ridiculous. But it is also the home of some breathtaking scenery (two-thirds of its 62 square miles is mountainous), a fashionable ski resort called Malbun, and a scattering of very good hotels and restaurants. Eventually, when it gets its act together, it will have one of the world's finest art museums, housing the bulk of Prince Franz Josef's $500 million art collection, the largest private collection in the world after the British royal family's. Because of political bickering, the opening date for the museum has been put back half a dozen times and it now looks unlikely to be unveiled before 1988. In the meantime, however, the Liechtensteinische Kunstsammlungen, or national museum, offers several Rubens paintings, which are supplemented with revolving displays from the prince's vast private stockpile. There's also in Vaduz one of the world's best stamp museums (almost a tenth of the national income is generated by postage stamps), which is a mecca for philatelists and has the virtue for the rest of us of being free and at least mildly diverting.

The real appeal here is fresh air and scenic grandeur. The uplands area around the village of Triesenberg is laced with footpaths that were once—and sometimes still are—cowpaths. Anyone with stout shoes, strong thighs, and a hankering for scenic vistas—not to mention an affection for the absurd—could do far worse. Hotels are generally small and welcoming and living costs appreciably less than in Switzerland.

Details: Liechtenstein can be reached by catching trains to Sargans or Buchs in Switzerland or Feldkirch in Austria and catching a connecting bus from there. The tourist office in Vaduz is very good and can help with any accommodation problems.

LUXEMBOURG

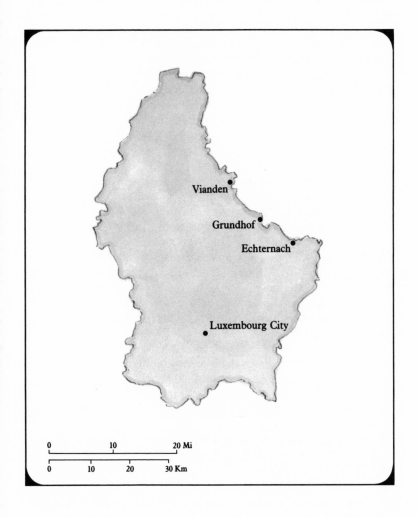

Vianden

Grundhof

Echternach

Luxembourg City

0   10   20 Mi

0   10   20   30 Km

Luxembourg's "Little Switzerland"

The Luxembourg tourist authorities like to refer to the countryside around the Valley of the Black Ernz (in French, Vallée de l'Ernz Noire) as the nation's Little Switzerland, but I wouldn't pack your skis. Although there is nothing even remotely alpine about the region, it is an area of outstanding natural beauty. And it offers a welcome and accessible respite of fresh air and woodland walks for anyone suffering from a severe overdose of urban sprawl. If you've just spent two weeks slogging through the crowded capitals of northern Europe, come here for a day or two of laid-back bucolic recuperation.

Echternach (pop. 4,200), a charming market town with narrow streets and geranium-filled windowboxes, makes a good base for exploring, as does the smaller town of Mullerthal a few miles away. But the real devotee of getting away from it all will head for the villages of Waldbillig, Haller, and Christnach in the valleys of the Ernz and Hallerbach rivers, or for the villages of Dillingen, Grundhof, and Weilerbach on the River Sûre (German: Sauer), which forms the border with Germany. There are miles and miles of excellent well-marked footpaths, which guide you through dark forests full of trilling streams, steep ravines, little stone bridges, and haunting rock formations.

From Grundhof, for instance, there's a beautiful (if sometimes steep) five-mile walk through the woods to Mullerthal (Miller's Dale). You can cover the ground in about three hours, but you're likely to find yourself distracted by such sights as the *Kasselt* (glorious views), the *Keltenhöhle* (site of prehistoric remains), and the *Adlerhorst* (a famous robber's cave that you enter by descending a ladder). For the less energetic, or those more pressed for time, an alternative walk from Grundhof is to Beaufort, which takes only about 1½ hours but leads you through some lovely woodland with a number of interesting rock formations and several small waterfalls. As a bonus, at the end there's an enchanting view of the fifteenth-century castle at Beaufort—one motorists never see.

Details: The tourist information office in Echternach, on Porte St. Willibord (Tel. 7 22 30), can provide you with maps and suggest an itinerary to suit your constitution. Small hotels and guesthouses are abundant so there's very little chance of getting stranded, but for those who don't want to risk it, many footpaths follow a circular route so that you are deposited back where you started.

Vianden

When Victor Hugo saw this village with its ancient church and hulking castle, he wrote: "Before long the whole of Europe will visit Vianden." Happily, he was wrong. Today Vianden, like the tiny country that contains it, remains almost as well off the beaten track as it did when Hugo first saw it more than a century ago. Anyone coming into the town from the direction of Luxembourg City will see instantly what attracted the great novelist. The view is spectacular: the castle perched on its hilltop and the small town piled at its feet like fallen boulders. Vianden itself, with its thirteenth-century gothic church and narrow medieval streets built almost perpendicularly on the hillside, is memorable though. But the castle provides its crowning glory. More than 1,000 years old, it is one of the two or three largest feudal fortresses in Europe; in its heyday up to 500 soldiers could be bedded down in the massive Knight's Hall. Now the property of the nation, the castle is slowly being restored after centuries of neglect. A chairlift from the village will take you 1,380 feet up the side of a mountain for knockout views of the castle, village, and the valley of the River Our. In the summer, particularly for the romantic, it's worth hanging around until nightfall when the castle is illuminated.

Details: Vianden is 30 miles from Luxembourg City near the German border in the north of the country. Also worth seeing in town is the house where Victor Hugo lived in 1871. Actually, it's a replica: the original was destroyed in the war, but the contents, including some of Hugo's paper and furniture, are all genuine. Handily, the local tourist office is in the same house. Vianden also has a small folklore museum and within walking distance are the remains of three castles— Falkenstein, Roth, and Sultzenbourg.

THE NETHERLANDS

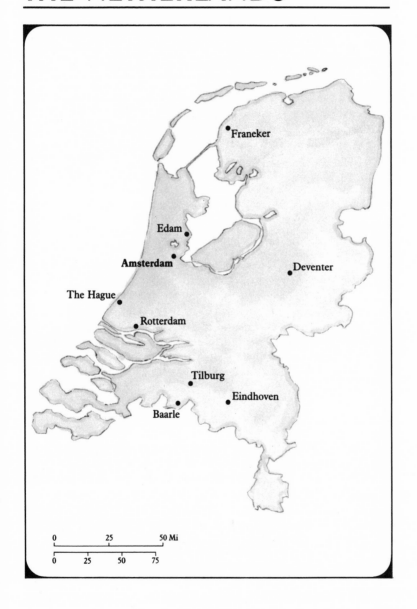

Franeker

Edam

Amsterdam

Deventer

The Hague

Rotterdam

Tilburg

Eindhoven

Baarle

0	25	50 Mi

0	25	50	75

Prof. Van der Poel Tax Museum, Rotterdam

I know what you're thinking, but you're wrong. However insurmountably numbing taxation might sound as a theme for a museum, the Prof. Van der Poel Museum, tucked away on one of Rotterdam's loveliest streets, is relentlessly fascinating. The professor was a Dutch tax official who spent decades assembling an incomparable collection of tax memorabilia, which he presented to the nation in 1937. Just three years later the whole collection was wiped out in a bombing raid on Rotterdam. With the unflappable zeal that marks his profession, Prof. Van der Poel set about assembling a new collection from scratch and in 1949 opened the present museum.

Almost every facet of the long and surprisingly bloody history of taxation is covered. There are ancient Roman tribute pennies, a denarius from the reign of Vespasian (used as a tax on urinals), a collection of porcelain commemorating a series of eighteenth-century tax riots, the arms and uniforms of early tax collectors, and weights and measures by which taxes were once assessed and levied, among much else. Everything you can think of has been taxed at some time or other, and it's all here, neatly arrayed over three floors, from early newspapers and matchboxes to wine, playing cards, beer, and even peat moss and raisins. One display case contains a small medal token, designed by Peter the Great, which was issued as a receipt to eighteenth-century Russians after they had paid a tax on their beards. The walls are lined with paintings and etchings from as far back as the sixteenth century relating to great moments in the history of tax collecting (yes, there are some) and the basement is devoted to the history of smuggling, with a small but intriguing collection of assorted objects, from shoes to cigarette packs, whose secret compartments failed to keep their secrets from the ever-vigilant customs officials. The wealth of material on display is staggering. Do stop by if you're in Rotterdam—it's not tax-deductible but it is free.

Details: The Prof. Van der Poel Tax Museum is at 14-16 Parklaan, a small boulevard in the heart of Rotterdam. It is open Monday through Friday from 9 A.M. to 4:30 P.M.

184

Torture Museum, The Hague

The Gevangenpoort (or Prison Gate) Museum in The Hague is an innocuous name for what is one of the more grisly diversions in Europe. It is, bluntly, a museum of torture; almost everything that was used to extract confessions and inflict pain from the fifteenth to nineteenth centuries can be found here, spread in awesome array over four floors. There are racks and wheels for stretching, guillotines for beheading, irons for branding, gibbets for hanging, and an alarmingly diverse and inventive assortment of thumbscrews, handscrews, and kneescrews, among much else.

For more than 400 years, from 1420 to 1828, the Gevangenpoort was the city prison. Heretics, debtors, and other offenders against the commonweal were dragged here, generally to be confined for years in abject filth and darkness. The cells have been preserved intact—note particularly the rather poignant carvings on the wooden sleeping stalls in the debtors' cell, notched up to mark the passing days—but the stench and despair must be left to the imagination. Whether you see it as a historical curiosity or as a stark reminder of humanity's almost limitless capacity for cruelty, you will find it a memorable detour.

Details: The Gevangenpoort Museum is in the central part of The Hague at 33 Bultenhof (tel. 070-460861). It is open Monday through Friday from 10 A.M. to 5 P.M. year-round and on Saturdays and Sundays from 1 P.M. to 5 P.M. during April through September.

Madurodam, The Hague

After their son, a Dutch resistance hero, was killed in 1945, a couple named Maduro decided to build a model village to his memory. One of the best and largest of its kind in Europe, Madurodam is perhaps an unlikely monument but a delightful place. This vast mini-metropolis is an entire Dutch city built with great skill and obsessive care to a scale 1/25th of actual size, and so sprawling that you must walk two miles of pathways to see it all. So convincing is the architectural detail on the little houses, churches, shops, and factories that you begin to suspect the whole was built by an army of three-inch-high craftsmen. Adding to the air of verisimilitude is the animation of many models — cars move along the roads, ships and barges ply the canals and waterways, planes taxi on the airport runways, a miniature band actually plays, and a funfair is in full swing. Even little windmills are used to regulate the water level in the miniature canals. At night, 50,000 tiny lights illuminate the village. All of this can prove a pretty severe test of your charm threshold and it's certainly not for everyone, but if you're traveling with children or at all drawn to miniaturizations, nothing in the world matches it.

Details: Madurodam is at 175 Haringkade in The Hague (Tel. 070-553900) and can be reached by buses or trams numbered 9, 22, 36, 65, and 89. It is open from April 1 to the first Sunday in October from 9:30 A.M. to 10:30 P.M. (11 P.M. in July and August). There's an admission charge of 15.50 guilders for adults and 3 guilders for children, but all proceeds go to charity.

Piggy Bank Museum, Amsterdam

Amsterdam is a city of museums, but none is more unexpected than the little Spaarpotten (Money Box) Museum on Raadhuisstraat. It contains 12,000 piggy banks and other money receptacles of every conceivable description, from all over the world and every period of history, all collected by a globetrotting director of the City of Amsterdam Savings Bank. Some, like a 500-year-old glazed savings pot from Indonesia, are very rare. And others, like those made of silver and gold, are very valuable — more valuable in fact than anything they could possibly contain. Many of the older ones are graced with delicate engravings, the summit of the craftmen's art. But most are simply clay or metal containers designed as simple keepsakes for children. The traditional pig shape predominates, but the containers run the whole gamut of possible shapes, from primitive earthenware turtles, scarcely recognizable as such, to mini-Taj Mahals, to convincing likenesses of Winston Churchill and Rembrandt's laughing cavaliers.

Among the most fascinating pieces are the mechanical ones — the demonic-faced nineteenth-century clown who greedily consumes a penny if you place it on his hand, or the seedy-looking magician who makes a coin disappear beneath his hat when you put it on his table. I wouldn't suggest you skip the Rijksmuseum for this one, but if you've got an hour to spare in Amsterdam, it's just a short stroll from Dam Square, the admission charge is only a guilder, and it's a lot of fun.

Details: The Spaarpotten Museum is at No. 20 Raadhuisstraat, a five-minute walk from Dam Square on the far side of NZ Voorburgwal. It is open Monday to Friday from 1 to 4 P.M.

Edam

Edam is perhaps the most agreeable and certainly one of the most underrated towns in Holland. The view from the Damplein, in the shadow of the seventeenth-century Town Hall, up the leafy main street with its tall, narrow houses and languid canal, must be one of the most quietly captivating anywhere. Tranquility is the keyword here: it suffuses the town like a dose of Valium. Even on the busiest days the most raucous sounds are the occasional dring of a bicyclist's bell and the gracious music of the carillon, the oldest in Holland, ringing out from the tower of St. Mary's Church. Side streets around the Damplein are a happy amalgam of old houses and interesting shops. Almost every turning provides an inviting prospect of canals, small white bridges, and ancient houses bursting with flowers.

If the weather lets you down or all the beauty palls, there's a wonderful haven in the Municipal Museum, housed in an old sea captain's residence overlooking the Damplein. Around the seventeenth century, Edam had a brief but memorable proclivity for producing strange people, and you will find them all commemorated here on canvas. There's Jan Claeszoon Clees (1570–1612), a local innkeeper whose 425-pound bulk made him the fattest man in Dutch history. Then there's a life-sized portrait of Kitty Kever (1616–33), an eight-foot-tall giantess. (A pair of her shoes, like small boats, are also on display.) And finally there's the aptly named Pieter Langebaard ("longbeard"), a local mayor whose red beard was, at ten feet, so long that he had to trail it over his arm. He used to show it at fairs to raise funds for the local orphanage. The museum is also noted for its unique floating celler. Because of erratic ground water levels, the cellar floor was built to stand free of the surrounding walls and thus can rise and fall with the springs below.

Details: Edam is on the E10, about 15 miles north of Amsterdam, which makes it an ideal excursion center even for those on a flying visit to The Netherlands. There's no train station, but frequent buses run from in front of the central station in Amsterdam. The municipal museum (Edams Museum) is open year-round from 1:30 to 4:30 on Sundays and on weekdays from 10–12 and 1:30 to 4:30. Closed Saturdays. For coffee or a light snack, try Theo Schilder's in the center of town under the sign of the hanging pretzel. But beware: the whole town is shut until 1 P.M. on Mondays.

Eise Eisinga's Planetarium, Franeker

In a simple house overlooking a canal in the heart of this little market town is one of the most remarkable museums I know of, the Planetarium of Eise Eisinga. At first sight it isn't particularly impressive. In the main room of the house, suspended on string from the high ceiling, are small globes representing the planets of the solar system as they were known in the late eighteenth century. Grooved tracks in the ceiling allow them to make a circuit around the room in exactly the time it takes them to circle the sun. You won't be knocked out. But go upstairs to where part of the wall has been cut away to reveal the elaborate mechanisms regulating it all and I think you'll find your polite interest deepening into an awed fascination.

Eisinga was an uneducated woolcomber who spent seven years from 1774–81 building the intricate clockwork mechanisms, working mostly at night by the light of flickering candles. Every bit, including even the nails, had to be fashioned entirely by hand. The fastest wheel moves only one millimeter every hour. The slowest has completed only six turns since 1781. None moves fast enough to be discernible and there is only the ineluctable ticking of the master mechanism, still spinning away after 200 years. Nothing I know of more grippingly demonstrates the vastness of the universe or the slowness of time than this curious contraption built two centuries ago in an obscure Dutch town. Allow at least 45 minutes for this one.

Even without its planetarium, Franeker would be a nice diversion. The town's central area with its Renaissance town hall and serene canal is relentlessly attractive and contains a surprisingly sophisticated range of shops. Old and new blend together effortlessly and everywhere is that incredible art at which the Dutch are unexcelled— pavement brickwork. Even the parking lots, where the bays are outlined in a contrasting shade of brick, look more like mini-plazas than places to park cars. Above all, for a quick meal there's an excellent restaurant, De Kaats, just across the canal from the planetarium. It serves an absolutely vast platter of fried eggs, sausages, bacon, ham, and bread for only about 10 guilders—surely the best food deal in northern Europe—in very friendly and agreeable surroundings. If you're traveling through northern Holland, try to put this one on your itinerary.

Details: The planetarium is at No. 3 Eise Eisingastraat in central Franeker. It is open Monday through Saturday from 9–12 and 1:30–6 from April 1 to September 30 and from 9–12 and 2–5 the rest of the year.

Museum of Moving Toys, Deventer

This must be every small child's dream—an old house devoid of furniture and filled with toys. If you're seriously interested in the history of play, you may be disappointed because the explanatory notes on the displays are only in Dutch. But if all you want is to recapture the pleasures of childhood for an hour or so, the Speelgoed-en Bliksmuseum, or Museum of Moving Toys, is the place to do it. Hundreds of playthings, mostly from around the turn of the century, are displayed over four floors. The name of the museum is a bit misleading—unless your idea of moving toys includes dolls and dollhouses, tin soldiers, and building bricks. But it's true that the bulk of the collection consists of almost every kind of tin wind-up toy ever made and a gloriously eclectic—and noisy—model train layout.

But the prize of the collection, for me at any rate, is to be found in a large display case upstairs. It's devoted to a certain type of Dutch building brick that was evidently very popular in its day. These consisted of an assortment of architecturally accurate pieces—buttresses, pillars, stones, and the like—packed with almost obsessive neatness into little boxes. By collecting enough of them, children could build a whole range of elaborate Victorian buildings. The ultimate goal was a three-foot-high gothic castle. One is on display at the museum and it's an absolute knockout—so marvelous and appealing and based on such a simple idea that you won't believe the company could ever have gone out of business. For a few minutes anyway I was six years old again. If you're anywhere near Deventer, seek this one out.

Details: Deventer (pop. 65,000) is an attractive old city, if a bit bleak and industrialized around the fringes. The Museum of Moving Toys is in the center of town just a few doors down from the VVV, the local tourist office, and is open Tuesday through Saturday from 10 to 12:30 and 2 to 5 and on Sundays from 2 to 5 only.

Cycling in Brabant

Probably no better way of seeing a country exists than by bicycle and there is no better country to see by bike than Holland. With its lack of hills and extensive system of paved bike paths running along-side almost every road in the country, it is a cyclist's paradise— which no doubt is why there are 9½ million bikes in Holland for a population of just 14 million people.

For tourists, the great problem of cycling tours in Holland, and elsewhere, has always been what to do with your luggage. The Dutch tourist office in Tilburg, in the heart of the little-known province of Brabant, has come up with a neat solution. It provides you with a bike, maps, route descriptions and itinerary, *and* ferries your luggage on ahead by van so that it's waiting for you at each overnight stop. Tours range from two to seven days and can be fixed at varying lengths to suit your stamina. All include breakfast and evening meals, overnight accommodation in a first- or second-class hotel, trailer, or tent (depending on how much you want to spend), and coupons for reduced rate admissions to attractions along the way. Most tours start at Oisterwijk, a lovely old town about six miles east of Tilburg, and meander through a gloriously tranquil landscape of woods, fens, streams, and farmland, interspersed with occasional unspoiled villages, like the carefully preserved town of Huesden, where there are almost always little museums and manor houses to explore and welcoming inns for refreshment. If you've got a few days to spare and a desire to see Holland up close, try this.

Details: Costs of tours range from about 200 to 600 guilders per person. Details can be acquired and bookings made through the Streek VVV, Spoorlaan 416a, 5038 CG Tilburg, Netherlands (Tel. 010- 311 335 1135). Ask for the brochure "King Cyclist in the Heart of Brabant."

De Efteling Amusement Park, Kaatsheuvel

European amusement parks are, on the whole, pretty dire. As a rule, if you see glittering lights and signs announcing "Fun for the Whole Family," or words to that effect, drive on and don't look back. But there are exceptions and one of the best—perhaps the very best— is De Efteling, near Tilburg. Spread over 375 acres, it has some of the most spectacular and scariest rides in Europe, including the continent's largest roller coaster. Its double corkscrew followed immediately by a neck-breaking bend will almost certainly part you from your lunch and your sensibilities. If you require further instant hysteria, try the Pirana, a swirling water ride, or the Halve Maen (Half Moon), a lurching, wildly swinging pirate ship, both guaranteed to leave you with all your internal organs seriously disorganized.

But there's also lots and lots here for quite small children, including an excellent and enchanting fairy tale forest with dioramas and animated models of Sleeping Beauty, Arabs on flying carpets, and the like, plus a steam railway, a puppet theater, playground, and wealth of gentle rides. For the whole family there's a first-rate ghost house and a boat ride called the Gondoletter, which meanders around a waterway whose banks are a quite spectacular carpet of flowers.

Throughout the park are a lot of nice touches not normally encountered—a talking litter bin that thanks you when you feed it rubbish, a free wading pool with a life-sized model elephant that squirts water over the delighted children, and handsome landscaping with an abundance of flowers such as you could only hope to find in Holland. In short, one of those rare places where the old slogan about offering something for everyone from age four to 84 really is true. Plan on a whole day here, especially if you're traveling with small children.

Details: De Efteling is at Kaatsheuvel, near Tilburg, and is open daily from 10 A.M. to 6 P.M. from March 31 to October 2. Children under three are admitted free. Everyone else pays 12.50 guilders, but the admission charge covers all the rides and other attractions inside.

The Most Confused Village in Europe, Baarle

For more than 500 years, the village of Baarle has been suffering an acute identity crisis. Although the community is comfortably inside The Netherlands, a good four miles from the Belgian frontier, only two-thirds of it is Dutch and the rest is Belgian. The discrepancy arose in 1479, when the Dutch Lord of Breda ceded several parcels of land to the Belgian Duke of Brabant. Since then despite all the political realignments of the last several centuries, from the Treaty of Westphalia to the setting up of a Belgian republic, the two countries have never been able to sort out the problem. Pockets of Baarle remain little Belgian enclaves, firmly cut off from their homeland.

As a consequence, this small town of about 6,500 people has two town halls, two police stations (but no jail), two schools, two post offices, even two names. The Dutch part is called Baarle-Nassau and the Belgian part Baarle-Hertog. Anomalies abound. The main market square is entirely Dutch, except for one inn, which is in Belgium. The zigzagging boundary lines run through several houses, so it is not unknown for husbands and wives to share a bed but sleep in separate countries. The residents of the split houses have to pay property taxes to two governments and have mailboxes at either end of their houses for the two different postal systems. One doctor, who was qualified to practice medicine in Holland but not in Belgium, was forced to dismantle his dispensary at not inconsiderable expense and move it a few yards back into his native land.

Until relatively recently, smuggling was big business in the town and it was not uncommon to see huge trucks being furtively unloaded of Belgian butter and cigarettes in the dead of night. With the setting up of the Common Market, many tax and price discrepancies were eliminated, but enough remain to make it worth your while to compare prices on the two sides of the local grocery store through which the boundary runs. Probably the most remarkable manifestation of this international insanity is to be found in the Cafe Het Hoeske on Stationstraat, where the pool table straddles the boundary. It is almost certainly the only place in the world where you can stroke the cue ball in one country and sink the eight ball in another.

Details: Baarle is about ten miles southeast of Breda on the main road between there and Turnhout in Belgium (see page 17). There's an hourly bus service from Breda (No. 32 line) and less frequent service from Turnhout (No. 645). Determining when you are in Belgian territory and when in Dutch is a constant challenge here. The local tourist office, just off the main square, has a helpful pamphlet in English, but you can also generally tell by looking at the color of the licence plates on cars parked outside the houses. Red and white ones are Belgian; yellow and black ones are Dutch.

Philips Evoluon, Eindhoven

In 1966 to celebrate its seventy-fifth anniversary, Philips, the Dutch electrical giant, gave its hometown a museum of science and technology, which it called Evoluon and built in the shape of a huge flying saucer. It stands in a pleasant park in the heart of town. However incongruous its appearance, it works marvelously well for display purposes. The visitor rises to the top level in a glass-encased elevator, where there is a bird's-eye view down onto the whole of the museum, and then descends, Guggenheim Museum fashion, down a circular ramp.

The intention of the museum is to show man's interaction with science and technology. The displays are, on the whole, about 20 years behind the times. There's little about microchips and computers, for instance, but masses about the marvels of color television, video telephones, and stereophonic music. That comment is made more in a spirit of observation than criticism. Stereophonic listening chambers may no longer strike us as one of the marvels of the age, but that isn't to say that sitting in one for a few minutes is any less relaxing or entertaining. Despite the slight archaic air about some displays, they are all well done and both the signs and taped commentaries are thoughtfully provided in English as well as Dutch. Many displays have buttons to push and handles to crank, which children always love, and the whole is successfully diverting. Don't travel miles out of your way, but if you are in the region of Eindhoven it's worth a couple of hours, particularly if you have restive youngsters on your hands.

Details: Philips Evoluon is on Noordbrabantlaan in Eindhoven and is open Monday to Friday from 9:30 to 5:30, Saturday from 10 to 5 and on Sunday from 12 to 5.

NORWAY

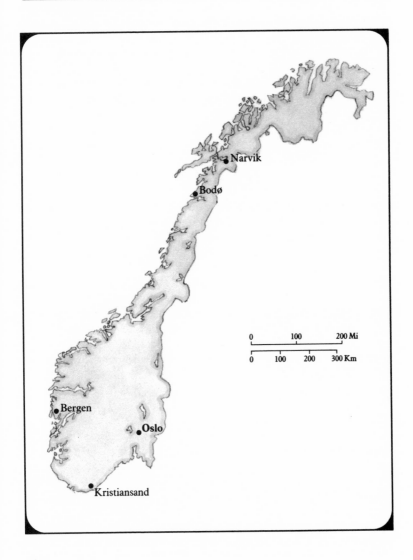

Holmenkollen Ski Jump, Oslo

At the height of summer, with a surprisingly warm Norwegian sun beating down on you, the idea of spending a day at a world-famous ski jump might seem an unlikely proposition. But you would be wrong. Few outings anywhere offer a more pleasing assortment of small pleasures than this one.

For thousands of Norwegians, Holmenkollen is nirvana. Every March, more than 100,000 spectators—a colossal number for a country of just four million people—flock the ten miles from central Oslo to watch the national ski jumping championships. But even in summer, with the snows long gone and the double-tiered spectators' stands deserted, Holmenkollen is eminently visitable. An elevator takes you the 183 feet to the top of the ski jump. From there the view across the fjord to Oslo—and, on a clear day, as far as Sweden beyond—is magnificent. More breathtaking still is the perspective down the ski jump itself: the idea of anyone voluntarily hurtling down that 10-story-high slide at 50 miles an hour or more in order to soar a couple of hundred feet out into space would be enough to make Evel Knievel giddy. Lower down the jump superstructure is a pleasant and inexpensive cafeteria from which the view to Oslo is equally impressive but less intimidating. Back on the ground is the Holmenkollen Ski Museum, opened in 1923, which houses the world's oldest collection of ski equipment, including the 2,500-year-old Øvrebø ski, the oldest in existence. A 4,000-year-old stone carving depicting a Norwegian skier shows just how deeply ingrained the sport is on the nation's history and psyche.

A good part of the pleasure in a trip to Holmenkollen comes in getting there. If you take the Frognerseteren line of the subway to the last station (a 30-minute ride from the National Theater in central Oslo), you can take a very pleasant 20-minute walk up a hill to the Tryvann Tower, the tallest structure in Scandinavia, with more panoramic views. On the way you'll pass the famous Frognerseteren Hovedrestaurant, which offers two dining rooms (one cheap, one expensive) and the atmosphere of a mountainside chalet. Try the reindeer burgers. Thirty minutes' walking from the Tryvann Tower will land you at the ski jump and its museum. About five minutes' walk downhill from the ski jump is Besserud station, where you can catch a subway back into town. This circuit is probably the most pleasant and scenic in the whole of suburban Oslo.

Henie-Onstad Art Center, Oslo

In the perhaps unlikely event that you've been wondering whatever became of Sonja Henie, the ice-skating star and sometime actress of the 1930s and 1940s, part of the answer at least can be found about 10 miles southwest of Oslo at the ponderously named but beautifully designed Sonja Henie-Niels Onstad Foundations Art Center. After hanging up her ice skates, Ms. Henie married Onstad, a Norwegian shipping magnate, and together they began accumulating one of the world's finest collections of twentieth-century abstract art. Today the fruits of that collection can be seen in the Oslo suburb of Baerum in the handsome museum they gave to the nation in 1961.

The fan-shaped building, constructed of hand-chiselled concrete and glass and set on a memorable site overlooking the Oslo Fjord, is one of the most elegant modern buildings in Scandinavia—and, at a cost of 70 million kronor, represents the largest private donation of any kind ever made in the country.

The permanent collection consists of about 300 paintings, including some of the best work by Matisse, Munch, Picasso, Bonnard, Léger, and Miró. There are also frequent visiting exhibitions, as well as films, concerts, ballet performances, and the like. Somewhat incongruously, there's also a room housing Ms. Henie's 600 ice-skating trophies.

Details: The Henie-Onstad Art Center is at Baerum (Tel. 54 30 50) and can be reached from central Oslo on buses numbered 32, 36, or 37. Alternatively, and much more pleasantly, you can travel by boat from Pier 3 in Oslo and see the city's fjord at the same time. The museum is open from 12 to 7 P.M. in winter and from 9 A.M. to 10 P.M. in summer (11 A.M. to 10 P.M. on Sundays).

Norway's "Lost" Valley, Setesdal

It's a strong-willed writer who can describe the Setesdal region without resorting to comparisons with Shangri-la. A deep, green valley of forests, waterfalls, and scattered turf-roofed farmhouses, cut off from the outside world by towering mountains, it is perhaps the nearest real-life equivalent to James Hilton's fictional paradise. For centuries this 60-mile-long sward of green along the River Otra in southern Norway was one of the most isolated and inaccessible areas of Europe. Only with the building of a modern through road in the 1950s was it finally given the chance to become part of the twentieth century. It's still making up its mind whether to join.

Setesdal's culture, traditions, and architecture are all still firmly rooted in the past. It is, for instance, the last place in Norway where you can still see older people dressed in the country's traditional folk costumes. But for the traveler its principal appeal lies in its excellent fishing for dwarf salmon in the sparkling Otra and landlocked Byglandsfjord—tackle can be rented throughout the region—and in its incomparable beauty. Although you can scarcely set a foot wrong wherever you go in the valley, three attractions are often overlooked yet worth seeing.

One is the Reiarfossen waterfall near Ose. It was named for a young man, Reiar, who boldly jumped his horse across it to win the hand of a beautiful young woman. Flushed with his success, he turned his steed around and tried to jump back to his beloved, but failed and was swept away to a hasty death and lasting fame. Whether or not you buy the story, the falls are impressive.

About 40 miles to the north is the medieval wooden church at Bykle, the oldest in the valley and one of the smallest in Norway. In 1826 an ambitious local artist covered every square inch of the interior with exquisite paintings of roses. But in the 1870s, the village priest, realizing his parishioners were more engrossed in the delicate murals than in his own ponderous sermons, tried to obliterate them. He managed to destroy a few, as well as some priceless medieval paintings, but not sufficiently to keep Bykle's diminutive church from having one of the most remarkable and fetching interiors in northern Europe.

At the nearby village of Flateland is the Rygnestad Farm, once the property of a certain Vond Asmund. The mountains that once cut off Setesdal from the rest of Norway also made it, until the last century, a haven for outlaws. Vond Asmund was perhaps the most famous. Today his property is still a working farm, owned by the nation but managed by his descendants. The barn, stable, corn mill, forge, and farmhouse have been preserved as they were almost 400 years ago. Visitors are welcome to poke around. Be sure not to miss the *nyeloft*, or storehouse. Up a dark and narrow flight of stairs is Asmund's treasure room. There you will find an astonishing assortment of items—tapestries, a carved bed, fine glass, Asmund's best clothes, and paintings of Queen Mary I of England and Philip of Spain—just as Asmund left them four centuries ago.

The Setesdal Valley remains secluded even today. Only two buses a day link its two dozen or so villages to the outside world. If you would like to see a part of Norway that few foreigners ever penetrate, this is the place to do it.

Details: The Setesdal Valley is just north of Kristiansand in southern Norway on Highway 12. The twice-daily bus trips, linking Kristiansand at the valley's southern end with Hardangerfjord to the north, take a half a day.

Hardangerfjord

The Hardangerfjord offers something for everyone—deep blue fjords, thundering waterfalls, glaciers, mountains, enchanting villages, and even the world's most attractive chicken coop. This last is at the village of Lofthus on the grounds of the Ullensvang Hotel. Originally, the tiny wooden structure was the summer studio of Edvard Grieg, the composer. Here he wrote parts of *Peer Gynt* and the whole of *Spring*. But a subsequent owner—obviously not a music lover—turned the cabin into a chicken coop. Today the cabin, containing Grieg's piano and other furniture, has been restored to its former glory and is open to the public. The keys are available at the hotel's reception desk. The cabin's attraction is not so much its checkered history as its idyllic setting on the banks of the Sorfjord (an offshoot of the larger Hardangerfjord). Grieg was in a position to be selective about his outlook and the view from his little hut is one of the best.

The most rewarding time to visit the Hardanger area is in the second half of May when the fruit trees for which the area is famed are coming to life. Then the valleys turn white and pink with flowering petals and the air is gloriously rich with the scent of apple and cherry blossoms. Fruit trees were brought to the area by Cistercian monks in the thirteenth century and there are still traces today of their presence. At Lofthus, for instance, look for the stone steps leading up the mountainside, laboriously hewn out of solid rock by the monks more than 800 years ago. A walk to the top takes you to Nosi (the Nose), a magnificent lookout point with a breathtaking view of the fjord and its mountains. The other great way to experience the fjord is on one of the ferries running between the waterside villages. Most call at Lofthus. In an area as rich in scenic beauty as

Norway, it's crazy to single out one place. But the Hardangerfjord can stand comparison with any other and has the additional virtue of being little known to the world outside.

Details: The Hardangerfjord area is about 30 miles east of Bergen. Lofthus makes an ideal base for touring the area, but there are hotels and guesthouses (called *pensjonats* and *gjestgiveris*) almost everywhere, as well as rooms in private homes (look for signs that say *Overnatting* or *Rum*). Lofthus is on the R7 road. There are no rail services to the village—the nearest rail connection is at Voss—but buses and ferries are frequent.

Narvik

The top tourist attraction of Scandinavia, according to the people who keep track of such things, is the midnight sun. And quite rightly—it's an unforgettable experience. The difficulty is finding the best place to watch it. Theoretically, all you have to do is get yourself above the Arctic Circle sometime between roughly late May and mid-July (times vary from place to place). But other considerations militate against many possible locations.

One is mosquitoes, which swarm across much of inland Scandinavia throughout the summer, enveloping the hapless like a blanket. Another is mountains; however glorious they may be by day, in many places they block out the sun at night. And the third is uncertain weather; it's a long haul to the Arctic Circle (about 450 miles from Stockholm or Oslo) and nobody wants to travel that sort of distance to find the sun hidden behind an unshifting mass of dark clouds.

One place that has miraculously escaped the first two problems, and generally avoids the third, is Narvik, about 100 miles inside the Arctic Circle on the northwest coast of Norway. Although no one would call it the St. Tropez of the North (its principal claim to fame is as an iron ore port), it's a pleasant enough town of 15,000 people with a good choice of hotels and guesthouses. More important, its location on a peninsula between two small fjords, the Rombaksfjord and the Beisfjord, gives it a host of excellent viewing points.

The most popular of these is the Fagernesfjell, a 4,100-foot mountain at the back of the town. A 15-minute cable car ride (open until about midnight in summer) will take you nearly to the top. Alternatively, you can seek out the town's beaches or follow the roads up into the hills overlooking the two fjords. Keep an eye out for the concrete fortifications left behind by the Germans after World War II. For those of us who grew up on Sgt. Rock comic books and "Combat" on TV, the chance to clamber through the tunnels and lookouts of an old German pillbox is irresistible. Just as important, they were always built in the spots with the most sweeping views.

In Narvik, daylight is uninterrupted from May 31 to July 14. Walking through empty, sleeping streets in broad daylight at two in the morning is a distinctly eerie experience. If you've ever wondered what it would be like to be the last person on earth, this will answer your questions. But the midnight sun is more than that. Because it dips almost to the horizon and then hovers there for a long time before gradually rising again, you get the world's longest and most spectacular sunsets and sunrises. That's what makes the long trek from the south—and a night without sleep—worthwhile.

Details: Norway provides no train services to Narvik, but, curiously, Sweden does, on a 26-mile line from Kiruna. The line isn't there as an act of charity, but to carry Swedish iron ore to freighters at Narvik. In fact, almost half of all the rail freight in Norway travels on these 26 miles of track. If you are not traveling up from Sweden, you can reach Narvik by bus or steamer from Bodø.

Bodø

An alternative to Narvik for those seeking the midnight sun is Bodø, a pleasant modern fishing port of 32,000 people about 30 miles north of the Arctic Circle and 70 miles south of Narvik. The view is even more spectacular than at Narvik, but, unfortunately, less reliable. Most of those who come to Bodø to see the midnight sun (it doesn't set here from early June to mid-July) trudge up Mt. Rønvik, a not very taxing walk, two and a half miles north of the city. There on a good night dozens—sometimes hundreds—of people spread out over the mountainside to watch the sun make its fiery circuit around Landego Island far out to sea. The hardier and less sociable press on from there, following a signposted path leading up to the 2,000-foot-high Lopsfjell, a two-hour walk. There the views are a bit more spectacular and infinitely more private.

But even if you arrive in Bodø to find it entrapped in thick mist or drizzle, one nearby natural phenomenon won't let you down: the Salstraumen maelstrom. Salstraum is a sound 22 miles south of Bodø between a narrow opening and the sea beyond. Four times a day, tides force a colossal 80 billion gallons of water through the narrow passage in an explosive, primieval clash between rock and water. Even from a safe distance, the thunderous, seething rush of water can be terrifying. The accompanying whirlpools and eddies are said to have provided Edgar Allan Poe with the inspiration for his story "Descent into the Maelstrom." It's not particularly easy to get to, but it does reward your efforts.

Details: The Salstraum inlet is about a 40-minute bus ride from Bodø, but services are not frequent; check the return times before setting out. If hitching or driving, follow the road from Bodø to Fauske, but take the branch road to Salstraumen at Tverlandet.

PORTUGAL

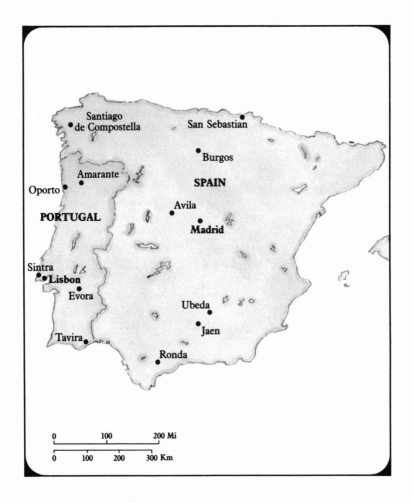

Sintra, near Lisbon

If you should ever come into a lot of money and begin casting around for the perfect place to live, consider putting Sintra high on your list. For centuries magnates and aristocrats from all over Europe have flocked here to escape the stultifying heat of the cities and idle away their summers in cool, airy villas scattered like dice among the densely wooded hillsides. Byron called the town "perhaps in every respect the most delightful in Europe" and I think he may have been right. Today it remains an elegant place, but a welcoming one, set among the steep slopes and ravines of the Sintra Mountains and filled with dark trees, fragrant foliage, and quiet corners. The town boasts two vast palaces and a ruined castle, two of the finest public parks in Europe, and tranquil—if sometimes steep—walks along the quiet roads and footpaths that provide panoramic views to Cabo da Roca, Europe's westernmost point, and the Atlantic Ocean beyond. Good restaurants and hotels are available—even at the height of summer getting a room here is seldom difficult—and there is easy access both to Lisbon, 14 miles to the east, and coastal resorts, a few miles to the west.

The main landmark in the center of town is the vast National Palace, or Paço Real, built in the fourteenth century by Joao I and for six centuries the summer residence of Portugal's kings. It contains some notable features, particularly its exquisite azulejo tiling, but in my opinion it's completely overshadowed by the lofty and sumptuous Palacio de Pena, or Pena Palace, Portugal's answer to the nineteenth-century excesses of Bavaria's King Ludwig. Sprawled across a hilltop site, the palace was built for King Ferdinand II (brother of England's Prince Albert) by a German architect named Baron Eschwege, who seems to have found inspiration in every architectural style known to man—moorish, gothic, renaissance, manueline, and baroque. It presents the visitor with a dazzling array of domes, battlements and balconies, towers, cupolas, and windows of every shape and size. The interiors, left unchanged since the last occupants departed in 1910, continue the kitschy excess with an enthusiasm that can only be called remarkable. The whole is a marvel, not to be missed.

Outside the palace is the much more subdued Parque de Pena, one of Europe's biggest and most splendid public gardens. But again there is a formidable challenge to its supremacy, this time from the nearby Monserrate Gardens, laid out in the nineteenth century by a rich expatriate Englishman. It's a masterpiece of landscaping, with lawns like golf greens and the world's most complete collection of ferns, some breathtakingly huge. There are 3,000 species of plants altogether, many of them quite rare. Also to be seen—as much for the fabulous views as for the remnants of stone—are the ruins of the Castelo dos Mouros, or Moorish Castle, near the Pena Palace.

About the only thing that can be said against the town is that it does get rather a lot of rain by Portuguese standards (hence its lushness). But if the sun is shining and you are anywhere near Lisbon, it can't be recommended highly enough.

Details: Sintra is less than an hour by train from Lisbon and the service is good. Buses to the nearby beaches depart from the train station though, perhaps even more appealingly, you can reach one of the best of the beaches, Praia das Macas, by tram in the summer. The tourist information office is in the Praca da Republica.

Tavira, Algarve

The Algarve runs for 150 miles along Portugal's southern coast and up around the rump of its western one. In almost every respect it is superior to Europe's other famous coastal stretches like the Costa del Sol and French Riviera—cooler, cheaper, less polluted, and less crowded. Although blemished here and there by package holiday resorts, it is still graced in large part by unspoiled fishing communities where tourists are regarded as a welcome but rather curious phenomenon. Of all the Algarve communities, none is lovelier than Tavira, a vaguely Moorish-looking town whose dazzlingly white buildings lead down to the Gilao River, spanned by a graceful Roman bridge and lined with palm trees behind which is tucked as inviting an assemblage of cafes and restaurants as you will find anywhere. Tavira is equally rich in churches—37 in all, none of any great note on its own, but all collectively adding to the town's charm. It is not perhaps a spot you would want to spend days and days exploring, but it's a marvelous place to wake up to in the morning and return to at the end of a long day at the beach. And the beaches here are very good.

None are at Tavira itself, but a mile or so south of town at Santa Luzia and Ilha de Tavira (Tavira Island) and farther up the coast around Cacela are some outstanding ones. Some sit on great sandbars, reached by ferries, where you can challenge breaking rollers on the seaward side or paddle around in calmer waters on the landward side—a useful option if you have small children or aren't a good swimmer yourself. For the more distant beaches you'll have to catch a bus, but unless you're an absolute fiend for early morning swimming, you'll probably come to regard the morning stroll to the bus stop on Tavira's handsome main square, predictably called the Praca da Republica, as one of the high points of the day.

Details: Tavira is on the south coast of Portugal, a few miles east of Faro. It's on the main southern rail line between Lisbon and Spain.

Evora

Evora is a town of 40,000 people and, it sometimes seems, about as many historic monuments. I don't suppose there's a place of its size anywhere in the world that packs a greater panorama of architectural treasures and intriguing attractions into a more compact area. Almost as an incidental matter it also happens to be a very handsome and agreeable town, home of an ancient university, and capital of the Alentejo, the region of Portugal that produces almost two-thirds of the world's cork.

Evora's most important monuments are handily clustered together on a sort of hilltop acropolis standing above the steep, maze-like streets of the Old Town. Probably the most famous—certainly the most macabre—is the Church of St. Francis (São Francisco), where the bones of 5,000 Franciscan monks, and a few nuns, are ranged around the walls and pediments with an air of fanatical tidiness—very similar to the Church of Santa Maria della Concezione in Rome (see page 166). Much more impressive, however, is the massive Romanesque cathedral, or Se, which dates from 1186 and, most unusually, is built of granite. Its Treasury is one of the richest in the world and contains, among much else, a solid-gold chalice weighing eight pounds and a small crucifix with 850 diamonds, more than 400 rubies, 180 emeralds from Brazil, and a pair of outsized sapphires. There's also a strikingly lovely thirteenth-century statue of the Virgin Mary, which opens up to reveal a triptych chronicling her life. For a small charge you can go up to the cathedral roof for a marvelous view of the town.

Just outside the cathedral is a second-century Temple of Diana, almost the only remnant of four centuries of Roman occupation of the town. It is the best preserved Roman monument in Portugal and was, curiously enough, the site of the local abattoir until 1870. Next door to the church is the Archbishop's Palace, now the home of perhaps the best regional museum in the country with a particularly strong collection of Renaissance paintings. Three other big buildings stand here—a seventeenth-century palace, which is still a private residence and not open to the public; the palace's church; and the Convento dos Loios, a former convent that has been converted into a splendid *pousada*, or state-owned hotel. And this is only one small corner of the town. Elsewhere are 31 monasteries and convents and at least as many churches, several very old and very lovely.

Amazingly, there would be even more ancient monuments but for a zealous sixteenth-century cardinal who tore down dozens of Roman temples and palaces for fear they might inspire a respect for paganism among the townspeople. The streets and little squares are a joy to wander through, especially if you know any Portuguese since they carry names like Square of the Unshaven Man, Avenue of Our Lord of Earthquakes, Street of the Cardinal's Nurses, and Square of the Sulking Child.

A very special trip.

Details: Evora is in south-central Portugal, about three hours by train from Lisbon and six from Faro.

Amarante

Very quickly after you arrive in Amarante you realize that it is unlike any other town in Portugal. Wander around a little and you will gradually discover that it is, in fact, unlike any other town anywhere. In both instances the reason derives largely from its inhabitation almost entirely by *maranes*—descendants of sixteenth-century Jews forced to convert to Christianity. Although the *maranes* eventually embraced Catholicism with some enthusiasm, they did it in a decidedly distinctive way, retaining a number of Jewish practices and adding a few peculiar ones of their own, mostly revolving around fertility rites. Don't expect to encounter orgies in the streets or naked virgins dancing around bonfires, but if you do come to town on the first Saturday in June, you can see townspeople exchanging, and nibbling on, little penis-shaped cakes.

But that, I hasten to add, is not all Amarante has to offer. Above all else it's a lovely little riverside town, where balconied houses jumble together and jut out over the fast-flowing waters of the Rio Tamega. An arched 1,800-year-old Roman bridge forms the focal point for a setting that is ineffably quaint and charming, best savored from the terrace of one of the many agreeable bars and restaurants lining the riverfront, where you can happily while away an evening growing intoxicated on both the cheap wine and picturesque setting.

By day, there's not a great deal to do except wander over to the Church of São Gonçala, a Moorish-style structure whose cloister walls are lavishly and attractively embellished with azulejos tiles. The church has a reputation as a healing center and its principal attraction, for me, is found in a side chapel full of votive offerings left by those whose maladies were miraculously cured by a visit here. The room is filled with wooden legs, jars crammed with gallstones and kidney stones, and wax models of other body parts that were either removed or rendered useful by a bout of fervent prayer. Also on the grounds, and scarcely less unexpected, is a small museum of modern art, devoted in large part to the works of Amadeo Sousa Cardosa, a native of Amarante whose primary claim to fame, I'm sorry to say, is that he once shared a Paris studio with Modigliani. Still, of its type the museum is very good.

Amarante's pleasures are, you will have gathered, rather modest ones and are unlikely to hold you for more than a day, if even that. But it is a beautiful place in a part of Portugal few outsiders penetrate and for that reason alone is recommended. As a further enticement, the four-hour trip by road or rail from Oporto is one of the most dramatic and memorable on the whole Iberian peninsula, leading through deep gorges and over narrow bridges along the banks of the Doura and Tamega rivers.

SPAIN

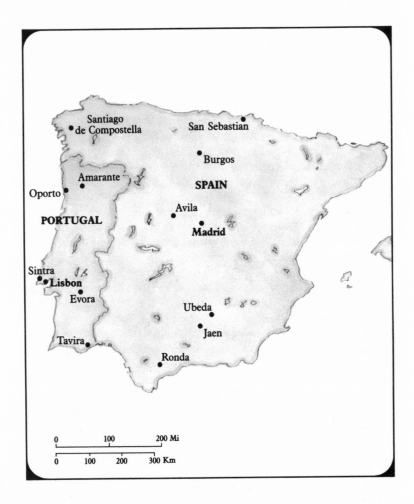

The Most Spectacular Road in Spain, Andalusia

I don't know if the Spanish have a nickname for the road from the Costa del Sol to Ronda, but I call it the Hail Mary Highway. Starting at the coast, it climbs steadily up through the jagged peaks and sheer sides of the Sierra da Ronda mountains. Narrow and tortuous, it offers a succession of majestic vistas and glimpses of villages clinging to the steep mountainsides as if by their fingernails, but also reveals some of the most dangerous-looking bends and sheerest plunges to be found anywhere on earth. You have only to peep over the edge once as you squeeze past an oncoming bus or fortress-like truck and even the most dedicated agnostic is likely to make fervent entreaties to God and wish he'd invested in a St. Christopher medal back in Malaga.

Eventually, after what seems like a lifetime of awed ecstasy mixed with deep terror, Ronda heaves in sight, sitting atop a rocky outcrop across a broad plain. It would be hard for anything not to be an anticlimax after this hair-raising journey, but Ronda rises, quite literally, to the challenge. This is no town in which to get drunk and go reeling through the streets at midnight—not unless you pack a parachute. A truly spectacular gorge called the Tajo, up to 1,000 feet deep, cuts through the town like a savage wound.

Three bridges span the chasm and houses cluster at the cliff's edge, poised like lemmings above the valley floor hundreds of feet below. In the late afternoon you can stand on one of the bridges and watch great vultures soaring on the thermals. The giddying look downward becomes all the more intense when you realize that during the Spanish Civil War many of the town's wealthier citizens were made to stand on the edge of the precipice and then gently nudged into the void. Hemingway vividly described the incident in *For Whom the Bells Toll*, just as he immortalized the local bullfight ring—the oldest in Spain, built in 1785—in *The Sun Also Rises*.

But Ronda is more than its gorge. The streets on the southern, older side of town are a tangle of narrow alleyways, as atmospheric as those of Cordoba, but infinitely less disturbed by intruders. There are several monumental buildings, including a cathedral and three former palaces, at one of which, the Casa del Rey Moro (House of the Moorish King), you can climb down 365 steps to the floor of the gorge. A magnificent place and an unforgettable journey. If you are traveling anywhere in southern Spain, don't miss this.

Details: Ronda (pop. 30,000) is about 20 miles due north of Marbella as the crow flies, but about 50 miles by road from either Malaga or San Roque. It is an ideal detour for anyone traveling to or from Malaga, Cordoba, Seville, or Granada, all of which can be reached from Ronda by bus or train.

The Paradores at Jaen and Ubeda

There are some very good reasons for including Jaen and Ubeda on any Spanish itinerary. Both are attractive and welcoming cities, easily reached from the main tourist centers like Madrid and Barcelona and yet little known to outsiders. Both have some very good restaurants and interesting diversions. But the really compelling rationale for seeking either place out is to spend a night or two in their incomparable paradores.

These government-owned hotels are generally, but not quite always, built in old castles, monasteries, convents, or palaces and are almost always a painstaking amalgam of old architectural features— baronial halls with vast wooden chandeliers, stone walls hung with tapestries, fireplaces you could park a car in—with more modern comforts like decent plumbing, air conditioning, and swimming pools. Most are notable not only for their architecture, but also for their settings, and all, including the modern ones, are spotlessly clean, extraordinarily efficient, and very good value. In short, apart from the siesta and the Spanish fly, they are Spain's greatest gift to happiness in the sack.

Paradores are always popular and can be difficult to get into without reservations. But the ones at Jaen and Ubeda are worth trying for, partly because of their relative proximity and partly because of the contrast they offer. Of the two, the parador at Jaen is unquestionably more spectacular. Built in what was once a Moorish fortress and later a palace for Castillian kings, it sits on a crag high over the town with views for miles and miles across plains of olive groves to the distant snowcapped Sierra Nevadas. Most rooms have balconies and four-poster beds and the common rooms have a scattering of suits of armor and other antiquities to add to the air of medievalism (which, it must be said, some people find a trifle cloying and contrived).

Even without its parador, Jaen would be well worth a visit. Stuck in the heart of Spain's olive country and capital of the province of Jaen, it is a handsome town of hilly streets with a splendid cathedral that was started in 1500 but took 270 years to finish. The prize treasure here is the *santo rostro*, or holy face imprinted on a hand-kerchief and said to have been used by St. Veronica to wipe the brow of Christ. There are also two good museums, the Museo Arqueologico and the Museo de Bellas Artes.

Ubeda, about 45 miles to the northeast and only about half the size of Jaen, provides an inviting, but less dramatic, contrast to Jaen's splendors. Although the town is full of notable old buildings—including the parador itself, housed in the sixteenth-century Palacio del Condestable—the real appeal here is just to wander through its quiet squares and narrow streets of whitewashed houses. The whole town is listed as a national monument and is a piece of medieval perfection, largely untouched by both time and tourism. The parador is built around a courtyard just off the town's main square, with airy, high-ceilinged bedrooms and all the antiques and other touches that make paradores unique. When you consider that this parador has just 25 bedrooms (all doubles), there's an exceptionally generous assortment of common rooms—two lounges, a library, a bar in the old wine cellar, and an excellent restaurant, which, as with all paradores, specializes in the local cuisine. Although you sacrifice the magnificent view you had at Jaen, you gain by having the life of the town—its bars and restaurants—literally just a few steps away in the Plaza de Vazquez de Molina.

Details: The Parador Nacional Castillo de Santa Catalina at Jaen is at Apartado de Correos 178 (Tel. 953-23 22 88). Rates range from 3,500 to 4,500 pesetas. The hotel has six single rooms. The Parador Nacional Condestable Davados in Ubeda is at Plaza de Vazquez de Molina 1 (Tel. 953-75 03 45). Bedrooms in all paradores have private baths. There are now almost 90 paradores scattered all over Spain. For details of others ask the Spanish National Tourist Office for its brochure *Paradores*. In all cases, reservations are strongly recommended—and they must be made with the individual parador.

Avila, Castilla la Vieja

The people of Avila are a bit blasé about their town wall. I suppose you get that way after 900 years. They consider the really big thing in town St. Teresa, who was born here in 1515 and made a name for herself by founding countless monasteries and reorganizing the Carmelite order of nuns. Though she was doubtless a good—nay, saintly — woman, she is a ubiquitous and rather tiresome presence in this town of 30,000 people in central Spain. You will be urged to see not only the font where she was baptized, but also the very first convent she founded, the convent where she was educated, the place where she was born (now — surprise, surprise — a convent) and endless other places where she sat, slept, worked, or prayed. All of these are very worthy and often even handsome, impressive, and moving. But I think you'd have to be a very good Catholic indeed to want to travel more than a few blocks to see them.

On the other hand, there is Avila's wall, which is even more historic than the saintly Teresa and rather more impressive. I realize that a wall might also seem a fairly feeble inducement to travel halfway across Spain, but it is an exceptionally awesome bit of engineering. Still completely intact after nine centuries, Avila's wall is the most perfect in Europe apart from the one at Carcassonne in France and infinitely less teeming with tourists and those who prey on them.

Seen from a distance, it gives Avila an enchanted, fairy-tale look and leaves you feeling as if you've stumbled on a piece of the Middle Ages miraculously preserved out in the middle of nowhere. From up close it is simply magnificent. The wall stands almost 40 feet high—a daunting height when you're in its shadow—and runs for about 1½ miles around the town, punctuated at regular intervals by 88 towers and nine gates. It was built in just nine years, from 1081–90, yet time seems not even to have breathed on it.

Unless you are heavily into medieval architecture, I wouldn't suggest a special trip for this one (but then, in fairness, I would probably say much the same of Carcassonne), but if you're near Avila on your way to somewhere else—traveling from, say, Madrid to Segovia or Salamanca—you'll enjoy the detour.

Details: Avila (pop. 30,000) is about 60 miles northwest of Madrid and can be reached by train from there. The best view of the town is on the road to Salamanca at a viewing spot near Los Cuatro Postes.

Santiago de Compostela, Galicia

If you were going to write a history of travel and tourism, Santiago de Compostela would be a good place to start. It was the subject of the very first guidebook, the *Calixtine Codex*, written in the early twelfth century by a Frenchman and giving the lowdown on food, routes, and places to see on the long trek from France to the remotest corner of Spain. But even by that time Santiago's tourism industry was centuries old. Throughout the Middle Ages it was the most important pilgrimage site in the world after Rome and Jerusalem, attracting up to 500,000 pilgrims a year, kings and peasants alike, from all over Europe. (Among the visitors were Chaucer's wife of Bath and St. Francis of Assisi.) If you had just spent several weeks traveling halfway across Europe, perhaps even risking your life, you might reasonably expect the long trip to end with a high point, and it does. The great cathedral at Santiago is a dazzling sight, then and now.

It was built as a shrine to St. James, the Apostle of Christ and patron saint of Spain, whose ashes were said to have miraculously drifted in a boat with neither sail nor rudder from the Holy Land to Galicia in the ninth century. The cathedral is a vast and slightly hectic mixture of styles—mainly baroque, gothic, and Romanesque. On its main front, which dates from about 1100, three bold towers rise up from a plain and asymmetrical base in an outburst of orna-mentation. You'd need a week to count the statues that peep out from every niche and balustrade. Nob-topped cupolas litter the upper extremities, making the roofline vaguely resemble an outsized chess set. It is a sight so stunning and glorious that you can easily imagine weary pilgrims sinking to their knees in the great square around you.

The cathedral's mixture of styles becomes a bit messy around the sides and back, though lurking here and there, particularly around the doorways, are some exquisite touches like the carvings of the Portico de la Plateria. But the greatest glory of the church, inside or out, is the Portico de la Gloria gracing the main entrance, carved by an obscure craftsman named Master Matthew, or Maestro Mateo. Its 130 figures are perhaps the finest pieces of Romanesque sculpture in existence. (A modest self-portrait of Master Mateo himself can be seen crouching in the shadows behind the central pillar.)

The interior provides a strikingly subdued contrast. The nave is almost Norman in its austere simplicity, though even here the eye is caught at the end by a sudden outburst of gilt: this is the indescribably ornate high altar, one of the most glorious in the world. Everywhere you turn you're confronted with a magnificent assemblage of carvings and statuary whose detail leaves you gasping. This is a place to linger over—but then so is the whole of Santiago. As the tourist pamphlet says, Santiago is not just a city of monuments; the city itself is a monument. Especially at night, to walk through its narrow, arcaded streets is to slip through the centuries. The city is also home of an ancient university and its 30,000 students make the bars and cafes oases of liveliness.

Details: Santiago de Compostela (pop. 68,000) is in the northwest corner of Spain in one of the least touristed parts of the country. It is on a main rail line, with links to most other parts of the country and down the Atlantic coast of Portugal to Oporto and Lisbon.

The Cathedral of Burgos, Castilla la Vieja

It is criminal to suggest it, and remiss even to think it, but if you haven't got the time to follow the famous pilgrims' route all the way across Spain to Santiago de Compostela, Burgos makes for a pretty fair compromise. Its mighty cathedral, the third largest in Spain, is very similar to Santiago's, at least superficially. Both stand commandingly over their towns, both pierce the sky with elaborate towers, and both induce gasps with their rich mixture of styles and wealth of decoration.

The cathedral at Burgos, which dates from 1222, begins at ground level in a determinedly gothic manner, but abruptly changes character at the top with two folly-like towers whose shape suggests nothing so much as a pair of Christmas trees made of stone. Inside, its florid ornamentation, particularly the famous grand staircase, the Escalera Dorada, stands in sharp contrast to the more simple majesty of the cathedral at Santiago. Here ornamentation clusters around every pillar and graces every wall. You cannot advance two feet without being halted by some new and fabulous piece of sculpture or wood carving. It's an impossible church to describe. H. V. Morton, one of the greatest travel writers and a man almost never at a loss for words, declined even to try, except to say that it seemed to grow richer each time he saw it.

With 17 chapels to explore, you could easily spend several days here. Whatever you do, don't miss the remarkable life-sized figure of Christ in a chapel to itself. Although the figure appears made of varnished wood, it is said to feel just like human flesh when touched. Its arms, legs, and neck are flexible, it wears a wig of real hair, and—a bizarre touch—its loins are covered with a satin petticoat.

Burgos' other claim to fame is as the birthplace of El Cid, Spain's greatest national hero. The cathedral contains the Cid's famous chest—which, according to tradition, was miraculously filled with treasure—and there's a statue of him outside.

Details: Burgos (pop. 107,000) is in north-central Spain and is on a main rail line between San Sebastian and Madrid.

SWEDEN

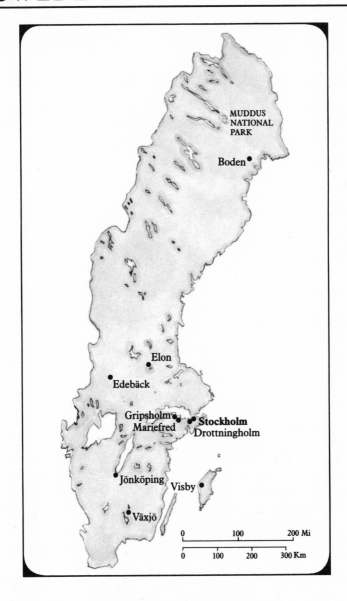

MUDDUS
NATIONAL
PARK

Boden

Elon

Edebäck

Gripsholm
Mariefred

Stockholm
Drottningholm

Jönköping

Visby

Växjö

0		100		200 Mi
0	100	200	300 Km	

Best One-Day Outing from Stockholm

Stockholm is a city of water. With a sea, a lake, and 25,000 islands scattered at its feet, it provides the starting point for some of the finest boat trips anywhere. The most rewarding, to my mind, is the three-hour cruise around the archipelago and up Lake Mälaren to the lovely little town of Mariefred (pop. 3,000). With its imposing seventeenth-century church, narrow streets, and idyllic lakeside setting, Mariefred is one of the most appealing and unspoiled places in Sweden, and easily deserving of a visit in its own right. But its glory is its massive medieval fortress, Gripsholm Castle, built by Gustav Vasa in 1537–44 on an island just offshore. In a nation awash with ancient castles, it is one of the best preserved and most beautiful. Gripsholm was last occupied by King Karl XV in 1864. After his departure it served for many years as a prison. Today it is a museum owned by the nation and, with almost 3,000 portraits lining its walls, effectively a national portrait gallery. Sixty of the 102 rooms are open to the public.

Mariefred is also home of Sweden's oldest inn, the Gripsholms Värdshus, on the lakeside overlooking the castle. Built in 1623, it has only seven rooms, so reservations are recommended. For railway buffs and children, there's an additional attraction in the summer: from Mariefred you can take a 40-minute ride on an old steam railway to the nearby town of Laggesta.

Details: Boat trips to Mariefred depart daily at 10 A.M. from June 1 to August 31 from the City Hall (Stadhusbron) dock in Stockholm. There's a restaurant aboard. By car, follow the E3 road south out of Stockholm; it's a 65 km drive. Gripsholm Castle is open daily from 10 A.M. to 4:30 P.M. from May 15 to August 31. Admission is Kr7 for adults and Kr3 for children. The steam railway runs every day from late June to late August, Sundays only in May, September, and October. Rates at the Gripsholms Värdshus (Tel. 0159 100 40) range from about Kr125-Kr200.

Yard-Wide Lane, Stockholm

Unless they are exceedingly rushed or woefully misguided, most visitors to Stockholm spend a good deal of their time in Gamla Staden (sometimes abbreviated to Gamla Sta'n), the city's Old Town. The home of the Royal Palace, the oldest church in Stockholm, and the city's stock exchange, the Old Town is a natural magnet for visitors. But easily overlooked among the quarter's warren of narrow streets and tiny courtyards is one of the more unusual local landmarks, Mårten Trotzigs Gränd, or Yard-Wide Lane. To an English-speaking passerby the name may seem somewhat odd because there's nothing even remotely grand about it. In fact, *grand* means *lane* in Swedish. Mårten Trotzigs Gränd is barely three feet wide, making it the narrowest street in Scandinavia, if not the world. To find it, walk down Västerlånggtan, a pedestrian precinct of boutiques and handicraft and antique shops. Past the Riksbank Building (built in 1670 and thought to be the oldest bank building in the world), on the left, you'll find it, an unimposing passageway connecting Västerlånggatan with the parallel street of Prästgatan. Nearby is Den Gyldene Freiden (Golden Peace) restaurant. Opened in 1721, it provides good food and old-world charm in abundance.

Sweden's "Lost" Theater, Drottningholm Palace

Anyone with an uncertain grasp of geography could be forgiven for mistaking Drottningholm Palace, seven miles west of Stockholm, for Versailles. The Dowager Queen Eleonora, who commissioned the palace in 1662, wanted it to look like Versailles and her wish was stunningly granted. Its scale is a bit more modest, but the ornate rococo building with broad avenues and geometric gardens is strikingly similar to the French original and the setting, on the shores of Lake Mälaren, is perhaps even more magnificent.

The palace has been the official residence of the royal family since 1980. It has always been a treasured part of the nation's heritage, yet for more than a century one of its most important features, its tiny eighteenth-century court theater, sat virtually unnoticed on the grounds.

Opened in 1766, for 26 years it was one of the most glittering spots in the world of the performing arts. But in 1792 with the assassination of its patron, the actor-king Gustav III, it abruptly fell into neglect. For the next century it was used successively as a granary, a dining hall for soldiers, and as a storehouse for lumber and vegetables. In 1921, a Stockholm professor who was searching the estate for a missing painting wandered into the forgotten theater. Among the cobwebs and detritus he found 30 original sets, trunk-loads of eighteenth-century costumes, and box after box of props. All had lain untouched for 129 years. The elaborate Italian-designed stage machinery—a marvel in its day because it allowed scenes to be changed without bringing down the curtain—was still in perfect working order. Even the original place cards, marking the seats for everyone in the royal household from the king and queen to the most menial member of the kitchen staff, were still in place. The professor had found a time capsule.

Now fully restored, the theater is the oldest in regular use in Europe and the best preserved seventeenth-century theater in the world. Every year from May to September leading companies like the Royal Stockholm Opera give 40 performances of operas, plays, and ballet in conditions just as Gustav III would have seen them in the 1700s. The original backdrops and props are used—when thunder is required, for instance, cannon balls are rolled across the roof—and musicians even dress up in period costumes. The effect is wholly convincing. Drottningholm is small and seats are never easy to come by, but the chance to watch a Haydn concerto or Rossini opera performed as their contemporaries would have seen them makes them worth trying for.

Details: Drottningholm Palace is open daily from 11 A.M. to 4:30 P.M. The best way to get there is by boat from in front of the City Hall in Stockholm, a pleasant 45-minute trip. For reservations and details of programs at the theater, write to Drottningholm Court Theater, Föreställningar, Box 27050, S-102 51, Stockholm. The cost of seats ranges from SKr30 to SKr150 and there is also a SKr15 booking fee. On the nights of performances, special buses are laid on. They depart from the Grand Hotel and from Vasagatan (opposite the Central Station) about 45 minutes before the performance time. Alternatively, you can catch a special theater boat from the City Hall jetty at 6 P.M.

Visby, Gotland

Visby is not a name that normally springs to mind when discussing
the world balance of power. A walled medieval city of about 20,000
people and capital of the island of Gotland, it is now a compact and
tidy and irrepressibly quaint little community. But in the twelfth
century, when the Hanseatic League was at its zenith, Visby was
one of the most powerful and prosperous cities on earth. With more
money at their disposal than they knew what to do with, the town's
burghers built churches—17 of them in Visby alone (though ten are
now in ruins) and 92 on the island as a whole. Most were built on
a scale more characteristic of cathedrals and none was erected more
recently than 1350.

Today Visby is the best preserved medieval city in northern Europe.
Its narrow streets of step-gabled houses are comfortably confined
within a two-mile-long wall dotted with 44 towers, each about 50
feet high. A walk along these ancient ramparts, particularly on a
moonlit night, will convince you that you've stepped through a time
warp. Although the twelfth century was its time of greatness, relics
in the town's excellent Historical Museum from ancient Greece,
Rome, and Minoa show that its importance as a trading power went
back much further.

Gotland is the largest island in the Baltic, although that isn't saying
a whole lot. It's only 78 miles long by 35 miles wide at its most
expansive, and its flatness and extraordinarily mild climate (roses
have been known to bloom in January) make it excellent cycling
country. Bicycles can be rented inexpensively all over the island.
Leaving Visby, you'll find a flat open landscape, a profusion of wild
flowers, quiet sandy beaches, and ancient churches at every turn.

Details: From the Swedish mainland there are daily ferries in summer from Nynashamn and Oskarshamn, both lasting about five hours.
Alternatively, but more expensively, you can fly to Visby from any
of about two dozen Swedish airports (30 minutes from Stockholm).
Although not many Americans visit Gotland, the place is very popular with Scandinavians and hotels can be a problem in July and
August, but the Visby Tourist Office at Färjeleden 5 (near the harbor)
should be able to find you a room in a private home.

The Swedish Glass Kingdom, Småland

Sweden's King Gustavus Vasa led a busy life. In between driving out the Danes, making himself king, fighting foreign wars, and introducing the Reformation into Sweden, he found time to do something of almost equally lasting importance for his country: In 1556, he imported some glassblowers from Venice and set them up in the province of Småland. Thus began Sweden's Glasriket, or Glass Kingdom, a region of glassmaking still unparalleled anywhere in the world. In an age of mass production and closely watched unit costs, this one small corner of south-central Sweden possesses some 30 glassworks producing exquisite items almost entirely by hand.

Most offer guided tours where you can watch craftsmen exercising skills and using implements that have scarcely changed in a thousand years. If that sounds a bit like a field trip for fourth-graders, don't be put off. There is an ineffable fascination in watching a team of skilled workers carefully turning a glowing red, 1,200-degree Centigrade glob into a translucent thing of beauty. The process may be elementary, but the products are masterly, and even the most stony-faced visitor (i.e., Daddy) invariably departs knocked out and with a new respect for vases, paperweights, and little bowls. It's worth noting that the more difficult pieces are usually executed in the morning.

The capital of the Glasriket is the ancient university town of Växjö; all 30 of the glassworks are within a 10-mile radius of it. In the town there's an excellent Glass Museum tracing the history of glassmaking from Roman times to the present. The museum houses a large collection of antique and modern glass from all over the world, which it supplements every summer with special exhibitions. It also organizes bus tours of the leading glass factories. Also in Växjö is the Emigrant Museum, chronicling the days in the nineteenth century when a quarter of the Swedish population—some 1.3 million people—emigrated to America. The museum contains Europe's largest archives and library on emigration. If you're trying to track down Swedish relatives, its staff is extremely helpful and efficient.

Details: Most glassmaking factories are open from about 8:30 A.M. to 3 P.M., though times can vary slightly from place to place. The three most popular are Lindshammar at Vetlanda, Kosta Boda at Kosta, and Orrefors in the village of the same name. Many factories close for the whole of July, but several, including the three above, leave some workshops open and some blowers at work for the benefit of tourists. All have shops selling their products at a fraction of what you would pay in New York.

The Swedish Match Museum, Jönköping

King Farouk of Egypt, a man who could afford to indulge an exotic whim or two, once had a plane diverted to Copenhagen when he learned that a rare matchbox he had long coveted had just come onto the market. Farouk was one of history's great phillumenists, or collectors of matchboxes, a hobby that evidently tends to grow on you. It almost goes without saying that the matchbox he bought came from the Jönköping factory of Johan Edvard Lundstrom, the father of the modern safety match.

In its day, Jönköping was the matchmaking capital of the world, with half a dozen factories cranking out matches by the billion. Although Sweden still produces a fifth of the world's matches, there are no longer any producing factories in Jönköping. The famous Lundstrom works live on, however, as the Swedish Match Museum, one of the most unlikely and quietly fascinating small museums in the country. Everything to do with the history of pyrotechnics, from ancient tinderboxes to the making of the modern match (take one aspen tree and chop it into 1.5 million pieces...), is on display here.

The early safety matches were hand-dipped, a laborious and frequently explosive process. But in 1864, a young Jönköping man named Alexander Lagerman invented the first machine for mass production. Lagerman's inventions, which were engineering masterpieces in their day and still look marvelously efficient to the modern eye, are on display in a separate room. Upstairs is an enormous collection of matches, boxes, labels, and other curiosities—a phillumenist's paradise. A visit to the museum may not change your life or inspire you to divert aircraft, but it won't fail to fascinate you.

Details: The Swedish Match Museum is at V Storgatan 18 A in Jönköping (Tel. 036 10 55 43) and is open daily except Sunday from 10 A.M. to 3:30 P.M.

Rafting on the Klarälven River, Värmland

You have to hand it to whoever thought up this one. Faced with the
need to get thousands of logs from Lake Vingängsjön to a paper mill
at Edebäck, 66 miles downriver, he hit on the novel idea of charging
tourists to do his work for him. Would-be Huckleberry Finns are
given a pile of logs, some rope to bind them, a sheet of instructions
for building a rudimentary raft about 15 feet by 10 feet (though you
are free to build something larger and more elaborate if you wish),
food, camping equipment, and fishing tackle if required, and a bit
of friendly encouragement. Then they are left to make of it all what
they can.

Building the rafts requires a little hard work, a good deal of
grunting, and a bit of cursing, but no special skills. Those who can't
face it can pay more for a raft already built. But for most people the
uncontained joy of casting off onto the water on a craft of your own
making without actually sinking is ample reward for a few hours'
intensive labor. And after that it's all downhill, so to speak. The
Klarälven is both wide and slow moving; its gentle current will
conduct you through the wilderness of Värmland at a stately one to
two miles an hour. Dipping a long pole into the river occasionally
is about all that's required of you in the way of navigational skills.
And even if you're not much good at that, the river's remoteness
ensures that your embarrassments will be private.

Apart from that, there is nothing to do but fish and swim and
laze and drink, scan the riverbanks for moose and beaver, and savor
the tranquility. Sheer bliss. It takes about five days to reach Edebäck,
but you can rent a raft for just one or three days if you prefer.

Details: River trips by raft can be arranged through HB Klarälv-
suthyrning, Pl 220, S-680 63, Likenäs, or Anders Wiss, Sundbergs-
vägen 13, S-685 00, Torsby. One warning: mosquitoes can be a
problem, so take a large stock of insect repellant.

Golfing at Midnight, Boden

For insomniac golfing enthusiasts, the Degerbacken Golf Course
near Boden, above the Arctic Circle in the far north of Sweden, must
seem a little bit like paradise. It is the northernmost golf course in

the world and the only one that can offer you 24 hours of daylight from late May to early August. During those several weeks, it's possible to golf right through the night—as many people actually do.

The course, which is over 18 holes and hilly, is described as medium difficult. It's not exactly famed on the PGA circuit—though since the summer of 1984 it has been the home of an international tournament, the Polaris Cup—but considering that its nearest competition is more than 100 miles away, standards are surprisingly high. The course is open throughout the night, but the clubhouse shuts at 9 P.M. So if you want to play into the wee hours with rented clubs, you'il have to come to some arrangement with the clubhouse keeper ahead of time.

If you are a really dedicated golfer, Degerbacken is a course to head for. Walking around in daylight when the whole world is sleeping is itself an uncanny experience. Sinking a 20-foot putt at three in the morning is simply indescribable.

Details: The Degerbacken Golf Course is about 15 miles north of Boden at Degerbacken (Tel. 0921-61071). A round costs SKr30 if you're 21 or older and SKr20 for those under 20.

Hiking in Swedish Lappland

The Swedes are an alarmingly energetic people. It may be all that winter darkness that does it, but at the first hint of spring there's nothing they like better than pulling on their hiking boots and heading off for a few days of vigorous rambling through the desolate, haunting vastness of the north country.

The northern region of Sweden, or Norrbotten, is one of Europe's last unspoiled open spaces and the Swedes are determined to keep it that way. A few exceedingly spartan mountain huts and a scattering of signposts and directional markers are about the only intrusions man has been allowed to make on the landscape. The air is pure, the rivers clean enough to drink from, and the rugged setting unbelievably beautiful. But the distance to creature comforts like cold beer and soft beds can be measured in tens of miles and the remoteness can be intimidating. More than that, if you don't know what you're doing, it can be dangerous.

For inexperienced hikers, the Muddus National Park, between Jokkmokk and Kiruna, is a good place to start. A 195-square-mile area of woodlands, bogs, and lakes, it requires no more than that you possess hard-wearing clothes, decent hiking boots, and a soupçon of common sense. A well-marked path runs for 50 kilometers through the heart of the park. Along it are six huts, which provide gas and utensils for cooking, mattresses, and a roof over your head, but little else. If you are staying the night, you'll need a sleeping bag and food. There's no electricity for lighting, but throughout the summer daylight lasts 24 hours. There's a charge of SKr30 to use the huts, but in many of them payment is on an honor system—you pay at the next manned hut you come to.

This obviously isn't for everyone, but if you like fresh air, exercise, and isolation, there's enough of it here to last you a lifetime.

Details: The Tourist Bureau (Turistbyrå) in Jokkmokk can provide details of routes through the Muddus National Park and information on huts. Some huts are sometimes locked and you may need to acquire the keys before you set out. Check before you go. If you're thinking of doing a lot of hiking, or of taking on a more challenging national park route, you should consider joining the Swedish Touring Club, or STF as it is more commonly known. Membership costs SKr80 a year, but it entitles you to reduced rates at the huts and the chance to join organized hikes led by the club. Write to the Swedish Touring Club, Box 7615, S-103 94, Stockholm.

SWITZERLAND

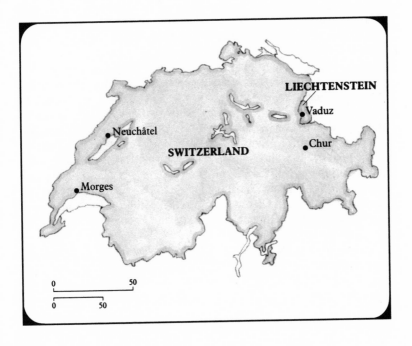

LIECHTENSTEIN

Vaduz

Neuchâtel

SWITZERLAND

Chur

Morges

0   50

0   50

Neuchâtel

I don't suppose any ancient town that enjoys a setting on a beautiful lake against a backdrop of mountains could ever really hope to remain off the beaten track. But insofar as it is possible, Neuchâtel has managed it. While the nearby towns of Lausanne, Geneva, and Fribourg have spent the last century diligently courting outsiders, Neuchâtel has been content to keep pretty much to itself, relying on the skills of its famed watchmakers for prosperity. It's a very pretty place, particularly in the Old Town, where a twelfth-century castle, now the seat of the cantonal government, overlooks the narrow streets and medieval buildings. At its feet is the Lake of Neuchâtel (Lac de Neuchâtel), the third largest in Switzerland, with views to the jagged, snowcapped peaks of the Bernese Oberland and the towering majesty of Mont Blanc. Although Neuchâtel lies along one of the boundaries where French and German influences run together in a generally amiable collision, the town itself is fiercely French-speaking. In fact, the French spoken here is said to be the purest not only in Switzerland but in all the French-speaking world, and it's not unusual for students from Paris and Bordeaux to come here to study their own language.

About all Neuchâtel has to offer the fidgeting tourist is a single large museum, by the Quai Leopold on the lake. It contains some interesting paintings, some Roman and prehistoric relics, and some odds and ends pertaining to Swiss culture. But the real attractions are the extraordinary mechanical figures built in the eighteenth century by local watchmakers. When activated, these little people not only move around in a convincing manner, but also play musical instruments, draw pictures, and write down words. Quite amazing. Unfortunately the figures are activated only occasionally (generally once a month on a Sunday), but do check while you are in town.

A number of village resorts line the west side of the lake, most of them quite busy, but on the eastern side is the much quieter, but no less inviting, little town of Estavayer-le-Lac (pop. 2,500), where fountains burble and the narrow streets contain appealing arcades. There's an excellent selection of small hotels, making it a tempting alternative to Neuchâtel. Before you head there, you might want to consider a trip in the opposite direction into the foothills of the Jura

Mountains hard up on the French border. Not only is this a simple and scenic journey, but you'll also find two very interesting museums. One is the Museum of Clocks at the Chateau des Monts, a country house at Le Locle, about 15 miles from Neuchâtel. Here a large and fascinating collection of clocks, watches, and other timepieces dates from the early seventeenth century. The delicate craftsmanship on these pieces, both mechanical and decorative, is astonishing. But even more amazing, I think, is the Museum of Man and Time at La Chaux-de-Fonds, about five miles away. Opened in 1974, it is built mostly underground and uses an imaginative layout to take you through the whole history of time measurement. More than 3,000 items are on display, ranging from the simplest primitive instruments using water or sand to the latest astronomical clocks. The purpose here is not only to show you what the different clocks look like, but also how they work, and the museum achieves its aim admirably with cutaway models, films (on three giant screens), and games. In a separate room you can watch craftsmen building and restoring old clocks. It is most fascinating. In 1978, the museum was voted European Museum of the Year.

Details: The Clock Museum at the Chateau des Monts at Le Locle is open daily, except Mondays, from July 1 to September 30 from 2 P.M. to 5 P.M., and on Sundays only from 2 to 5 the rest of the year. The Museum of Man and Time, at 29 rue des Musées in La Chaux-de-Fonds, is open every day but Monday throughout the year from 10 A.M. to noon and from 2 to 5 P.M. In Neuchâtel, the local museum, called the Musée d'Art et d'Histoire, is on 2 rue des Beaux-Arts, and is open every day but Monday from 10 to noon and from 2 to 5. It is also open on Thursday evenings from 8 to 10 P.M.

The Military Museum at Morges

When you consider that the Swiss adopted their policy of neutrality as long ago as 1515—just 23 years after Columbus discovered America—the idea of their possessing a military museum of note is perhaps a little surprising. There are in fact nine museums in Switzerland devoted wholly or in large part to exploits on the battlefield, but the best—and one of the best anywhere—is the Musée Militaire Vaudois, housed in an imposing thirteenth-century castle in the lakeside town of Morges, near Lausanne. Here, spread through 20 rooms, you'll find a vast and neatly laid out array of cannons, swords, guns, uniforms, suits of armor, crossbows, banners, and everything else related to the ancient art of killing people for king and country. Even if, like me, you are not particularly drawn to slaughter and carnage, you can't help being fascinated by the craftsmanship and ingenuity that went into some of these ancient instruments of destruction. A Swiss grenade launcher of 1750 must not only have surprised the hell out of those aimed at, but it was also quite a handsome piece of engineering, as was the prototype French machine gun of 1871, which looks a bit like a cross between a cannon and a watering can. Less intimidating, but no less fascinating, are the 120 or so scale models of cannons, field guns, and ammunition wagons, all scrupulously crafted. But the prizes of the collection are the 8,000 lead and pewter soldiers collected by a perennial boy-at-heart named Raoul Gérard that trace the whole long pageant of European military apparel from prehistory up to 1939. Most of the pieces are tiny— less than four centimeters high—but are hand-painted with the most exquisite care and detail. Absolutely fascinating.

Details: The Musée Militaire Vaudois in Morges is open weekdays from 10 A.M. to noon and 1:30 P.M. to 5 P.M., and on Saturdays, Sundays, and public holidays from 1:30 to 5. Closed from mid-December to the end of January. Morges is about ten miles west of Lausanne on the main road and rail routes to Geneva.

Chur, Grisons

Chur is one of those European towns that a lot of travelers pass through—in this case mostly skiers en route to one of the 20 mountain resorts nearby—but few actually stop to see. To be sure, the town's industrial fringes don't seem to offer much promise for the place. But wander into the town's center, to the Altstadt, and you'll find an area of cobbled streets, medieval buildings, and hushed courtyards as alluring and timeless as any in Europe. Only the cosmopolitan range of goods on sale in the ancient shop windows (Chur is said to be the most sophisticated shopping center between Milan and Zurich) disturbs the illusion that you have stumbled into the Middle Ages.

Chur is the oldest town in Switzerland and one of the most historic—though it must be said that much of the history is of purely local interest—and capital of the polyglot canton of Grisons (German:

Graubünden), where French, German, and Italian influences mingle with the native Romansch, a complicated dialect (actually several complicated dialects) that sounds like Portuguese and is based on Latin. The linguistic competition is reflected in the fact that Chur has five official names (the French *Coire*, Italian *Coira*, Romansch *Cuera* or *Cuoira*, and German *Chur*) and local schoolbooks have to be printed in up to seven languages and dialects.

There's plenty to see in Chur—most notably the Rhaetian Museum, which specializes in Romansch culture and history, and the handsome twelfth-century Catholic Cathedral of St. Lucius, worth at least a flying visit to view its magnificent high altar—yet the town's principal value is as a base for discovering and enjoying the nearby area. Within easy striking distance are an astonishing 150 valleys, countless mountain villages and resorts, and miles and miles of scrupulously signposted and meticulously maintained footpaths. You could in fact walk all the way to Geneva by footpath from here.

Chur stands near the Rhine at the foot of the gorgeous Schanfigg Valley, up which you can follow a dead-end road or rail line some 16 miles to the old resort of Arosa, a beautiful place with pleasant lakes, where you can fish or rent a rowboat, and ride a cable car that will take you up Mount Weisshorn (8,600 feet) for unforgettable views. Up the next valley are the more famous resorts of Klosters and Davos, where the mountains rise like walls and the beauty is simply intense. From here you have the option of pressing on to the canton of Ticino and into Italy. To the west of Chur is the less well-known resort of Flim-Waldhaus, where there are walks through larch woods, more expansive views, and a small lake, Caumasee, fed by warm springs that make swimming a possibility here when elsewhere in Switzerland it would be insanity. A few miles to the north of Chur is Liechtenstein. But that's only the briefest of rundowns on this area's possibilities. So long as you don't linger in the industrial town of Landquart or in the suburbs of Chur itself, you can hardly set a foot wrong wherever you go.

The final attraction of Chur is that it's on the route of the Glacier Express, the famous but costly train trip that runs right through the Alpine heartland of Switzerland over some of the most breathtaking landscape in the world. The 7½-hour journey from St. Moritz to Zermatt, takes you through 91 tunnels and over 291 bridges. It's a masterpiece of engineering and an unforgettable experience—but if you're traveling on a Eurailpass or Youthpass, note that you will have to pay the full fare between Zermatt and Desiritis.

Details: Chur (pop. 33,000) is on the main rail line from Zurich and about two hours from there by train. On the sidewalks of the town you'll notice red or green footprints painted at intervals. These mark off walking tours, each of about an hour's duration, of the town's main sights. The local tourist office, at the interestingly named address of No. 6 Ohostrasse, can provide you with an English-language pamphlet to serve as your guide.

ATTRACTIONS BY SUBJECT

ATTRACTIONS FOR CHILDREN

Aalholm Castle, Denmark
Bakken Amusement Park, Denmark
Curiosities, Museum of, England
Deutsches Museum, West Germany
De Efteling Amusement Park, Netherlands
Eise Eisinga's Planetarium, Netherlands
Evoluon, Netherlands
Garden of Monsters, Italy
Schloss Hellbrunn, Austria
Legoland, Denmark
Madurodam Model Village, Netherlands
Moving Toys Museum, Netherlands
Piggy Bank Museum, Netherlands

CASTLES, HISTORIC HOUSES

Amboise, France
Augustburg Palace, West Germany
Benrath, Schloss, West Germany
Capodimonte Palace, Italy
Chinon, France
Clos-Lucé, France
Craigievar Castle, Scotland
Drottningholm Palace, Sweden
Egeskov Castle, Denmark
Hardwick Hall, England
Hellbrunn, Schloss, Austria
Herrenchiemsee, Schloss, West Germany
Hochosterwitz, Austria

Hvittrask, Finland
Nazionale, Villa, Italy
Olavinlinna Castle, Finland
St. Michael's Mount, England
Snowshill Manor, England
Tratzberg, Schloss, Austria
Vianden, Luxembourg
Ward, Castle, Ireland

MUSEUMS AND GALLERIES

Armoury Museum, Graz, Austria
Bomann Museum, Celle, West Germany
Bottle Ship Museum, Aerøskøbing, Denmark
Bread Museum, Ulm, West Germany
Burrell Collection, Glasgow, Scotland
Capodimonte Palace, Naples, Italy
Clock and Watch Museum, Vienna, Austria
Clock Museum, Le Locle, Switzerland
Curiosities Museum, Arundel, England
Decorative Arts Museum, Saumur, France
Deutsches Museum, Munich, West Germany
Gallen-Kallela Museum, Helsinki, Finland
Glass Museum, Vaxjo, Sweden
Hammerich's House, Aerøskøbing, Denmark
Henie-Onstad Art Center, Norway
Horse Museum, Saumur, France
Hunterian Art Gallery, Glasgow, Scotland
Kettle's Yard Art Museum, Cambridge, England
Leonardo da Vinci Museum, Amboise, France
Maritime Museum, Buckler's Hard, England
Match Museum, Jönköpping, Sweden
Military Museum, Morges, Switzerland
Mushroom Museum, Saumur, France
Musical Instruments Museum, Brussels, Belgium
Oriental Museum, Durham, England
Orthodox Church Museum, Kuopio, Finland
Piggy Bank Museum, Amsterdam
Planetarium of Eise Eisinga, Franeker, Netherlands
Plantin-Moretus Museum, Antwerp, Belgium
Playing Cards Museum, Turnhout, Belgium
Poster Museum, Lahti, Finland
Press Museum, Aachen, West Germany
Printing Museum, Mainz, West Germany

Quaker Museum, Jordans, England
Roman Settlement, Saalberg, West Germany
Seurassari Open Air Museum, Helsinki, Finland
Ships' Figureheads Museum, Isles of Scilly, England
Silkeborg Museum, Silkeborg, Denmark
Ski Museum, Oslo, Norway
Soane Museum, London
Tax Museum, Rotterdam, Netherlands
Theater Museum, Drottningholm, Sweden
Time, Museum of Man and, La Chaux-de-Fonds, Switzerland
Tobacco Museum, Vienna, Austria
Tobacco and Cigar Museum, Bunde, West Germany
Torture Museum, The Hague, Netherlands
Toulouse-Lautrec Museum, Albi, France
Toys, Musem of Moving, Deventer, Netherlands
Violin Museum, Mittenwald, West Germany
Wallpaper Museum, Kassel, West Germany
Wine Museum, Speyer, West Germany

INTERESTING AND ATTRACTIVE TOWNS AND RESORTS

Aachen (Aix-le-Chapelle), West Germany
Aeolian (Lipari) Islands, Italy
Albi, France
Amarante, Portugal
Avila, Spain
Baden-Baden, West Germany
Bad Homburg, West Germany
Bodø, Norway
Bonifacio, Corsica
Castle Combe, England
Cefalu, Sicily
Celle, West Germany
Chinon, France
Chios, Greece
Colmar, France
Echternach, Luxembourg
Edam, Netherlands
Evora, Portugal
Glengarriff, Ireland
Hallstatt, Austria
Honfleur, France
Karpathos, Greece
Kinsale, Ireland

Le Puy, France
Lübeck, West Germany
Lucca, Italy
Narvik, Norway
Orta San Giulio, Italy
Portmeirion, Wales
Quimper, France
Ravello, Italy
Rocamadour, France
Scilly Isles, England
Sintra, Portugal
Skyros, Greece
Snowshill, England
Spa, Belgium
Speyer, West Germany
Sylt, West Germany
Symi, Greece
Tapiola, Finland
Tavira, Portugal
Todi, Italy
Urbino, Italy
Visby, Sweden
Zagorochoria, Greece
Zitsa, Greece

PLACES OF SCENIC BEAUTY

Aran Islands, Ireland
Athos, Mount, Greece
Bowland, Forest of, England
Charente, River, France
Gargano Peninsula, Italy
Glendalough, Ireland
Hallstatt, Austria
Hardangerfjord, Norway
Herm, Channel Islands
Kefalonia, Greece
Klein Walsertal, Austria
Konigssee, West Germany
Liechtenstein
"Little Switzerland," Luxembourg
Mittenwald, West Germany
New Forest, England
Orta, Lake, Italy

Ridgeway Path, England
Rocamadour, France
St. Michael's Mount, England
Scilly Isles, England
Setesdal Valley, Norway
Sorrentine Peninsula, Italy
Vikos Gorge, Greece

GARDENS AND PARKS

Abbey Gardens, Scilly Isles, England
Bergpark Wilhelmshohe, Kassel, West Germany
Birr Castle, Ireland
Bodnant Gardens, Wales
Bomarzo Gardens, Italy
Garinish Island, Ireland
Monet's Garden, Giverny, France
Père Lachaise, Paris, France
Powerscourt, Ireland
Vikos National Park, Greece
Villandry, France
Windsor Great Park

CHURCHES, CATHEDRALS, MONASTERIES

Albi Cathedral, France
Athos, Mount, Greece
Brou, Church of, France
Burgos Cathedral, Spain
Catherine, Church of Ste., France
Corentin, Cathedral of St., France
Durham Cathedral, England
Meteora, Monasteries of, Greece
Nea Moni Monastery, Greece
Rennes-le-Château, Church of, France
Santiago de Compostela, Spain
Speyer Cathedral, West Germany
Tournai Cathedral, Belgium
Ulm Cathedral, West Germany

ACTIVITIES

Bicycling in Belgium
Bicycling on Bornholm, Denmark
Bicycling in The Netherlands

Concerts at Sutton Hall, England
Cruising the River Charente, France
Golfing in Ireland
Golfing at midnight, Sweden
Hiking in Lappland, Sweden
Hiking the Ridgeway Path, England
Horseback riding in the New Forest, England
Horse and wagon tours of Samsø Island, Denmark
Opera at Savonlinna, Finland
Rafting on Klaralven River, Sweden

USEFUL ADDRESSES

WHERE TO RENT VACATION COTTAGES, VILLAS, OR APARTMENTS IN EUROPE

At least a couple of hundred companies can offer you rented accommodations all over Europe. But beware: at many of them that rustic-sounding cottage so compellingly described in the brochure will prove on arrival to be a jerrybuilt plywood affair with all the comforts and esthetics of an army barracks, standing amid monotonous rows of others exactly like it. If what you're looking for is a stone-built former farmhouse standing alone in glorious countryside, you're much more likely to find it at any of the following addresses. But even here you should find out as many details as you can beforehand: whether there's heating, whether you'll need to provide your own bed linen, whether there are any shops or pubs within walking distance.

Great Britain

English Country Cottages, Claypit Lane, Fakenham, Norfolk, N221 8AS.

Forestry Commission, 231 Corstorphine Road, Edinburgh, EH12 7AT, Scotland (forest cabins and cottages, mostly fairly remote, owned by a government agency).

Character Cottages, 34c Fore Street, Sidmouth, Devon, EX10 8AQ.

The Holidays Secretary, The National Trust for Scotland, 5 Charlotte Square, Edinburgh, EH2 4DU (Scottish cottages owned by conservation society).

The Landmark Trust, Shottesbrooke, Maidenhead, Berkshire (highly recommended; see main text, page 120).

Denmark

Dantourist A/S, Hulgade 21, DK-5700 Svedborg (wide range of properties, most of them built especially for holidaymakers, throughout Denmark).

Ireland

Lismore Travel, 106 East 31st Street, New York, N.Y. 10016.
O'Shea Tours, 195 South Broadway, Hicksville N.Y. 11801.

France

Gîtes de France, 178 Piccadilly, London, or Federation Nationale des
    Gîtes Ruraux de France, 35 Rue Godot-de-Mauroy, 75009 Paris (1,500
    graded properties throughout France).
Vacances en Campagne, c/o DePetris & Stewart, 500 Fifth Avenue, New
    York, N.Y. 10036, or Box Cottage, Sutton Pulburough, Sussex, RH20
    1PS, England.

All over Europe

Villas International, 214 East 38th Street, New York, N.Y. 10016.
At Home Abroad, 405 East 56th Street, New York, N.Y. 10022.

SPECIAL INTEREST VACATIONS

Boating (yachts, barges, canoes, etc.)

Great Britain

Hoseasons Holidays, Sunway House, Lowestoft, Suffolk. (Self-driven
    river cruisers and barges).
Blakes Holidays, Wroxham, Norwich, Norfolk (Self-driven river cruisers
    and barges).
Floating Through Europe, Inc., 271 Madison Avenue, New York, N.Y.
    10016 ("hotel" barge tours of the Thames and Avon rivers; expensive
    but cosseted).

Ireland

Celtic Canal Cruisers, Tollamore, Co. Offaly, Ireland.
Emerald Star Line, St. James's Gate, Dublin 8.
Hoseasons Holidays (see address under Great Britain).
Blakes Holidays (see address under Great Britain).

Denmark

Dantourist A/S, Hulgade 21, DK-5700, Svendborg, Denmark.

France

Holiday Charente (highly recommended; for address and details, see main
    text, page 49).

Hoseasons Holidays (see address under Great Britain).

Blakes Holidays (see address under Great Britain).

Floating Through Europe, Inc. (see address under Great Britain).

Austria

Platzgummer Michael Hochsteg 579, A-6290 Mayrhofen, Austria (guided canoe trips down the River Ziller).

Greece

Neptune Cruising, 3 The Square, Hamble, Hants., England (motorized sailboats).

Italy

Peter Stuyvesant Travel, 35 Alfred Place, London WC1 (flotilla motorboat tours around Sardinia).

Belgium and The Netherlands

Floating Through Europe, Inc. (see address under Great Britain).

Cycling

Great Britain

East Anglia Cycling Holidays, Yoxford, Suffolk.

Denmark

Dansk Cykelferie-Dantourist, Hulgade 21, DK-5700, Svendborg, Denmark.

East Anglia Cycling Holidays (see address under Great Britain).

Netherlands

See main text, page 190.

Cooking

France

La Varenne Ecole de Cuisine, 34 Rue St. Dominique, 75007 Paris (traditional and nouvelle cuisine; courses in English).

Haute Cuisine Bordelaise, 12 Place de la Bourse, 33076 Bordeaux (wide range of courses, but not for beginners).

En Famille Agency (Overseas), Westbury House, Queen's Lane, Arundel, Sussex, England (cooking and living in French homes).

Italy

Marcella Hazan School in Bologna, c/o P.O. Box 285, Circleville, N.Y.
10919 (English-language courses on Italian cuisine; expensive but very
good. Special one-week courses in Venice at Hotel Cipriani in April
and October).

Cigahotels, 67 Jermyn Street, London SW1 (three- or five-day courses at
Hotel Gritti, Venice).

Great Britain

Ken Lo's Kitchen, 14 Eccleston Street, London SW1 (Chinese cooking in
London).

Leith's School of Food and Wine, 36a Notting Hill Gate, London W11
(one-week courses from July to September on a wide range of cuisines;
relatively cheap and very popular).

Arts

Great Britain

Galleon Travel, 52 High Street, Sevenoaks, Kent (wide variety of
painting courses and tours).

West Dean College, Chichester, Sussex (extremely wide variety of
traditional and lesser-known crafts in a beautiful country house setting:
highly recommended).

Crafts Advisory Committee, 12 Waterloo Place, London, SW1Y 4AV
(clearinghouse for information on craft centers and workshops
throughout Britain).

Flatford Mill Field Centre, East Bergholt, Colchester, Essex, C07 6UL
(painting courses; especially good for beginners).

The Barn Studio, Horn Street, Winslow, Buckinghamshire, MK18 3AL
(painting and drawing for experienced artists and beginners).

Dove Workshops, Barton Road, Butleigh, near Glastonbury, Somerset
(pottery courses for all levels).

Austria

Austrian Airlines, A-1107 Vienna, Fontanastrasse 1 (wide variety of
courses in various arts all over Austria; instruction generally in
German).

Geraser Sommerakademie, A-2093 Geras/Stift (wide range of courses in
twelfth-century monastery; particular emphasis on restoration and
little-known arts like glass-staining).

Denmark

Bornholms Kongresbureau, Bornholm (seven-day weaving courses on island of Bornholm).

Galleon Travel (for address see Great Britain).

Italy

Accademia di Belle Arti "Pietro Vanucci," Piazza San Francesco al Prato 5, Perugia (painting and sculpture).

Istituto per l'Arte e il Restauro, Palazzo Spinelli, Borgo Santa Croce 10, Firenze (art restoration workshops in Florence).

Horseback riding, pony trekking, etc.

Great Britain

Ponies of Britain, Brookside Farm, Ascot, Berkshire (complete list of approved riding and trekking centers in Britain; price £1).

Riding in the New Forest (see main text, page 97).

Riding in the Lake District, Troutbeck Hotel, Troutbeck, Cumbria, CA11 OSJ (escorted treks, suitable for beginners).

France

Rofe Travel, 17 Princes Arcade, Jermyn Street, London (horse-drawn caravans in Brittany).

Cox & Kings Travel, 46 Marshall Street, London W1V 2PA (horseback riding in the Dordogne).

Austria

Austrian Airlines, A-1107 Vienna, Fontanastrasse 1 (horseback riding in the Hausrack Forests or around Lake Neusiedl).

Italy

A.N.T.E., Largo Messico 13, Rome (information on more than 40 approved riding centers in Italy).

INDEX

245